97 Things About Ethics Everyone in Data Science Should Know

Collective Wisdom from the Experts

Bill Franks

Beijing · Boston · Farnham · Sebastopol · Tokyo

97 Things About Ethics Everyone in Data Science Should Know

by Bill Franks

Copyright © 2020 O'Reilly Media, Inc. All rights reserved.

Published by O'Reilly Media, Inc., 1005 Gravenstein Highway North, Sebastopol, CA 95472.

O'Reilly books may be purchased for educational, business, or sales promotional use. Online editions are also available for most titles (*http://oreilly.com*). For more information, contact our corporate/institutional sales department: 800-998-9938 or *corporate@oreilly.com*.

Acquisitions Editors: Jonathan Hassell, Andy Kwan	**Proofreader:** Penelope Perkins
	Indexer: WordCo Indexing Services, Inc.
Development Editor: Nicole Taché	**Interior Designer:** David Futato
Production Editor: Christopher Faucher	**Cover Designer:** Karen Montgomery
Copyeditor: Arthur Johnson	**Illustrator:** O'Reilly Media, Inc.

August 2020:   First Edition

Revision History for the First Edition

2020-08-06:   First Release

See *http://oreilly.com/catalog/errata.csp?isbn=9781492072669* for release details.

978-1-492-07266-9

[LSI]

Table of Contents

Part I. Foundational Ethical Principles

Part II. Data Science and Society

Part III.   The Ethics of Data

Part IV. Defining Appropriate Targets & Appropriate Usage

Part V.   Ensuring Proper Transparency & Monitoring

Part VI.   Policy Guidelines

Part VII.   Case Studies

Preface

The intersection of ethics with the world of analytics and data science is a topic that I have become passionate about in recent years. I've written a variety of blogs and papers on the topic. I've also spoken about the need for attention to ethics at numerous public conferences and at many private meetings with corporate clients. What I discuss is based upon my concerted and ongoing effort to learn what others are thinking and saying about the ethics of analytics. I also receive feedback during these interactions that enables me to continue to evolve my own viewpoints as I recognize gaps in my thinking.

What I have consistently found in my interactions is that people are very receptive to giving ethics more attention once their eyes have been opened to the fact that the need for ethical consideration is much broader and more important than they realized. The vast majority of the examples I've seen where something unethical occurred with analytics and data science were not driven by anyone operating with bad intent. Rather, it is usually the case that the ethics of the situation simply weren't thought through well enough, if at all.

When O'Reilly approached me about partnering on this project, I knew it was something I had to do. I was excited about the opportunity to see what hundreds of other people had to say about ethics. I firmly believe that as more of these types of conversations about ethics occur among members of the analytics and data science community, we can continue to make progress toward ensuring that analytics and data science are done in as ethical a manner as possible. The key is to get people's attention so that they are awakened to the need to give proper focus to ethical considerations. The goal of this book is to be a catalyst for this awakening—to help readers fully understand the importance of applying proper ethics to analytics and data science initiatives. Curating the final submissions that made it into the book was a tremendous learning experience for me, and I hope that readers will find the final outcome to be of value as well.

As you read the book, you will find a wide range of opinions and writing styles. That was intentional. To the extent that two entries have conflicting views, it provides an opportunity for you to ponder which view you find more compelling and why. My colleagues and I did not write this book to tell you precisely what is and isn't ethical. Rather, the book provides perspectives from others in the community so that you can continue to refine your own ethical guidelines.

The book's title is *97 Things About Ethics Everyone in Data Science Should Know*. Who, exactly, is "everyone in data science"? That description should be interpreted broadly. Certainly, anyone involved in the definition, creation, or usage of analytics and data science processes will benefit from the book. This includes people in both technical and business-facing roles. Students or people considering a career change into the field will also benefit. However, the content is not deeply technical or hard to understand. As a result, people who simply have an interest in understanding how ethics intersects with data science will find this book of value as well, regardless of their job role or educational background.

Why Now?

While the need for ethics in analytics and data science has always been present, a couple of recent trends have helped to finally push the topic to the forefront. The first trend is what I focused on in my book *The Analytics Revolution* (*http://www.theanalyticsrevolutionbook.com*) (Wiley). Namely, we have entered an era in which analytical processes are being fully automated and embedded into decision processes. Humans are now often relegated to creating analytics and data science processes and then monitoring their performance, while the important decisions are automated. This automation has led people to be more concerned and suspicious about what is actually happening within those processes, and it quickly leads to a discussion about ethics. This is especially true when models are applied to sensitive areas such as credit scores, health care, or risk assessment.

The second trend driving focus on ethics is the rise of artificial intelligence (AI). Not only are myriad AI processes being embedded and automated as part of the first trend, but AI processes are also quite opaque by nature. This opaqueness makes people uncomfortable and forces discussion around what is happening within the AI algorithms and why. This again quickly turns into an ethics discussion. As AI becomes more sophisticated and continues to impact our lives on a daily basis, people want to know that it is being used in an appropriate manner.

Ethics Are "Fuzzy"

Ethics are, unfortunately, much fuzzier than we'd like to think. If you ask a hundred people, "Is the ethical choice typically clear?" most will quickly respond with a firm "yes." However, once we are challenged to think more deeply about the question, it soon becomes obvious that ethical decisions are not as clear cut as we allow ourselves to believe. While it is often easy to identify "the rule" that should be followed for a given situation, it is also just as easy to identify one or more exceptions to that rule.

Let's take a relevant example from the analytics and data science space. One of the central points of the European Union's General Data Protection Regulation (GDPR) is the right to be forgotten. This means that I can tell organizations that I no longer want them to keep any data they may have about me, and they have to delete that data. It sounds very unambiguous, doesn't it? If I ask to have my data deleted, then companies must comply under penalty of law.

Well, it isn't that simple. There are many cases in which exceptions make sense from a legal and/or an ethical perspective. What if I have a warranty in place for a product? If I ask to be forgotten, can the manufacturer keep just enough information to service the warranty until it expires, or does my request also invalidate the warranty (since the company would no longer have a record of me or my purchase)? Is the ethical path to follow the law to the letter or to give customers a choice based on the trade-offs that they may not have considered? The point is that no matter how "clear and unambiguous" GDPR or any law may be, it will never account for every situation. Unusual situations will in turn require judgment about what the ethical action is.

In the extreme, consider an ethical guideline shared by virtually every society in the history of humanity: we should not kill another person. Few would argue that this isn't a good and ethical rule. However, we can find many exceptions even to this universally accepted rule. To name just one example, if someone breaks into my home and is trying to kill me, is it OK for me to kill that person in self-defense? Most individuals and legal systems say "yes," and many have a range of other exceptions, such as war and capital punishment. If something as clear and unambiguous as "do not kill" has exceptions, how can we not expect to deal with exceptions in our data science and analytics work?

Once we are forced to admit that there is an exception to a rule or that a rule doesn't apply cleanly to a specific situation, we must consider what other exceptions might exist and whether the rule fairly applies to that situation. We are then forced to make an ethical judgment. We must focus on keeping ethical considerations in mind as we plan, build, and implement analytics and data science processes.

Take Ownership of Ethics!

The analytics and data science community must lead and take ownership of the ethics of the analytics and data science processes we produce. Ideally, this book can be one point of reference along the way. But your approach cannot simply be to do whatever you desire until your organization's legal team says "stop" or a public outcry occurs. Unfortunately, our laws haven't caught up with much of what is possible today. As a result, analytics and data science organizations are often faced with situations in which an action may be legal by default (because no law addresses the situation) yet could be widely viewed as unethical. The diligence and judgment of an organization's analytics and data science experts are often all that stand between an unethical idea and its implementation.

As many of the opinions in the book urge, analytics and data science organizations should be intentional in their pursuit of doing only ethical work. Codes of ethics, ethical review boards, ethics violation tip lines, and other related approaches can help to keep an organization on the side of ethical actions. Simply ensuring that people are thinking about ethics every day and at every step of a project will cause unethical decisions and actions to become less common. It is impossible to make a perfect decision every time, but putting focus on being ethical can drive a lot of progress. Also worth noting is that, given the fuzziness of many situations, you can expect that some people will disagree with where you have drawn your ethical lines no matter where you draw them. So be sure you can defend your decisions with both logic and conviction (while also being fully transparent) if those decisions are questioned.

If there is one takeaway from this book, it should be that *you can't wait for someone else to take the lead when it comes to ensuring that your analytics and data science activities are ethical.* You must step up and help take the lead yourself! Be intentional about considering ethics every day, and you will sleep well at night while protecting the integrity and reputation of both yourself and your organization.

How the Book Is Organized

We most often hear ethical concerns raised in the context of model scores having bias in terms of gender, race, and so on. While that certainly is a critical area to focus on, there are ethical considerations throughout the entire process of building, deploying, and using a data science or analytics application. You'll find a wide range of interesting scenarios and solutions discussed throughout the book that cover both expected and unexpected territory.

Rather than simply throwing 97 submissions at readers, we decided to group the entries into some high-level themes. This provides a couple of benefits for you as a reader. First, if there is a certain aspect of ethics that most interests you—for example, policy guidelines—you can quickly go to that section. Second, organizing submissions in this way makes it easier to compare and contrast views about a given theme by having those views in close proximity. Each submission is a stand-alone opinion, and each section of the book is independent of the others. There is no need to read the book in a typical front-to-back fashion. Feel free to skip around to the sections and submissions that most interest you.

The sections in the book are as follows:

- **Part I:** Offers reminders of core ethical foundations that we should account for as we apply ethics to our analytics and data science work

- **Part II:** Ties together general societal ethical norms with analytics and data science requirements

- **Part III:** Contains targeted discussions of the ethics behind the collection and usage of the data that feeds analytics and data science processes

- **Part IV:** Addresses the front-end definition of what a process aims to do and/or the back-end application of results

- **Part V:** Offers insight into how we can make what a process is doing understandable and ensure it operates ethically over time

- **Part VI:** Provides guidance on how to structure policies to encourage ethical actions

- **Part VII:** Includes discussions of industry-specific or use case–specific examples

Astute readers will notice there are actually 98 essays in this book and not 97 as the title indicates. We had so many good submissions that, during the final selection process, we decided it was better to provide readers a bonus viewpoint than to force the list to 97. We believe you can get value from them all!

I hope you find that this compilation of opinions helps you succeed in keeping your own analytics and data science initiatives ethical. Enjoy!

—Bill Franks

O'Reilly Online Learning

 For more than 40 years, *O'Reilly Media* has provided technology and business training, knowledge, and insight to help companies succeed.

Our unique network of experts and innovators share their knowledge and expertise through books, articles, and our online learning platform. O'Reilly's online learning platform gives you on-demand access to live training courses, in-depth learning paths, interactive coding environments, and a vast collection of text and video from O'Reilly and 200+ other publishers. For more information, visit *http://oreilly.com*.

How to Contact Us

Please address comments and questions concerning this book to the publisher:

O'Reilly Media, Inc.
1005 Gravenstein Highway North
Sebastopol, CA 95472
800-998-9938 (in the United States or Canada)
707-829-0515 (international or local)
707-829-0104 (fax)

We have a web page for this book, where we list errata, examples, and any additional information. You can access this page at *https://oreil.ly/97-things-ethics-data-science*.

Email *bookquestions@oreilly.com* to comment or ask technical questions about this book.

For news and information about our books and courses, visit *http://oreilly.com*.

Find us on Facebook: *http://facebook.com/oreilly*

Follow us on Twitter: *http://twitter.com/oreillymedia*

Watch us on YouTube: *http://youtube.com/oreillymedia*

Acknowledgments

I'd like to thank first and foremost all of the people who took the time to contribute submissions for the book. Given the unique format of this book, it would literally not have come to be without all the contributors. I was very impressed with the breadth and quality of the submissions that we received. To the extent that this book is considered a success, that success rests primarily on the shoulders of the contributors.

I'd also like to thank the O'Reilly team for their support from start to finish. After I was approached about partnering on this project and agreed to do it, it didn't take long for me to realize that I wouldn't be on my own. The support from the team in processing submissions, coordinating with all of the authors on edits, and working through the final formatting was terrific. I was assigned an experienced and professional team who made the process as painless as possible.

Last, I'd like to thank everyone in the analytics and data science community who has contributed to the discussions around ethics that have helped to shape my own views, and that I am sure also helped shape the views of the contributors in the book. Without the strong dialog in the community that has taken place, the ideas in this book would not be as well formed and complete as they are.

PART I

Foundational Ethical Principles

Our civilization operates under broad ethical frameworks. This section contains viewpoints that remind us of some of these foundational ethical principles that we must not neglect.

The Truth About AI Bias

Cassie Kozyrkov

Chief Decision Scientist, Google Cloud

No technology is free of its creators. Despite our fondest sci-fi wishes, there's no such thing as AI systems that are truly separate and autonomous...because they start with *us*. Though its effect can linger long after you've pressed a button, all technology is an echo of the wishes of whomever built it.

Data and Math Don't Equal Objectivity

If you're looking to AI as your savior from human foibles, tread carefully. Sure, data and math can increase the amount of information you use in decision making and/or save you from heat-of-the-moment silliness, but how you use them is still up to you.

Look, I know sci-fi sells. It's much flashier to say "The AI learned to do this task all by itself" than to tell the truth: *People used a tool with a cool name to help them write code. They fed in examples they considered appropriate, found some patterns in them, and turned those patterns into instructions. Then they checked whether they liked what those instructions did for them.*

The truth drips with human subjectivity—look at all those little choices along the way that are left up to people running the project. *What shall we apply AI to? Is it worth doing? In which circumstances? How shall we define success? How well does it need to work?* The list goes on and on (*https:// oreil.ly/FkHtg*).

Tragicomically, adding data to the mix obscures the ever-present human element and creates an illusion of objectivity. Wrapping a glamorous coat of math around the core doesn't make it any less squishy.

Technology always comes from and is designed by people, which means it's no more objective than we are.

What Is Algorithmic Bias?

Algorithmic bias refers to situations in which a computer system reflects the implicit values of the people who created it. By this definition, even the most benign computer systems are biased; when we apply math toward a purpose, that purpose is shaped by the sensibilities of our times. Is AI exempt? Not at all. Stop thinking of AI as an entity and see it for what it really is: an excellent tool for writing code.

The whole point of AI is to let you explain your wishes to a computer using examples (data!) instead of instructions. Which examples? That depends on what you're trying to teach your system to do. Think of your dataset as the textbook you're asking your machine student to learn from.

Datasets Have Human Authors

When I've said that "AI bias doesn't come from AI algorithms, it comes from people," some folks have written to tell me that I'm wrong because bias comes from data. Well, we can both be winners...because people make the data. Like textbooks, datasets reflect the biases of their authors.

Consider the following image.

What do you see?

- Bananas
- Stickers
- Bananas on shelves

Was your first thought "bananas"? Why didn't you mention the plastic bag roll, or the color of the bananas? This example comes from Google's AI Fairness training course and demonstrates that although all three answers are technically correct, you have a bias to prefer one of them. Not all people would share that bias; what we perceive and how we respond is influenced by our norms. If you live on a planet where all bananas are blue, you might answer "yellow bananas" here. If you've never seen a banana before, you might say "shelves with yellow stuff on them." Both answers are also correct.

The data you create for your system to learn from will be biased by how you see the world.

This Is No Excuse to Be a Jerk

Philosophical arguments invalidating the existence of truly unbiased and objective technology don't give anyone an excuse to be a jerk. If anything, the fact that you can't pass the ethical buck to a machine puts more responsibility on your shoulders, not less.

Sure, our perceptions are shaped by our times. Societal ideas of virtue, justice, kindness, fairness, and honor aren't the same today as they were for people living a few thousand years ago, and they may keep evolving. That doesn't make these ideas unimportant; it only means we can't outsource them to a heap of wires. They're the responsibility of all of us, together.

Fairness in AI

Once you appreciate that *you* are responsible for how you use your tools and where you point them, strive to make yourself aware of how your choices affect the rest of humanity. For example, deciding which application to pursue is a choice that affects other people. Think it through.

Another choice you have is which data to use for AI. You should expect better performance on examples that are similar to what your system learned from. If you choose not to use data from people like me, your system is more likely to make a mistake when I show up as your user. It's your duty to think about the pain you could cause when that happens.

At a bare minimum, I hope you'd have the common sense to check whether the distribution of your user population matches the distribution in your data. For example, if 100% of your training examples come from residents of a single country, but your target users are global...expect a mess.

Fair and Aware

I've written a lot of words here, when I could have just told you that most of the research on the topic of bias and fairness in AI is about making sure that your system doesn't have a disproportionate effect on some group of users relative to other groups. The primary focus of AI ethics is on distribution checks and similar analytics.

The reason I wrote so much is that I want you to do even better. Automated distribution checks go only so far. No one knows a system better than its creators, so if you're building one, take the time to think about whom your actions will affect and how, and do your best to give those people a voice to guide you through your blind spots.

Introducing Ethicize™, the fully AI-driven cloud-based ethics solution!

Brian T. O'Neill

Founder and Principal, Designing for Analytics

License our latest AI automation platform now, and get a free "Ethics Power Boost" for your next analytics or data science solution for just an additional $2.5M!

That's half off the standard price of $5M, but it's for a limited time only.

Why not make your solution ethical right out of the box with no extra effort?

For the next 30 days, annual platform subscribers can select free 1-day shipping, or you can choose to run the platform in our Ethix™ Cloud for just $49,999 per month. Ethicize™ your solution with an AI-powered system that will completely revolutionize the way you deliver ethical data science and analytics solutions, all with no extra human labor, monitoring, or additional development time. How is this possible? Because Ethicize™ itself is also AI-powered!

Look, talking to customers and real people—especially people you don't even know—takes real time. That's time your technical, product, or solutions teams could spend mining the data warehouse for new AI opportunities. Conversations with individuals don't *scale*, and you can't design to the whims and needs of every single person anyways.

Just imagine having one-on-one conversations with people to understand their problems, latent needs, concerns, and attitudes toward your solution. Who has time for that when your competitors are out there pushing models to production, poaching your senior data scientists, and powering forward with an AI strategy that must be better than yours?

Ethics used to be a hassle, but now your team can Ethicize™ your new product, platform, or solution with just one click!

Look around: you've hired the PhDs. You've got talented analysts and data engineers, and you've made a significant investment in cloud this year. The digital natives will tell you that speed wins. Are you really going to sit around and conjure up hypothetical scenarios of AI gone wrong? Your competitors aren't doing that! While you're sitting in design jams and conducting empathy-driven research with real people who may not even be your customers, the competition is out pushing code into production and delivering incredible customer value.

Let us shoulder the burden of your ethics considerations with an easy add-on solution that requires *zero* human intervention whatsoever.

If you're like a lot of companies out there, designing a solution with ethics in mind is insurance. You need to protect yourself from future risk; after all, you don't want the equivalent of gorilla accusations (*https://oreil.ly/AlLF5*) coming back at your company, right? Sure, you could exercise the problems you're solving with a diverse group of skills, departments, and people, create design prototypes, and evaluate them with real people before going to production, but how can you possibly cover all the potential risk scenarios out there?

You can't.

That's why we've launched Ethicize™—a simple, bolt-on solution to your future ethics problems that is 100% AI-powered. It's like insurance for your data science solution, and it requires almost *zero* human intervention whatsoever. After all, the people leading your data teams are expensive employees. You want them focused on developing models and solutions, right? They're not trained ethicists or designers. Of course, you could simply start to apply human-centered design as a means of building empathy into your solution from the start, but that too takes time, and your data is just sitting there like gold waiting to be mined and shaped into customer value. Lean says you should launch and get feedback. And even if there is an issue with your integration with Ethicize™, since you're using Agile, it shouldn't take long to address any ethics problems that arise, right? That's why you're using two-week sprints!

So you can do ethics the hard way, if you want—or you can just click "Add to Cart," and Ethicize™ will get to work integrating ethics into your solution in minutes. The choice is up to you!

"Ethical" Is Not a Binary Concept

Tim Wilson

Senior Director of Analytics, Search Discovery

When considering the capture, processing, or use of data, companies are instructed to ask themselves, "Is this ethical?" The implication in the framing of the question is that the answer is either "yes" or "no." In many cases, that is fine, but in many more cases, the answer is not nearly as cut and dried as the question implies.

Is it ethical to secretly collect personal data about someone without their knowledge and then to sell that data to multiple third parties for use in targeted marketing? No.

Is it ethical to ask a person to consent to tracking for the sole purpose of analyzing and improving their experience on a website, and then to honor their consent (or lack thereof)? Yes.

Is it ethical to give a person the option to opt out of being tracked and then, if they do not opt out, to track their behavior and use that data to market to them with targeted banner ads on other sites as they browse the internet? It's complicated.

In the case of regulations like the GDPR in the EU, this sort of tracking would be a clear regulatory violation and could subject the organization to a sizable fine. But a regulatory violation does not necessarily make it unethical. (It is also a violation of GDPR to prevent someone from accessing a website if they do not consent to being tracked; a case could be made that this would be perfectly ethical—the company incurs costs to create and maintain a website, so the company should be able to place whatever constraints it wants on allowing access to that content—but this would in actuality be a regulatory violation.)

There is also a gray area when it comes to the varying beliefs and perceptions across the many different people who would be the target of this tracking.

One person, or a large group of people, may be entirely unconcerned with being tracked, may be annoyed by "consent" pop-ups that have to be responded to when visiting a website, and may prefer to have advertising presented to them that is more relevant than ads simply targeted at a mass population. ("I would rather see an ad for hiking gear, as I like to hike, than to see an ad for diapers, since my kids have been out of diapers for over a decade.") This person or group would see the hypothetical "opt out" scenario as entirely ethical: it gives them what they want (a website-browsing experience with fewer interruptions and more relevant ads) at a low "cost" (organizations collecting data regarding their behavior without their explicit consent).

Another group of people may hold a completely different view: they do not trust corporations to collect, store, and use any form of data about them. They *want* to be informed any time they are going to be tracked, and they want to have the opportunity to explicitly allow or disallow that tracking (and not just the tracking, but also the current and future use of any data that is collected). For this group, the "opt out" scenario is clearly *unethical*.

This ambiguity crops up again and again in the real world when it comes to making decisions about data collection and use: the answer to the question "Is this ethical?" will differ based on who is asked and how they are asked. The classic litmus test for a data ethics decision is, "If what we are doing or planning to do with this data were to be published on the front page of the *New York Times*, would it cause negative PR for the company?" The reality is that there is almost no collection of data that would entirely pass *or* entirely fail this test: human beings are complex creatures with complicated feelings about the data they generate and the organizations that can capture and use it.

Cautionary Ethics Tales: Phrenology, Eugenics, ...and Data Science?

Sherrill Hayes

Director, PhD in Analytics and Data Science,
Kennesaw State University

Phrenology, from *phren* meaning "mind" and *logos* meaning "knowledge," was the study of the shapes and contours of the skull as indicative of human mental faculties and character traits. It was developed initially by Franz Joseph Gall (1758–1828) and grew to an internationally recognized science and practice throughout the 19th century. A related area of science that emerged in the 19th century and continued throughout the 20th century was eugenics. Although these practices once had scientific support and popular appeal, both have been wholly debunked. So what do these discredited pseudosciences have to do with data science ethics? When we consider the methods, applications, and zeitgeist of their day, some eerie echoes reverberate across time to provide a cautionary tale.

So What Did Phrenologists and Eugenicists Do?

Phrenologists used scientific instruments such as tape measures and calipers to record the size and map the contours of people's heads. They believed the brain was an organ that grew or atrophied from natural predispositions or repeated use, and thus the size, shape, and bumps of a person's head reflected the growth of the brain underneath. They used their measurements of these features, along with behavioral observations, to infer certain aspects of personality and character.

Eugenicists used similar techniques but measured the whole body, focusing especially on physiological differences. Grounding their work in a form of "social Darwinism," they inferred that these measurements pointed to the superiority or inferiority of certain racial characteristics, and they encouraged processes like selective breeding to improve population health. For well over a hundred years, the "sciences" of phrenology and eugenics were well regarded as attempts to understand human behavior and physiological variation, especially since they were supported by seemingly unbiased scientific measurements.

So What Was the Problem?

Although phrenology and eugenics had accurate measurement tools and well-documented findings, the results were based on false assumptions, poorly collected data, and nonrepresentative samples. Although phrenologists constructed their models empirically, the underlying mental faculties that they inferred from those measurements were created by studying friends whom they believed had those faculties (convenience samples) and were tested on inmates of jails and asylums (biased samples). Eugenicists also were selective in the groups they compared, primarily using the tools and findings to support the deeply held stereotypes and racist ideologies of the time (confirmation bias). Ultimately, eugenics research became the foundation of Nationalsozialistische Rassenhygiene, or "National Socialist racial hygiene," of Germany's Nazi regime, which led to the deaths of nearly 10 million individuals who were supposedly inferior. Although we can now look back on these methods and critique them, it is also easy to understand how individuals at the time may have believed these conclusions, which were shrouded in the cloak of science.

What About Data Science?

Data science is a quantitative science based on massive amounts of continuously created data, analyzed quickly by complex algorithms, apparently at population-level scale, and free of a priori assumptions. It is easy to see why it is gaining widespread acceptance across business and society. Data scientists spend a great amount of time developing models and drawing conclusions from apparently "naturally occurring" phenomena, which in most cases are the trails that we leave in our digital lives. Not unlike the bumps on our heads, the length of our legs, or the shape of our noses, these digital trails are things that tell us something important about ourselves as humans in a society...right?

In his book *Everybody Lies*, Seth Stephens-Davidowitz convincingly and compellingly illustrates how Google Trends data offers insights into almost Freudian-like subconscious human behavior.[1] This is part of the power of data science—it can tell us things about ourselves that even we may not be aware of (or are too scared to admit to). On the other hand, Cathy O'Neil, in her book *Weapons of Math Destruction*, argues that AI and predictive algorithms are only as good as the data fed into them, and more often than not, the results of these apparently unbiased algorithms and models are nothing more than a replication of existing social inequities.[2] Rather than giving us information to predict the unknown, O'Neil provides examples of ways that data science techniques penalize, marginalize, and disenfranchise those who are already at risk in our society. Many others have also uncovered the faulty assumptions underlying AI algorithms designed more for efficiency than accuracy; the racial and gender bias of some facial recognition algorithms; online advertising that shows high-income jobs to men more often than to women; crime predicting and criminal sentencing algorithms that discriminate against the poor and people of color; the opacity of the secondary data market that unfairly discriminates against people in the insurance and credit market; and hiring algorithms that have violated the Americans with Disabilities Act.

Just like craniometer or femur length measurements, data science tools may be accurate in what they measure, but the conclusions drawn may be no better than equating an enlarged lobe in rear section 21 to "amativeness." Unless data scientists collaborate with subject matter experts when developing their data and methods, their conclusions could be based on faulty assumptions or on insufficient or biased data. The major problem? AI algorithms involve complex mathematics and computer programming beyond the understanding of most people, but people trust them because "numbers are unbiased." The complexity of data science methods often means it is difficult to interrogate algorithms, leaving them shrouded in the invisibility cloak of science. Excessive belief in something because it is done scientifically is *scientism*, not science.

---

1 Seth Stephens-Davidowitz, *Everybody Lies: Big Data, New Data, and What the Internet Can Tell Us About Who We Really Are* (New York: Dey Street Books, 2017).

2 Cathy O'Neil, *Weapons of Math Destruction: How Big Data Increases Inequality and Threatens Democracy* (New York: Crown, 2016). *https://weaponsofmathdestructionbook.com*.

Conclusions

Although organizations, professional bodies, academic institutions, and even policy-making bodies have attempted to create ethical guidelines (e.g., GDPR and the California Consumer Privacy Act) for the collection and uses of data to limit the risks to individuals and protected groups, these efforts mostly fall into the category of "reactive" ethics. The impact of these efforts is as of yet as unclear as many of the algorithms and statistical techniques they are attempting to influence.

It is imperative that data scientists become intentional about collaborating with other scientists, scrutinize the data they use, develop ethical codes to follow, and be open to critique of their methods. This is essential to avoid being painted into the same corner of scientism and logical fallacies that helped bring down other, less rigorous scientific movements of the past. Otherwise, we may find our textbooks and framed data visualizations in the dusty antique shops of the 22nd century.

Leadership for the Future: How to Approach Ethical Transparency

Rado Kotorov

CEO, Trendalyze Inc.

Aside from identifying ethical issues, organizations need to be prepared to address their role and their employees' role in making moral decisions. I do not believe that companies should have an obligation to teach their employees ethics. I am a firm believer that a business's purpose is to deliver goods and services in an efficient and profitable way. In this respect, I side with Milton Friedman's article "The Social Responsibility of Business Is to Increase Its Profits" (*https://oreil.ly/NhctK*). Leave moral and ethical education to the family, educational institutions, and religious and other belief-based organizations.

Yet we live in a technologically complex world in which moral and ethical issues are quite complex and confusing. Ignoring them by closing our eyes is not the right choice. I believe that companies have the duty to acknowledge the moral and ethical concerns of employees. Employees also have the right and obligation to raise such concerns.

The juxtaposition of balancing a business's obligation to efficiency and profitability and acknowledging workforce concerns around ethics has led me to conclude that establishing full ethical transparency in organizations is the best route forward. Financial transparency has produced miracles for organizations, leading to more accountability and better performance. Similarly, ethical transparency will help employees and organizations make choices that they can proudly defend, thus alleviating everyone from the burden of moral dilemmas.

Let's briefly examine two common ethical practices.

1. Playing God

This type of choice is well known in ethics and involves someone making decisions about the lives and deaths of other people, most frequently in exchange for some larger social benefit. These are typically known as utilitarian decisions. For example, imagine a programmer being tasked with developing the rules system for an autonomous car. Naturally, the programmer will try to save as many lives as possible in the event of an accident. But where this is not possible, how would the rule be constructed to choose between two individuals? What if the choice was between a man and a woman, or between a child and an adult? Another example is when decisions are made to eradicate species in nature. Imagine a bioengineer being tasked with creating a gene that eradicates all malaria-carrying mosquitoes. How are such choices made? Both of these dilemmas are created by advances in technology and thus have rarely been taught or examined by the institutions that have traditionally instilled ethics.

2. Moral Blinding

Moral blinding poses a different issue. Technologies can be developed in a way that completely obfuscates their purpose and final use from employees. For example, a data scientist may be asked to build a psychographic profiling algorithm for a marketing recommendation system that will match site visitors with vacation packages, when in fact the algorithm will be used for political profiling to influence voter choices. Companies may do so to protect trade secrets or because they know that the moral issues can be a distraction in the work process or a deterrent to finding employees. Sooner or later, employees will discover the real issues, and some of them may not be able to cope with the moral burden.

The question, then, is: should moral blinding be allowed? My position is that it should not. If an employee is developing an accident choice algorithm for autonomous cars, they should know that, because they are hardcoding a life-and-death choice. They should not be told that they are building an algorithm for a video game. Or if they *are* told that, they should also be told that the company may license the algorithm to autonomous car manufacturers. This will certainly affect how the algorithm is built, or whether the employee will even build such an algorithm.

How Should Companies Tackle Such Issues?

Within the framework of ethical transparency, companies and employees have three key obligations:

- Disclose potential ethical issues in the workplace
- Research and educate employees on ethical issues
- Document their individual and mutual stances on ethical issues

These three rules provide a framework for discussion. Today, most ethical problems will be created in the companies that produce new technologies. Hence, the discussion needs to start there and then be extended to engage society. Tech leaders have to step up and be ethical leaders, as they know best what their technologies can and cannot do.

I acknowledge that the industry is entering some uncharted waters and that ethical issues in the tech world are new. Some of the ethical issues we will face will test our human beliefs, but no progress has ever been made over the centuries without tackling hard issues. Open and structured dialogue has to take place for tech ethics to evolve.

Rules and Rationality

Christof Wolf Brenner

Consultant, Know-Center GmbH

In Isaac Asimov's famous science fiction stories, a hierarchical set of laws acts as the centerpiece to ensure ethical behavior of artificial moral agents. These robots—part computer, part machine—can efficiently handle complex tasks that would otherwise require human-level minds to complete.

Asimov argues that his ruleset is the only suitable foundation for the interaction between rational human beings and robots that adapt and flexibly choose their own course of action. Today, almost 80 years after the first iteration of the laws was devised in 1942, die-hard fans still argue that Asimov's laws are sufficient to guide moral decision making. However, looking at the ruleset as finalized by Asimov in 1985, it becomes clear that, applied exclusively, these laws might not produce what we would call "good decisions":

Zeroth Law
> A robot may not harm humanity, or, by inaction, allow humanity to come to harm.

First Law
> A robot may not injure a human being, or, through inaction, allow a human being to come to harm.

Second Law
> A robot must obey the orders given it by human beings, except where such orders would conflict with the First Law.

Third Law
> A robot must protect its own existence, as long as such protection does not conflict with the First or Second Law.

Asimov's autonomous ethical agents can assess situations and act accordingly based on a combination of information about the world that they process and the aforementioned laws, which are imprinted in their artificial brains. However, as conflict between different laws arises, the robots are also able to reflect, reason, and reach sensible conclusions. This tiny and often overlooked detail provides a first inkling of how static rulesets might not be able to sufficiently support moral decision making on their own, and that Isaac Asimov was most likely aware of that. At the very least, even though he strongly promoted the exclusive application of the laws, his plots usually revolve around fringe cases in which no clear decision could be reached and therefore further reasoning would be required. Consider, if you will, accidents involving autonomous vehicles in a setup similar to the famous trolley problem:

> A fully autonomous car—a robot in Asimovian terminology—is transporting a human being (A) to its desired destination. Suddenly, in a twist of fate, some living being (B) appears on the road. The artificial intelligence (i.e., the computer) that controls the vehicle (i.e., the machine) must come to a decision within a fraction of a second: take evasive action or continue straight ahead. If it does try to dodge B, the vehicle skids and hits a tree, A dies, and B survives. If not, A survives, but B dies. For simplification purposes, we shall assume that collateral damage is negligible or identical in both cases.

Based on this fringe scenario, we can derive two major issues with Asimov's laws. First, if the robotic car had to decide between harm to human beings and harm to nonhuman beings, the nonhuman beings always lose. This results in speciesist robots—that is, robots that have a bias for or against a being because of its species. If B were a group or one of the last of a kind of animals, we surely should at least consider the implications of running them or it over.

Second, the laws are not tailored to support decision making when different levels of harm to humans may occur. If all potential outcomes of a scenario were to involve harm to a human being, the ruleset would not be able to guide us to a decision: if all alternatives comply with the rules, they are equally good. If the outcome would involve either one human losing an arm or another human losing both arms, there would be no preference. Rather, Asimov's laws are designed purely to prioritize groups of human beings or humanity as a whole over everything else. Even if it were easy for us to rationally argue for one course of action over another, the robot would not be able to do so if it were only following the laws.

If Asimov's laws were to be taken as the basis for ethical decision making by robots, they would additionally need to be able to rationally argue for better outcomes or against worse outcomes in fringe cases. Rationality would need to be the glue between the laws. But then why use static laws in the first place? Wouldn't it be easier to just use our own rationality to decide what acts are good?

Understanding Passive Versus Proactive Ethics

Bill Schmarzo

Chief Innovation Officer, Hitachi Vantara

Several friends have challenged me to get involved in the AI ethics discussion. I certainly do not have any special ethics training. But then again, maybe I do. I've been going to church most Sundays (not just on Christmas Eve) since I was a kid, and have been taught a multitude of "ethics" lessons from the Bible. So, respectfully, let me take my best shot at sharing my thoughts about the critical importance of the AI ethics topic.

What Is AI Ethics?

Ethics is defined as the *moral principles* that govern a person's behavior or actions—the principles of "right and wrong" that are generally accepted by an individual or a social group. "Right or wrong" behaviors are not easily codified in a simple mathematical equation. And this is what makes the AI ethics discussion so challenging and so important.

To understand the AI ethics quandary, one must first understand how an AI model makes decisions:

1. The AI model relies on the creation of "AI rational agents" that interact with the environment to learn the *rewards and penalties* associated with actions.

2. The rewards and penalties against which the "AI rational agents" seek to make the "right" decisions are framed by the *AI utility function*.

3. To create an "AI rational agent" that makes the "right" decision, the AI utility function must comprise a holistic definition of *"value"* that includes financial/economic, operational, customer, societal, environmental, and spiritual values.

Bottom line: the "AI rational agent" determines "right" and "wrong" based on the definition of "value" as articulated in the AI utility function.

Simple, right?

It isn't the AI models that scare me. My experience to date is that AI models work great. But the thing is, AI models will strive to optimize exactly what humans have programmed them to optimize via the AI utility function.

And that's where we should focus the AI ethics conversation, because *humans tend to make poor decisions.* Just visit Las Vegas if you doubt that statement. The effort by humans to define the rules against which actions will be measured sometimes results in unintended consequences.

The Ramifications of Unintended Consequences

Shortcutting the process of defining the measures against which to monitor any complicated business initiative is naive...and ultimately dangerous. The article "10 Fascinating Examples of Unintended Consequences" (*https://oreil.ly/sExdR*) details actions "believed to be good" that ultimately led to disastrous outcomes, including:

- The SS *Eastland*, a badly designed and ungainly vessel, was intended to be made safer by adding several lifeboats. Unfortunately, the extra weight of the lifeboats caused the ship to capsize, thereby trapping and killing 800 passengers below the decks.

- The Treaty of Versailles dictated surrender terms to Germany to end World War I. Unfortunately, the terms empowered Adolf Hitler and his followers, leading to World War II.

- The Smokey Bear Wildfire Prevention campaign created decades of highly successful fire prevention. Unfortunately, this disrupted normal fire processes that are vital to the health of forests. The result is mega-fires that destroy everything in their path, even huge pine trees that had stood for several thousand years through normal fire conditions.

One can mitigate unintended consequences and the costs associated with false positives and false negatives by *bringing together diverse and even conflicting perspectives* to thoroughly debate and define the AI utility function.

Defining the AI Utility Function

As mentioned earlier, to create a "rational AI agent" that understands how to differentiate between "right" and "wrong" actions, the AI model must work off of a holistic AI utility function that contemplates "value" across a variety of often conflicting dimensions—for example, increase financial value, while also reducing operational costs and risks, *and* improving customer satisfaction and likelihood to recommend, *and* improving societal value and quality of life, *and* reducing environmental impact and carbon footprint.

And ethics *must* be one of those value dimensions if we are to create AI utility functions that can lead AI to the right decisions. This brings us to a very important concept: the difference between *passive ethics* and *proactive ethics*.

Passive Ethics Versus Proactive Ethics

When debating ethics, we must contemplate the dilemma of passive ethics versus proactive ethics. And it starts with a story that many of us learned at a very young age—the parable of the Good Samaritan.

The story is of a Jewish traveler who is stripped of his clothing, beaten, and left for dead alongside the road. First a priest and then a Levite come by, but both cross the road to avoid the man. Finally, a Samaritan happens upon the battered traveler and helps him. The Samaritan bandages his wounds, transports him to an inn on his beast of burden to rest and heal, and pays for the traveler's care and accommodations at the inn.

The priest and the Levite both operated under the passive ethics philosophy of "do no harm." Technically, they did nothing wrong. The Samaritan operated under the proactive ethics philosophy of seeking to "do good."

The "do no harm" mindset is totally insufficient in a world driven by AI models. Our AI models must embrace proactive ethics by seeking to "do good"; that is, every AI model and the AI utility function that guides the operations of the AI model must proactively seek to do good.

There is a *huge* difference between "do no harm" and "do good," as the parable of the Good Samaritan well demonstrates.

Summary

Let's consider a simple ethics test that I call the "Mom test." Here's how it works: if you were to tell your mom of a decision or action you took in a particular matter, would she be proud of or disappointed in your choice? That simple test would probably minimize many of our AI ethics concerns.

As humans define the AI utility function that serves to distinguish between right and wrong decisions, we *must* understand the differences between passive ethics and proactive ethics.

Be Careful with "Decisions of the Heart"

Hugh Watson

Professor of MIS, Terry College of Business, University of Georgia

Today, companies and government organizations are increasingly using advanced analytics like deep learning to partially or fully automate decision making. Analytics is employed to make lending decisions, recommend probation or prison sentencing, screen job applicants, and more. While these algorithms can result in faster, cheaper, more efficient, and even fairer decision making, they are not without risk. Cathy O'Neil, in her influential book *Weapons of Math Destruction* (Crown), and others argue that algorithms can increase inequality, deny services and opportunities, and even threaten democracy.

The conversation between the Tin Woodman and the Scarecrow in *The Wonderful Wizard of Oz* by L. Frank Baum provides an interesting perspective on the need for including "heart" as well as brains (i.e., algorithms) when automating decisions:

> *"I don't know enough,"* replied the Scarecrow cheerfully. *"My head is stuffed with straw, you know, and that is why I am going to Oz to ask him for some brains."* *"Oh, I see,"* said the Tin Woodman. *"But, after all, brains are not the best things in the world."* *"Have you any?"* inquired the Scarecrow. *"No, my head is quite empty,"* answered the Woodman, *"but once I had brains, and a heart also; so, having tried them both, I should much rather have a heart."*

When decisions can significantly affect people's lives, the decision-making process should include "heart" as well as brains. The applications that are developed should be free of bias and not unfairly discriminate against classes of people; comply with the increasingly complex set of laws and regulations; not damage a company's brand; and allow individuals to opt out and/or obtain an explanation of why a decision was made and seek remediation.

When building models, be careful not to introduce unintentional errors and biases, as can happen with a poor selection of model training/testing data. For example, a prescreening bias can occur when using data that has biases that were baked into previous processes (e.g., a college admissions model that uses only the data of students who were admitted in the past). You must know how to handle categorical data that has only a small percentage of observations in a category of importance. Also, you should be sure to constantly monitor a model's performance for accuracy and how it affects different classes of people.

The EU's GDPR, which took effect in May 2018, and the California Consumer Privacy Act (CCPA) of January 2020 both place limitations on how personal data can be used and shared. GDPR requires opt-in authorization to collect any personal data; any requests to use personal data must be specific and unambiguous; the collection and use of personal data must be for a specific, well-understood business purpose; and citizens have the right to have their personal data deleted (the so-called right to be forgotten). Article 22 of GDPR states that "[individuals] shall have the right not to be subject to a decision based solely on automated processing." CCPA has similarities to GDPR, but with a focus on consumer privacy rights and company-required disclosures to customers. For example, companies must have a link on their websites titled "Do Not Sell My Personal Information."

Some uses of algorithms are legal but are bad for business. An oft-cited example is Target using predictive modeling to identify women who are likely pregnant and then sending them pregnancy-related coupons. The blowback occurred when a 16-year-old girl received such coupons and her father complained that the coupons promoted teenage pregnancy (later he learned that she was indeed pregnant). The story was told in the *New York Times*, *Fortune*, and other widely read publications and tarnished Target's brand.

People should be able to ask for and receive an explanation of why a decision was made. The US Public Policy Council of the Association for Computing Machinery (ACM) and the ACM Europe Policy Committee, working both separately and together, codified seven principles for ensuring that personal data and algorithms are used fairly. The fourth guiding principle is the need for explanation—the ability to communicate, when asked, an algorithm's logic in human terms. Individuals should also be able to challenge an automated decision and/or learn what can be done to remediate it. This requirement can be challenging because of the "black-box" nature of some of the most powerful predictive models (e.g., deep learning) and can lead to the use of models that have slightly less predictive power but are more explainable in human terms (e.g., decision trees).

To meet the demand for the legal and ethical use of algorithms, especially those that involve decisions of the heart, data scientists need to adopt a broader perspective on what their responsibilities are, and companies need to expand their governance (e.g., people, committees, and processes) to include their legal staff and businesspeople who are in touch with the customer.

Fairness in the Age of Algorithms

Anna Jacobson

Candidate for Masters in Data Science, UC Berkeley

Of all the exciting work taking place in the field of data science, the machine learning algorithm (MLA) is one of the advancements that has garnered the most popular attention—and to many, it is the area of data science that holds the most promise for the future. However, as with all powerful technologies, MLAs also carry the risk of becoming destructive forces in the world.

Early applications of MLAs included email spam filtering, image recognition, and recommender systems for entertainment. In these low-stakes settings, the cost of any errors is low, usually a minor inconvenience at worst. However, the cost of errors in MLAs has dramatically increased as they have begun to be applied to human beings, such as in predictive policing. Despite the apparently objective process of training MLAs, it sometimes results in algorithms that, while computationally correct, produce outputs that are biased and unjust from a human perspective. And in high-stakes settings, MLAs that produce unfair results can do enormous damage.

Fairness is an elusive concept. In the practice of machine learning, the quality of an algorithm is judged based on its accuracy (the percentage of correct results), its precision (the ability not to label as positive a sample that is negative), or its recall (the ability to find all the positive samples). Deciding which of these three measures is the best proxy for fairness is not always straightforward, and improvements in one metric can cause decreases in others.

Fundamentally, MLAs are only as fair as the data itself. If the underlying data is biased in any way, its structural inequalities may not only be replicated but may even be amplified in the algorithm. ML engineers must be aware of their own blind spots; all the small decisions they make about their training data can be as impactful as their engineering techniques. Even more problematic, however, is that societal problems such as discrimination and exclusion are deeply rooted in the world around us—and consequently, they are inherent in the data that we extract from the world.

Achieving algorithmic fairness, it seems, is as difficult as achieving fairness in human-led systems. Human systems are biased in all of the ways that algorithmic systems are biased—and humans are additionally biased in ways that machines cannot be. However, algorithmic systems can be both less visible and less transparent: often, people are unaware that an algorithm is being used to make a decision that affects them—and even if they are aware, the algorithm is presented as a complex, unknowable "black box" that is impossible to see, much less understand.

Three clear steps must be taken to improve algorithmic fairness:

1. First, we must do better to ensure the quality of the data being used to train the algorithms. For instance, all subjects should have an equal chance of being represented in the data, which means that additional effort may be required to obtain data from traditionally underrepresented groups. Models also must be retrained periodically with new data to start to root out historical biases, despite the added expense that this incurs.

2. Second, within the field of machine learning, processes must be standardized across the industry to eradicate as much bias as possible from the engineering process. This should include a variety of approaches, including unconscious bias training for engineers similar to the training that intelligence analysts routinely undergo; engineering protocols akin to the protocols of scientific research, such as rigorous peer review; and independent post-implementation auditing of algorithmic fairness in which the quality of an algorithm is judged not only by standard engineering metrics but also by how it impacts the most vulnerable people affected by it.

3. Third, MLAs must be brought into the light in our society, so that we are all aware of when they are being used in ways that impact our lives; a well-informed citizenry is essential to holding the groups that create and use these algorithms accountable to ensure their fairness. We are constitutionally guaranteed the right to due process and the right to equal protection; we should interpret these rights to include the right to know what data about ourselves is being used as input and the right to access any output that is generated about ourselves when MLAs are used in constitutionally protected contexts.

Taking these steps will require profound changes throughout our society, by many stakeholders and across many domains. In a world governed by laws and conventions that never envisioned the power of the MLA, the responsibility to strive for fairness in machine learning systems belongs to everyone who works in or with them. As MLAs become more prevalent in our society, it will become increasingly critical that the humans in the loop address this issue to ensure that this technology fulfills its promise to do good rather than its potential to do harm.

References

- Vyacheslav Polonski, "Mitigating Algorithmic Bias in Predictive Justice: 4 Design Principles for AI Fairness," Towards Data Science, November 23, 2018, *https://oreil.ly/TIKHr*.

- Gal Yona, "A Gentle Introduction to the Discussion on Algorithmic Fairness," Towards Data Science, October 5, 2017, *https://oreil.ly/NbVOD*.

- Moritz Hardt, "How Big Data Is Unfair," Medium, September 26, 2014, *https://oreil.ly/kNrtx*.

- Julia Angwin, Jeff Larson, Surya Mattu, and Lauren Kirchner, "Machine Bias," ProPublica, May 23, 2016, *https://oreil.ly/b41AW*.

- Hugo-Bowne Anderson, "Weapons of Math Destruction (with Cathy O'Neil)," November 26, 2018, in *DataFramed*, podcast, 55:53, *https://oreil.ly/5ScpO*.

- Kate Crawford and Jason Schultz, "Big Data and Due Process: Toward a Framework to Redress Predictive Privacy Harms," *Boston College Law Review* 55, no. 1 (January 29, 2014), *https://oreil.ly/X_W8h*.

- "Statement of Concern About Predictive Policing by ACLU and 16 Civil Rights Privacy, Racial Justice, and Technology Organizations," American Civil Liberties Union, August 31, 2016, *https://oreil.ly/_hZHO*.

- Sam Corbett-Davies, Emma Pierson, Avi Feller, and Sharad Goel, "A Computer Program Used for Bail and Sentencing Decisions Was Labeled Biased Against Blacks. It's Actually Not That Clear," *Washington Post*, October 17, 2016, *https://oreil.ly/cQMJz*.

- Mark Puente, "LAPD to Scrap Some Crime Data Programs After Criticism," *Los Angeles Times*, April 5, 2019, *https://oreil.ly/JI7NA*.

Data Science Ethics: What Is the Foundational Standard?

Mario Vela

Principal Data Scientist, US Cellular Corp

To address the question of ethics in any arena, including data science, we first need to ask ourselves what standard should be used to define what is "good" and what is "bad." The importance of knowing such a standard is fundamental, since choosing the wrong standard can generate false definitions of what is "good" and "bad," with a variety of consequences in society and, in this case, in the practice and use of data science. Hence, the standard must be absolute, because if it changes, then the meaning of "good" and "bad" is lost, and we fall into moral relativism.

Peter Kreeft suggests that, to talk about ethics, we must ask ourselves: what is the moral standard that we use in our daily lives?[1] If we cannot readily answer such a question, we should embark on the search for the answer using logic and reason. Kreeft argues that, to answer this type of question, we have two options: either our core moral values are objective, or they are subjective; they are discovered as scientists discover the laws of physics, or they are created as the rules of a game or a piece of art. He also notes that premodern cultures believed that core moral values are objective, and it is only in recent times that society started to believe that those core moral values are subjective and human-made and can be changed over time. The latter scenario is called *moral relativism*, a widespread and dangerous ideology in modern times.

Regardless of which option we believe, there are significant consequences to the goal of achieving a good set of moral rules for data science. For instance, if we believe moral values are objective, we should "find" them, but if we believe they are subjective, then we must "create" them.

---

1 Peter Kreeft, *Ethics: A History of Moral Thought* (Recorded Books, 2004).

For data science, the practical implications are that we should take a position about ethics regarding objective or subjective moral values. If we decide that moral values are objective, we should identify the unchanging core moral values and build our ethical analytics practices around them. In contrast, if we say that moral values are subjective, then we need to create those moral values and agree on using them among the community.

Each option has challenges, but we know only one must be true. Subjective moral values immediately move us into a dangerous moral relativism, which can be abused by interested groups and expose adoption issues, since not all interested parties might agree on them. On the other hand, objective moral values present the challenge that, in order not to fall in a subjective approach, these moral principles need to be discovered and cannot be *created* by humans. They necessarily need to exist independent of us, and because of that, they present the benefit of being unquestionable and provide less resistance for adoption. Hence, this search should take us into metaphysical research and inquiry.

I want to propose that it is in this metaphysical inquiry that we will find not only the necessary objective ethical standard for our data science practice but also a beautiful and fulfilling encounter—a personal encounter that will transform our lives and provide clarity on topics as complex as ethics in data science.

Understand Who Your Leaders Serve

Hassan Masum

Senior Director of Analytics, Prodigy Education

You may have good intentions when it comes to ethics and technology. But you will find it difficult to put your good intentions into practice if your leaders don't truly serve the people you want to help.

That's why it is important to *understand who your leaders serve*. Are the leaders of your organization self-centered, or are they servant-leaders? Do your leaders treat the people your organization serves as exploitable resources or as partners to help thrive? When trying to answer questions like these, take time to understand what your leaders say and do.

If the leaders at the top of your organization serve the same people you want to help (which hopefully includes your team and your clients or customers), then you have some hope of putting ethics into practice. (You will rarely find that *easy*, but it may at least be *possible*.) If not, then you will have to continually swim against organizational currents to stay ethically afloat.

If your leaders truly serve the people you want to serve, then applying values can help you and your leaders to serve more effectively. Some values that are particularly relevant to data scientists include transparency, rationality, intellectual humility, and constructive skepticism. If you are a master at living values like these, then show or teach those values to your colleagues. Be humble: a value that is critical to you may be optional in someone else's context, even when you both serve the same people.

Understanding the "values chain" from yourself on up will clarify your likely ethical operating space. Ask yourself: do I understand the values my organization is living by, and how these values will help or hurt us and the people we serve? What are the essential values I'd like to see in my organization to help it survive long-term and help me feel proud of working here? Can I collaborate with others to promote essential values that are being overlooked? If not, do I want to work here?

At some point your ethical environment may be a factor in prompting you to switch jobs or search for a more values-aligned opportunity. You may feel that you want your energy and talent to serve values you agree with. If you feel strongly about this, then ask questions about culture and ethics when seeking or creating a new opportunity. What would your interviewer's organization *not* do, even if it was profitable and legal? What governs and guides the organization beyond the goal of maximizing short-term profits? How does it align business success with serving its users' best interests? How would you answer these questions as an entrepreneur yourself?

Even if you feel your leaders mean well in principle, they (and you) are influenced by the broader environment within which your organization lives. A common influence is from the omnipresent financial pressures in a profit-maximizing and competitive landscape. When and why should you say "no" when a legal but ethically debatable "yes" could help you grow your business or defend it against competitors?

To tackle pressures like these, you may wish to seek perspectives from outside your organization. Have others faced similar issues, and if so, how did they handle them? Is there an industry, academic, or nonprofit group you could join that could help you navigate the shoals of ethical decision making? Is a sector-wide solution needed to set algorithmic standards or advocate for better regulation that stops a race to the bottom? Or is the logical scope society-wide, suggesting political and civic coalitions?

As your scope of concern widens, you may feel overwhelmed. One way to handle that is to focus on the ethical scale you feel most engaged with (whether that is your team, organization, specialization, sector, or society) and seek others who feel similarly.

Whichever scale you focus on, there are some critical questions to answer: what is your system for, and who does it serve? How is this being embedded into rules, incentives, and algorithms? (See Tim O'Reilly's book *WTF? What's the Future and Why It's Up to US* [Harper Business] for context.)

Whether building a human team or an AI or analytic solution, you can make better choices if you understand who your leaders serve—and who *you* should serve when it is your turn to lead.

PART II

Data Science and Society

This section shows how societal norms intersect with the ethical issues we face when pursuing analytics and data science initiatives. The submissions help to put ethical data science in a broader context.

Unbiased ≠ Fair: For Data Science, It Cannot Be Just About the Math

Doug Hague

Executive Director, School of Data Science at UNC Charlotte

As I have been thinking through the ethical implications in data science, one thing has become glaringly obvious to me: data scientists like math! Nothing very surprising there. But as we go about our work building models and making great predictions, we tend to reduce the conversation about ethics to mathematical terms. Is my prediction for Caucasian Americans the same as for African Americans? Are female predictions equivalent to male ones? We develop confusion matrices and measure the accuracy of our predictions. Or maybe the sensitivity (true positive rate) or the specificity (true negative rate) is important, so we balance that for various subgroups. Unfortunately, mathematicians have shown that while we may be able to balance the accuracy, specificity, or other measures of bias for real datasets, we cannot balance them all and make perfectly unbiased models. So we do the best we can within the framework we are provided and declare that our model is fair.

After studying the issues and applications, I assert that models that balance bias are not fair. Fairness really does not pay attention to mathematics. It pays attention to individual viewpoints, societal and cultural norms, and morals. In other words, fairness is defined by social systems and philosophy.

For example, in criminal justice, recidivism models predict whether a person arrested will commit another crime if released on bond. As an indicted individual, you believe that the false positive rate should be as low as possible so you are not kept in jail when you should not be. The average citizen, however, wants the false negative rate as low as possible to minimize the number of people who are let out and go on to commit a new crime. Balancing these two is a trade-off that both sides will say is not fair. And we have not even started to discuss the bias in the data and in the system that has resulted in disproportionately higher numbers of African Americans being incarcerated.

As one considers the ethical implications of data science, one quickly gets to debating the cultural and moral norms of the society that the model is being deployed into. As a data science team deploys a model, those cultural norms must be considered. Philosophies of utilitarianism and its derivatives are prevalent within Western society; here, the role of overall good is debated, and the balance between individual good and common good is discussed. Different philosophical constructs are favored in other cultures and geographies. Understanding which cultures a model will touch and how and where it will touch them is important to reaching for fairness for the deployed model.

Understanding the system within which a model is deployed is just as important. As models are deployed, they enter an operational system. Depending on the specifics of the situation, there frequently are decisions that get made after the model prediction. Often data scientists develop and measure model accuracy based on what mathematics predicts. However, measurement of the entire system and decisions that occur *after* the model prediction are just as important. Additionally, human-in-the-loop models are often held up as being even more accurate; however, are they also less biased and fairer? With a human in the loop, bias may creep back into decisions. Also, if there is more than one decision maker, different people will bring different levels of information as well as cultural differences. Each of these differences can easily result in system bias and fairness issues even if the model was tuned and prepared to be as fair as possible. Framing the operations and measuring performance should occur for both the model outcome as well as the system outcome. I believe many lawsuits over fairness and discrimination occur because both sides frame the situation differently. Each side is "right" within their framing, but which frame will a jury conclude to be fair?

As responsible data scientists, we should expand our ethical considerations beyond the mathematical bias of our model to include cultural and societal definitions of fairness, and our model deployment should consider framing the outcomes of the system and not just the model predictions.

Trust, Data Science, and Stephen Covey

James Taylor

CEO, Decision Management Solutions

Trust is a big deal when it comes to data science. "Black-box" algorithms, concerns about bias, and a sense that data scientists may know everything about the data but nothing about the business all undermine trust in data science models. Indeed, building data science models that can and will be trusted is regarded as a critical issue for many data science teams.

Stephen Covey once wrote a famous list about trust—the 13 behaviors of a high-trust leader. Five of these behaviors relate very specifically to leadership (talk straight, demonstrate concern, right wrongs, show loyalty, keep commitments), but the others provide a great framework for building trust in data science.

Listen First

Perhaps the most important way data science teams can build trust in their models is to begin listening to their business partners—that is, asking businesspeople how they decide and how they would *like* to decide, and really listening to their answers. If business partners feel heard, then they are much more likely to trust the solution the data science team creates. Working with them to develop a decision model, for instance, creates a shared understanding of the decision and a sense of being heard.

Extend Trust

Data scientists who want their models to be trusted need to extend trust to their business partners. Businesspeople can be wrong about what moves the dial, about what the threshold should be, about what customer segments the company has, and about much else besides. Data scientists should resist the temptation to just assume that the data can answer all these questions without input from the business experts. That would give the impression that the businesspeople's expertise is not trusted and make it harder to deliver trusted data science. Begin by extending trust.

Clarify Expectations

Before building a data science model to influence the decision, make sure expectations are clear. If the data science will fit easily into the current decision, improving its accuracy, say so. If the data science is likely to disrupt the current approach and require significant organizational change, then say that. Use the decision model to clarify expectations for the use of the data science being developed.

Confront Reality

Do not pretend that the organization will change the way it makes decisions just because the data science team tells it to. The reality is that many decisions are constrained by regulations, driven by policies, and motivated by goals and objectives. A new data science result may be able to improve the decision making "in theory," but to improve it "in practice" you must confront reality. A shared understanding of the decision-making approach, in the form of a decision model, is key.

Create Transparency

Transparency in data science—explainable AI—is well established. Real success will also require transparency about how the data science will be used. You must be able to show how the score is used to change decision making and impact business results. A clear, shared understanding of the decision making that wraps around the data science is key.

Deliver Results

Lift and model accuracy are not results. Improved business outcomes are results. The data science team's job is to improve business results, which means improving the way decisions are actually made and not just producing a data science output. Deliver the result your business partners care about. Use the decision model to put data science results in a business context.

Practice Accountability

Be accountable to your business partners. Remember that they have other things to do besides work with you, and other projects they must support.

Do not forget that they have business objectives to meet and that the data science needs to help them meet those objectives. Be accountable to the business problem, not just to the analytic solution.

Get Better

One of the most important lessons in data science is that continuous improvement is key. Don't try to develop a perfect model. Develop a minimum viable data science product and get it into production to see how it affects business outcomes. Capture data about how decisions were made and how the data science was (or wasn't) used. See how well this worked out in business terms. Improve the data science. Repeat. Don't ride off into the sunset when you have built a model; focus on how you can help the business get better now and in the future.

Trust is important in data science. To build trust, you must listen first, extend trust, clarify expectations, confront reality, create transparency, deliver results, practice accountability, and get better.

Ethics Must Be a Cornerstone of the Data Science Curriculum

Linda Burtch

Managing Director, Burtch Works

We've all seen the headlines: companies gathering personal data without permission, accidentally deploying discriminatory algorithms, or selling access to private data, as well as other examples of corporate data culture gone wrong.

In my other piece for this book, I address the responsibility of the corporate side when it comes to addressing the work culture that creates these types of ethical issues. This led me to wonder: how can we instill more ethical consideration into the data science community at large to prevent these types of disasters?

Ethics has long been part of the curriculum for those pursuing finance degrees and MBAs more generally, and in the past few years especially, we've seen more of these courses in data science master's programs and even in online learning programs. In my view, to address the growing ethical quandaries that this age of seemingly boundless personal data provides us with, ethics needs to be made a cornerstone of any quantitative learning program, including traditional academic degrees, data science boot camps, MOOCs (massive open online courses), and everything in between.

I know, I know. The math, statistics, and computer science curriculum for a data scientist is already overflowing, and the scope of learning is daunting. And I'm aware that adding more to the aspiring data scientist's academic plate is a big ask. However, data scientists must develop an understanding of the bigger picture for projects that they're working on, and of the ramifications their work may have for different groups. Algorithms that are not developed with existing social factors in mind can easily end up reinforcing the discriminatory practices that they might reveal if examined by a discerning data scientist. We've already seen how these situations can play out in notably sensitive areas such as health care, where privacy is paramount and access to care is not always equitable.

Data ethics programs must also address current legislation and considerations for the collection of personal data: are people aware of what data is being collected? Do they know how their data is being used? Do they have an option to opt out? Is their data being responsibly stored and protected? Is their data being sold to third parties without their consent?

Legislation in the digital age has been notably behind in this area, and in some cases this has led companies to simply ignore potential ethical ramifications because there are no existing laws. But for future generations of data scientists who will be tomorrow's business leaders, instilling this responsibility and big-picture thinking into their learning curricula will teach them to start thinking about these problems from the very beginning.

How can data scientists be expected to provide responsible analysis and insights to their companies if they are not taught how to consider all the potential angles in these situations? Even as laws and public opinions on privacy have evolved, they are certainly not keeping pace with the development of technology that can do great harm if left unchecked.

Additionally, instilling these types of critical thinking skills in regard to ethics will give data scientists the information they need to make more informed decisions about how to direct company strategy. I've repeatedly said that those who have a well-developed understanding of analytics should be in charge of running companies, and that understanding should include how analytics can be used responsibly to further a business's goals without opening the business up to potential scandal down the line.

As more of the world grows to depend on digital resources, the amount of data available for us to exploit is growing exponentially, and that growth shows no signs of stopping. I have no doubt that in five or ten years there will be even more ethical tangles for us to sort through, as we continue to integrate different data sources and find new ways to uncover the information we seek from data. Whether we navigate this process successfully will depend on whether quantitative professionals have been armed with the knowledge and ethical mindset necessary to critically evaluate the directions we're taking every step of the way. Developing this base of knowledge must start with the data science curriculum.

Data Storytelling: The Tipping Point Between Fact and Fiction

Brent Dykes

Author and Senior Director, Insights & Data Storytelling, Blast Analytics

Data and narrative have always had an interesting working relationship. While they are often intertwined, they are sometimes viewed as opposites. For example, if something is seen as "anecdotal," it is often approached with a hint (or maybe a heavy dose) of skepticism. Because it is based on personal experiences or accounts, anecdotal information is viewed as being less true or less reliable than factual information. Even the word "story" can be used as a synonym for a lie or misleading information. Because stories are typically more emotive in nature, they can be perceived as being manipulative.

On the other hand, facts have mostly enjoyed a reputation for being pure, trustworthy, and unbiased. When people demand "just the facts," they seek a higher standard of truth that is indisputable and untarnished by opinions or beliefs. However, in our current post-truth era, the reputation of factual information is now being threatened by falsehoods masquerading as "alternative" facts. Data that would never have been questioned in the past is now mistrusted simply because of who shared the information or because of its misalignment with the preferred messaging.

In combination, data and narrative can form a formidable union, each strengthening the other in areas where it is weak. In a post-truth environment, we must be even more disciplined in how we craft and tell stories with data. Even though data storytelling has been mostly associated with data visualization, narrative remains a critical pillar of data storytelling. How we form a story around our data is what will make our insights more engaging, persuasive, and memorable. However, we can encounter a tipping point at which the narrative can subjugate the numbers, and the facts can turn into fiction. If we want to share insights in a reliable, ethical manner, we must be mindful of the ways in which we can potentially cross this fact/fiction threshold.

Ideally, a data story should be the product of analysis or research. In other words, the data story is built on an evidence-based foundation. Problems can emerge when the narrative is formed before any data is involved. Rather than weaving a narrative around a related set of observations and insights, you're tempted to select only facts that fit the desired story. When the data must support a predetermined narrative, you may inadvertently or intentionally do the following:

- Limit yourself to a narrower dataset
- Massage the numbers so they align with your message
- Leave out context that could have clarified the data
- Misconstrue what the numbers actually mean
- Visualize the data in misleading ways
- Exclude or discredit conflicting data that undermines your narrative
- Overlook key discrepancies in the supporting data
- Rely on acceptable data from potentially questionable sources

Verifying a hypothesis or a hunch with data is different than cherry-picking facts to justify a decision or support an agenda. When you already have an intended storyline in mind (e.g., we made the right business decision), you have less flexibility to listen to what the numbers are really saying (e.g., it wasn't the best decision). The path your data story can take is more rigid, and its destination is fixed. Unless you're open to adjusting your narrative based on what the data reveals, you could potentially undermine the integrity of your entire data story.

If a narrative is unduly influencing the direction and selection of the data, your data story can inadvertently switch from being factual to being fictional. At that moment, the data becomes a dubious adornment rather than a sharp instrument within your data story. With data storytelling, the facts should always guide the narrative, not the reverse. Whenever data and narrative come together in the right way, they can form powerful, compelling data stories that are ethically sound—not fictional accounts that distort and mislead but factual ones that guide and inspire.

Informed Consent and Data Literacy Education Are Crucial to Ethics

Sherrill Hayes

Director, PhD in Analytics and Data Science,
Kennesaw State University

A key element to ethics of any kind is the idea of "informed consent" from the participants who are giving of themselves for the benefit of others. Informed consent is a central part of research ethics for any federally funded research or for the research that takes place inside most universities and colleges, but it is typically not required in research undertaken by private companies.

In the case of data ethics, it has not always been clear that individuals understand (or are even interested in) the terms and conditions they accept when downloading a new app or cookies on their web browser. Although "click-thru" consent has become an accepted way to pass legal tests, it does not always pass the ethical test of ensuring that people have an understanding of those terms and conditions. Thanks to initiatives like GDPR in Europe and the CCPA in the US, people are more aware of hidden terms and conditions and have ways of opting out of certain types of tracking. While people are happy to click "OK" to get things "for free," they have limited understanding that they are "paying" by giving access to their data, which is being used and/or resold to pay for their access. At the moment, there are still only limited options for those who want access to certain apps or materials on the web but choose to opt out. Effectively, opting out of sharing your data at this stage means you likely have no access to certain websites, apps, and other materials.

Given the broad impact that data science tools and technologies already have in people's everyday lives, it seems necessary that children and youth are exposed to these ideas and are able to effectively offer (or withdraw) their consent. This move will require developing formal curricula for secondary and postsecondary education that include a strong component of "data literacy." Ellen Mandinach and Edith Gummer define "data literacy" as

> the ability to understand and use data effectively to inform decisions….These skills include knowing how to identify, collect, organize, analyze, summarize, and prioritize data. They also include how to develop hypotheses, identify problems, interpret the data, and determine, plan, implement, and monitor courses of action.[1]

Developing a strategy for integrating data literacy into high school and college curricula presents two key challenges. First, data science is strongly quantitative and related to existing subjects like mathematics and statistics, which are classes that many students already find challenging and may opt out of when given the chance. Jennifer Priestley proposes a "Hierarchy of Data Science," wherein data scientists *must* learn the basics of mathematics as a starting point needed to appreciate core concepts from statistics and computer science, and then must develop the necessary skills related to modeling and classification and refine their ability to communicate results.[2] Second, the implications for people's individual, social, political, and economic lives extend far beyond learning mathematical formulas and programming languages, so these concepts need to go across all of the curriculum. To assist educators, I propose the following framework for helping to understand data literacy and integrate it into and across curricula:

Data Aware

> The first stage represents an awareness that the technology with which you are interacting is producing data. Individuals may be competent users of technology and yet not aware of the "data trails" they are creating through their interaction with technology. Individuals at this level need to develop some entry-level proficiency related to social media (social studies); the Internet of Things, or IoT (science and engineering); and data marketplaces (economics, mathematics). These individuals also need some statistical and computer science knowledge to understand the nature of data collection, coding fundamentals, basic statistical techniques (e.g., descriptive statistics, visualizations), and research design. To help them learn this information, students should be given case studies

---

1 Ellen B. Mandinach and Edith S. Gummer, "A Systemic View of Implementing Data Literacy in Educator Preparation," *Educational Researcher* 42, no. 1 (January 1, 2013): 30, *https://doi.org/ 10.3102/0013189X12459803.*

2 Jennifer Priestley, "Maslow's Hierarchy of Data Science: Why Math and Science Still Matter," Data Science Central blog, February 12, 2019, *https://oreil.ly/SFmnZ.*

---

in textbooks and could be assigned project-based learning (PBL) opportunities to work with teachers across subjects. This type of learning is appropriate for most high school and most early undergraduate curricula.

Data Informed

The second stage represents the ability to understand different forms of data. This includes recognition of data that is "structured" and "static" (e.g., survey data, transaction data) and of data that is "unstructured" and "in motion" (e.g., images, voice data, text data, sensor-based data). Basic skills such as organizing and cleaning data and more advanced techniques like data mining, text mining, and scraping should also be introduced. Recognition of different forms and analyses has implications for presentation of data to both academic and nonacademic audiences. This is appropriate for most undergraduate curricula and professional training.

Data Literate:

The third stage represents a deeper knowledge and understanding of the methodological strengths, weaknesses, and potential issues of various data forms, collection techniques, and analytical methodologies. Individuals move beyond packages (e.g., SAS, SPSS) to develop their own models and programs. This third stage is appropriate for advanced undergraduate students, graduate students, and academic researchers.

This data literacy model should complement existing disciplinary training in theories, research design, and qualitative research since these provide breadth and context. In addition, students should develop a deep appreciation for ethical treatment of the people represented by the information in the data. Developing this ground-up approach should help mitigate some of the ethical and research-quality issues emerging as a result of the shortcuts (e.g., one-year certificates, online courses) created to fill the data science skills gap. In skipping the science, methods, and ethics and going directly to analytical modeling and visualization, little if any consideration is given to how the algorithms embedded in "point and click" software actually work. Frequently, these exercises generate meaningless outputs—or worse, algorithms (unintentionally) built on biased data that have dire consequences for individuals, groups, and/or whole communities of people.[3] As more educators

---

3 Cathy O'Neil, *Weapons of Math Destruction: How Big Data Increases Inequality and Threatens Democracy* (New York: Crown, 2016). *https://weaponsofmathdestructionbook.com.*

incorporate data literacy strategies into their high school, undergraduate, and graduate curricula, this simplistic framework will require further modification; however, this should be a start for a dynamic conversation.

First, Do No Harm

Eric Schmidt

Global Director, Data & Analytics, Coca-Cola

It is October 2019, and I am presenting at a data science conference at the Historic Academy of Medicine in Atlanta, Georgia. Unceremoniously tucked away in a corner of the men's room is a bust of Hippocrates, the father of professional ethics, and a plaque with the Hippocratic oath. The basic gist of the Hippocratic oath is *primum non nocere*, or "first, do no harm." That is a pretty good generalization and represents an ethical framework that has stood for millennia. As a new profession, data science is just beginning to define our ethical framework.

As I stared at Hippocrates's bust, I wanted to ask him: who defines ethics? Leaders of technology companies have been at the center of the public stage in this discussion, but I wonder if they are leveraging the wealth of established philosophy on ethics. Rather than inventing new frameworks, what could Larry Page, Sergey Brin, Mark Zuckerberg, Steve Jobs, Larry Ellison, Bill Gates, Jeff Bezos, or Jack Ma learn about data privacy or other modern ethical dilemmas from Socrates, Confucius, Hobbes, Locke, Kant, and Nietzsche? For example, Hobbes and Locke might argue over social contract theory to sway Zuckerberg toward more or less absolute government regulation. If we leave data science ethics to the technocrats and allow corporations to follow their nature, would they drive society to ruthlessness, as Hobbes might argue? Certainly, we can find evidence of this ruthlessness in corporate behavior.

In most professions, practitioners define ethics. "Attorney-client privilege," "protect and serve," "seek the truth," "do not reveal your source," "serve the people": these are all mottos that encapsulate a profession's ethical code. While these codes might have some basis in the historical philosophy of ethics, professions develop their ethics with feedback from society, updating as standards evolve. The resulting ethical code is only as good as the practitioners' interpretation of society. Further, ethical codes are effective only if professionals enforce them, and history has shown that doesn't always happen. If we let data science practitioners define ethics for the field, would the members live up to and self-enforce those codes?

Maybe an ethical code is not even needed for the data science field. After all, how can math be unethical? $2 + 2 = 4$, does it not? The equation does not care what inputs it is given; it objectively adds two numbers without bias. However, machine learning is more complex, and one argument is that data scientists may inadvertently create biased models if they use incomplete or nonrepresentative training data. In my opinion, that is an efficacy issue, not an ethics issue.

If machine learning or artificial intelligence is not innately good or evil, then we should consider the application of data science. For example, we might consider using data science to identify a precancerous person for the purpose of marketing life insurance or recommending a medical checkup. Which use case is ethical? Are both cases acceptable as long as we save the patient's life? If ethics is really about the application, then practitioners can simply adopt the ethics where it is being applied. The field may not need its own framework.

Perhaps the ethical question is who should have access to data science methods. In the 1990s, the technology race was all about computing power. The US government restricted exports of high-performance computers under the Export Administration Act of 1979 for national security reasons. Apple Computer used this situation to great effect when it released the Power Mac G4, "the first desktop supercomputer," in 1999. The premise, which may have been more marketing than reality, was that G4 exports should be restricted to prevent rogue nations from using the computer to develop nuclear or other advanced weapons. Building on that premise, should advanced data science methodologies be restricted to prevent rogue actors, organizations, or nations from doing harm? That would seem to be counter to the open source culture of data science, but as Locke might argue, voluntary sacrifice of some freedoms may be needed to ensure other more important freedoms. Ethics is hard and probably comes at some cost.

A final thought: my question to Hippocrates's bust still stands. Who should define ethics for data science—corporate leaders, the field of application, practitioners, or maybe an open source ethics AI? Given the complexity of today's world, getting ethics right is a big challenge. A good place to start might be a simple golden rule like the one Hippocrates laid out for the medical profession a few thousand years ago: first, do no harm.

Why Research Should Be Reproducible

Stuart Buck

Vice President of Research, Arnold Ventures

Today's sciences—especially the social sciences—are in a bit of turmoil. Many of the most important experiments and findings are not reproducible. This "reproducibility crisis" has significant implications not just for the future of academic research and development but also for any business expecting increased returns from investing in innovation, experimentation, and data analysis. Business needs to learn from science's mistakes.

As Vice President of Research at Arnold Ventures, I have close knowledge of this ongoing crisis, because I have funded a good deal of these "second look" efforts. Here's an unhappy sample of what we funded and found:

- In 2015, the journal *Science* published the results of the largest replication project ever performed: the Reproducibility Project in Psychology (*https://oreil.ly/9_Sqm*), in which hundreds of researchers around the world attempted to replicate 100 psychology experiments from top journals. Only about 40% of the findings could be successfully replicated, while the rest were either inconclusive or definitively not replicated.

- In 2018, the Social Sciences Replication Project (*https://oreil.ly/U2IzY*) attempted to replicate 21 social science experiments that had been published in the journals *Science* and *Nature* between 2010 and 2015. Only 13 of the 21 experiments could be replicated successfully, and even then, replication revealed that the "effect size"—the magnitude of the declared discovery—was typically about half of what had originally been claimed.

As John Ioannidis of Stanford University told the *Washington Post*, "I would have expected results to be more reproducible in [top] journals."

Beyond these well-known replication projects, researchers have documented reproducibility problems in the research literature on economics (*https://oreil.ly/vVjIY*), finance (*http://www.nber.org/papers/w20592*), marketing (*https://oreil.ly/h4i8Y*), management (*https://oreil.ly/-9bLK*), organizational sciences (*https://oreil.ly/JASK4*), and international business (*https://oreil.ly/WLi8-*). Indeed, after analyzing over 2,000 business experiments, Ron Berman, professor of marketing at the Wharton School at the University of Pennsylvania, and his colleagues estimated (*https://oreil.ly/tSg0-*) that 42% of the effects found to be significant were actually false positives.

Scientific establishments worldwide have taken these findings seriously and are acting on them. For example, the US Congress officially asked the National Academies of Sciences, Engineering, and Medicine to produce a major national report (*https://oreil.ly/PVU3E*) (it's still in progress) with suggestions about how to fix the reproducibility problem in scientific and engineering research.

Digital innovators from Alibaba to Google, Facebook to Netflix, Microsoft to Amazon have already actively embraced large-scale, rapid experimentation as integral to their innovation efforts. But every organization seeking authentic insight from experiment and data analysis needs to be wary of the problems that have made scientific research unreliable.

Indeed, I would argue that research and data analysis can often be unethical without a strong focus on reliability and reproducibility. Ethical problems in research and data analytics can arise in at least two ways:

- If your company does an A/B experiment on its customers but in a way that doesn't offer concrete details about what's better or worse for the customers (A or B), then the customers have been subjected to an experiment for no purpose. Indeed, if one of A or B is worse than the other in some way, you won't know which, and you may continue to subject customers to a subpar experience.

- If you use data analysis to make decisions about employees, customers, and so on, but you don't do so in the most rigorous way possible, you can be misled into doing things that are worse for people. To take one of many possible examples, if a large company uses in-house data to develop an algorithm to screen applicants before hiring, or to measure employee performance, but doesn't rigorously screen for racial and gender bias that can arise in subtle ways, the algorithm could subject the company to legal liability for employment discrimination.

Part of the reproducibility problem in science comes down to education, training, and familiarity with good statistical practice. Make sure that your team has at least one person on staff, or a consultant, who is up to speed on current best practices for research. The reproducibility crisis in science has led to many important lessons about how to structure experiments, how to do data analyses, and so forth. Heed those lessons, and not only will you make better and more informed decisions, but you'll also be less at risk of acting unethically toward customers and employees.

Build Multiperspective AI

Hassan Masum and
Sébastien Paquet

Sr. Director, Analytics, Prodigy Education
Applied Research Scientist, Element AI

How AI and data science are deployed is decided by their makers and owners —but other stakeholders are impacted and are sometimes harmed.

If you care about avoiding harm, you have to consider multiple perspectives when deploying data science and AI. You must step into someone else's shoes by asking: if I were that person, how would this system impact my life?

The impacts of a new technology can be unintended and complex, even for a seemingly benign goal such as connecting people. The creator or any single actor cannot see the whole picture. But every actor deeply understands their own situation and can therefore assess how a given technology serves or harms them.

Learning from stakeholders' opinions and lived experiences has long been part of responsible technology discourse (in ideas like "implementation research" and "diffusion of innovations"). That accumulated experience remains relevant in the data science age.

With this in mind, how can you incorporate more points of view in data science and AI development? Here are people whose perspectives you should consider incorporating, and questions they are likely to care about:

Users think: "Does this AI lessen my problems? Is it safe for me and fair to me? What kind of person will it help me to be?"
> As the UK government's design principles (*https://oreil.ly/osClX*) and Digital Service Standard (*https://oreil.ly/Ig9pY*) emphasize, start with user needs. Keen users may be especially candid with their feedback; ditto for desperate or frustrated users who crave better solutions. Invest time and empathy to get at users' deeper issues and desires.

People who care think: "How is this AI helping or harming a user who is my friend, colleague, or loved one?"
> Those who know a person well can often assess what helps or harms them. For example, to understand how a child is affected by AI, you could speak with the child's parents, siblings, friends, and teachers.

Impactees think: "How will this AI affect me? Is it harming me even though I never asked for it?"

Nonusers of an AI can still be affected by it, as with citizens punished by algorithms that limit their eligibility for benefits or parole. Such citizens could benefit from policies like Article 22 of the EU's General Data Protection Regulation (*https://oreil.ly/sJAc4*), which specifies a right for people to express their point of view on automated decisions that impact them, to contest such decisions, and to obtain human intervention. Before implementing data science at scale, map out who would be impacted and how that impact might in turn affect others.

Skeptics think: "Why can't this AI be improved or abandoned? Who were the idiots who built it?"

Seek constructive skeptics: the most insightful people who *don't* buy your vision. When skeptics seem unconstructive, you can still seek to understand their emotions and worldview.

Regulators and civil society think: "Is this AI operating lawfully? Is it safe and fair? How can it serve the public interest and balance different peoples' interests?"

Support effective regulatory and civil oversight that serves the public interest. Help oversight to work better, such as by sharing impact information for your AI, or by codeveloping standards and algorithmic accountability. (You'll have to decide which countries' regulatory agencies and ethics to support.)

Data scientists and AI makers think: "Have I considered my responsibilities as a creator, my biases and constraints, and others' perspectives? Will this be legal, safe, and trusted and improve the world?"

Reflect on *your own* perspective. Why are you creating this new technology? What shapes your motives, including your work, finances, culture, and personality? What obligations hinder you from satisfying users' and impactees' needs? Can you improve your empathy for and understanding of others?

Doing all this is hard in the onslaught of daily responsibilities. But making the time to take a more expansive view of what you build helps to reduce risk, delight customers, and make the world a better place.

Listening to diverse stakeholders can be tough but rewarding. So can engaging them in diverse ways, such as through surveys, interviews, and ethnographic research. If you can do this and build truly multiperspective AI, then you will have a better chance of introducing innovations that generate long-term user and social value.

Ethics as a Competitive Advantage

Dave Mathias

Cofounder, Beyond the Data

As a former-attorney-turned-analytics-person, my view on ethics has changed. Instead of looking at ethics as something that is a compliance item, I look at it as a strategy and a competitive differentiator. High data and analytics ethics can truly be a competitive advantage for organizations. Of course, this higher ethics threshold must be genuine and align with an organization's culture, but if it does, and the organization takes up this higher ethical bar, then there are a variety of benefits it may be able to reap.

First, in the war for talent, ethics can be a competitive advantage in hiring. Companies like Google and Microsoft have recently faced ethical pushback from their employees and received bad press over work the companies undertook.

Second, customers and partners are looking for companies to be more transparent and ethical in how they harness data. Customers are tired of reading the fine print. They are tired of the bait and switch. They are tired of companies asking for forgiveness, not asking for permission. Organizations that recognize this and raise their data and analytics ethical bar will be able to differentiate themselves from their competitors and, at the same time, may be able to be more resourceful and analytics-focused and thus save costs.

Third, brands will be increasingly impacted by the ethics of how they use data. A brand that has shown a propensity for high analytics ethics should likely have higher brand affinity. Further, when mistakes arise, there will be an audience more forgiving of the brand.

Recently, I have been thinking more about the importance around ethics and analytics with Dr. Bonnie Holub and in connection with my interviews of chief data officers and chief analytics officers in preparation for our upcoming book. Having higher ethical standards can't just happen in a day and on a whim. Instead, there must be a change that occurs from the top down and from the bottom up in both support and recognition. This includes aligning these ethical standards with the authentic culture of the organization. There may be a desire to modify an organization's culture from both the top down and the bottom up, but recognition of this need and a plan to conduct this change are essential to make it effective.

One thing organizations may seek to do is to establish their Data Principles. Basically, think of Data Principles as your organization's bylaws or manifesto on how it uses data and analytics. Data Principles should include the ethical framework your organization seeks to have around harnessing data. The concept is taken in part from Ray Dalio's book *Principles* (Simon & Schuster), in which he explains the personal and professional principles to which he partly attributes his success. Assuming your organization has high ethics in analytics as an agreed part of its strategy, incorporating high ethics explicitly in your Data Principles is important. Of course, those principles need to be well communicated and need to encourage holding truth up to power. These Data Principles should not be developed in a vacuum but instead should have broad input, buy-in, and communication.

Even with Data Principles in place, an organization has to ensure that people, process, and procedures are aligned to empower everyone to support a high level of ethics. The most important part of this is ensuring that everyone realizes ethics is their responsibility and is not left to compliance, attorneys, and others. Incorporating both empowerment and broad engagement around ethics and its importance can allow you to truly differentiate your organization based on ethics.

Algorithmic Bias: Are You a Bystander or an Upstander?

Jitendra Mudhol and
Heidi Livingston Eisips

Founder and CEO, CollaMeta
Adjunct Faculty, San Jose State University

Automated Decision Systems (ADS) are used in many human endeavors, from ad targeting and credit scoring to child welfare and criminal justice. ADS impact us daily, but we seem oblivious to the pervasive influence of algorithms on our lives: up to 87% of Americans are identifiable from their zip code, birthday, and gender.[1]

A well-designed algorithm can bring positive socioeconomic change; for instance, machine learning is at the heart of many medical imaging and drug discovery innovations.[2] Still, ADS may be amplifying bias on an unprecedented scale, while giving it the garb of scientific objectivity. In *Automating Inequality*, Virginia Eubanks "exposes how US institutions, from law enforcement to health care to social services, increasingly punish people—especially people of color—for being poor."[3]

We face a choice: either act to address algorithmic bias or turn a blind eye. Psychologists call the latter *bystander apathy*.

1 Latanya Sweeney, "Simple Demographics Often Identify People Uniquely" (Data Privacy Working Paper 3, Carnegie Mellon University, 2000), *https://oreil.ly/RONis*.

2 Hongming Chen, Ola Engkvist, Yinhai Wang, Marcus Olivecrona, and Thomas Blaschke, "The Rise of Deep Learning in Drug Discovery," *Drug Discovery Today* 23, no. 6 (2018): 1241–50, *https://doi.org/10.1016/j.drudis.2018.01.039*.

3 Virginia Eubanks, *Automating Inequality: How High-Tech Tools Profile, Police, and Punish the Poor* (New York: St. Martin's, 2018).

Understanding Bystanderism

Research in the late 1960s revealed that the greater the number of people present at an emergency, the lower the likelihood of receiving help.[4] Scott Lilienfeld et al. cite William Glassman and Marilyn Hadad's 2008 research that showed that bystanders "are typically quite concerned about the victim but are psychologically 'frozen' by well-established psychological processes, such as pluralistic ignorance, diffusion of responsibility, and sheer fears of appearing foolish."[5]

Bystander apathy is attributed to the *diffusion of responsibility theory*: when in the presence of others, individuals feel less personal responsibility and are less likely to take action; conversely, the smaller the group, the more likely a person is to take action.

Diplomat Samantha Power coined the term *upstander*, which has come to mean "a person who speaks or acts in support of an individual or cause, particularly someone who intervenes on behalf of a person being attacked or bullied." An upstander does two vital things: they support the target of the bullying, and they influence the bully to stop.

Are You a Bystander or an Upstander?

We are at a crossroads: do we remain mute witnesses to algorithmic injustice, or do we do something? From demand to supply, conception to creation, data collection, training, and testing to deploying production models, serving customers, and identifying targets, each individual/enterprise in the ADS value chain has the potential to become an upstander. Those collecting and labeling training data can acknowledge, address, and eliminate bias both in the methodologies and in the data pool. Developers can think carefully about accountability, explainability, transparency, and the consequences of design choices. Private entities or agencies building or deploying such products may

---

4 Bibb Latané and John M. Darley, "Bystander 'Apathy,'" *American Scientist* 57, no. 2 (1969): 244–68, https://www.jstor.org/stable/27828530?seq=1; Bibb Latané and Judith Rodin, "A Lady in Distress: Inhibiting Effects of Friends and Strangers on Bystander Intervention," *Journal of Experimental Social Psychology* 5, no. 2 (1969): 189–202, https://oreil.ly/7iCPZ.

5 William E. Glassman and Marilyn Hadad, *Approaches to Psychology* (London: Open University Press, 2008), as cited in Scott O. Lilienfeld, Katheryn C. Sauvigné, Steven Jay Lynn, Robin L. Cautin, Robert D. Latzman, and Irwin D. Waldman, "Fifty Psychological and Psychiatric Terms to Avoid: A List of Inaccurate, Misleading, Misused, Ambiguous, and Logically Confused Words and Phrases," *Frontiers in Psychology* 6 (August 3, 2015): 1100, https://oreil.ly/Mc-cb.

use frameworks—such as AI Now's Algorithmic Accountability Policy Toolkit—for guidance.[6]

Other systemic challenges, such as climate change, teach us that only wide-ranging institutional reforms have sufficient impact. In high-emitting countries like the United States and Australia, individual households voluntarily reducing emissions by an average of 25% would drop national emissions by only 5%.[7] Meaningful change is possible when national and local governments enact laws and enforce well-researched, evidence-based policies. The same holds true for algorithmic bias and data transparency.

While successfully eradicating algorithmic bias is daunting, the upstander role fortunately has some momentum behind it. Research by Marco van Bommel et al. shows that introducing an *accountability cue* eliminates feelings of anonymity and increases the chances of offering help.[8] Data ethics can actually be a vital competitive advantage to enterprises.[9] GDPR and similar regulations can be allies in this fight.

The Time to Be an Upstander Is Now

Human psychology and human ingenuity both drive the global economy. As Cathy O'Neil points out, "It's up to society whether to use that intelligence to reject and punish [the vulnerable]—or to reach out to them with the resources they need."[10] Pervasive bias creates high socioeconomic costs. Being an upstander represents an opportunity, not a liability. The opportunity lies in asking penetrating questions around fairness and accountability, empowering civic and organizational activism, and committing to the leadership required to achieve better societal outcomes.

---

6 AI Now Institute, "Algorithmic Accountability Policy Toolkit," October 2018, *https://ainowinstitute.org/aap-toolkit.pdf*.

7 Carol Booth, "Bystanding and Climate Change," *Environmental Values* 21, no. 4 (2012): 397–416.

8 Marco van Bommel, Jan-Willem van Prooijen, Henk Elffers, and Paul A. M. Van Lange, "Be Aware to Care: Public Self-Awareness Leads to a Reversal of the Bystander Effect," *Journal of Experimental Social Psychology* 48, no. 4 (2012): 926–30.

9 Gry Hasselbalch and Pernille Tranberg, *Data Ethics—The New Competitive Advantage* (Copenhagen: Publishare, 2016), *https://dataethics.eu/da/projekter/bog*.

10 Cathy O'Neil, *Weapons of Math Destruction: How Big Data Increases Inequality and Threatens Democracy* (New York: Crown, 2016). *https://weaponsofmathdestructionbook.com*.

Data Science and Deliberative Justice: The Ethics of the Voice of "the Other"

Robert J. McGrath

Chair, Department of Health Management and Policy,
University of New Hampshire

Data science—by which I refer to the collective whole of methods largely predicated on forms of artificial intelligence (machine learning, deep learning, technological learning in general)—has pervaded society with well-documented effects, both positive[1] and negative.[2] And it continues to engender many discussions weighing the two and the ultimate benefit to society.[3]

---

1 Sonja Marjanovic, Ioana Ghiga, Miaoqing Yang, and Anna Knack, "Understanding Value in Health Data Ecosystems: A Review of Current Evidence and Ways Forward," *Rand Health Quarterly* 7, no. 2 (January 2018): 3; L. Nelson Sanchez-Pinto, Yuan Luo, and Matthew M. Churpek, "Big Data and Data Science in Critical Care," *Chest* 154, no. 5 (November 2018): 1239–48; Stuart J. Russell and Peter Norvig, with John Canny et al., *Artificial Intelligence: A Modern Approach*, 2nd ed. (Upper Saddle River, NJ: Prentice Hall/Pearson Education, 2003), 1081.

2 Rebecca Wexler, "Life, Liberty, and Trade Secrets: Intellectual Property in the Criminal Justice System," *Stanford Law Review* 70 (2018): 1343–1429; Soroush Vosoughi, Deb Roy, and Sinan Aral, "The Spread of True and False News Online," *Science* 359, no. 6380 (2018): 1146–51, *https:// doi.org/10.1126/science.aap9559*; Jack Smith IV, "'Minority Report' Is Real—and It's Really Reporting Minorities," Mic, November 9, 2015, *https://oreil.ly/qpT_Z*; Jack Nicas, "How YouTube Drives People to the Internet's Darkest Corners," *Wall Street Journal*, February 7, 2018, *https://oreil.ly/ ceaey*.

3 Luke Muehlhauser and Anna Salamon, "Intelligence Explosion: Evidence and Import," in *Singularity Hypotheses: A Scientific and Philosophical Assessment*, ed. Amnon Eden, Johnny Søraker, James H. Moor, and Eric Steinhart (Berlin: Springer, 2012); Eliezer Yudkowsky, "Artificial Intelligence as a Positive and Negative Factor in Global Risk," in *Global Catastrophic Risks*, ed. Nick Bostrom and Milan M. Ćirković (New York: Oxford University Press, 2008), 308–45; Nick Bostrom, "The Superintelligent Will: Motivation and Instrumental Rationality in Advanced Artificial Agents," *Minds and Machines* 22 (2012): 71, *https://doi.org/10.1007/s11023-012-9281-3*.

But it is here, at this intersection of society and technology, that a more foundational contemplation may be needed. Often cited in these examinations of the effects of data science are the outcomes, or the unanticipated consequences of actions, such as with the ethics of algorithmic development or their alteration as learning progresses. These arise in the cases of systematic bias, such as with minority biases, racial biases, or other structural biases, which if not addressed will propagate in the autonomous learning process. But what is lost in this examination is the actions themselves and how technology replaces not only human activity but also parts of the collective voice.

Collective decision making is the foundation of all social structures, of all societies. It is the collective identity that weaves its way through all social relationships, including political structures, justice structures, community supports, law, and civic duties.[4] But when algorithms replace human voices—such as with machine learning on preferences in purchasing, voter sampling, predictive case law, or virtually any human action when taken in the aggregate—that nonhuman voice or voice of "the other" is essentially counted in the collective voice of how those goods, services, and civic structures ought to be allocated and construed. Some might argue that it is not citizens but their use of technology and the benefits it provides that are making civic choices, and thus collective voice is enhanced. However, others might argue that if the choices themselves are limited as a result of the predictive process, then the deliberative process has fundamentally been hindered along the way. Such quandaries have led to some asking whether it is ethical frameworks or questions of foundational justice models, such as social and deliberative justice, that need to be considered when informing the work of data scientists.[5]

These are the foundational issues relegated to theories of justice upon which ethics resides. Questions of how, why, and toward what ends rest firmly in this space of foundational civic voice and the value given that voice. The question lingers: what if that voice has no human face?

---

4 Bernard Yack, "Community and Conflict in Aristotle's Political Philosophy," *The Review of Politics* 47, no. 1 (1985): 92–112. *https://oreil.ly/HwRf_*.

5 Ben Green, "Data Science as Political Action: Grounding Data Science in a Politics of Justice," Computers and Society, Cornell University, last modified January 14, 2019, *https://arxiv.org/abs/1811.03435*.

Spam. Are You Going to Miss It?

John Thuma

Vice President, FIS Data Solutions Group

With the California Consumer Privacy Act, or CCPA, the laws around personal data and ethics are going to change dramatically. Signed by Governor Jerry Brown in 2018 and put into effect in January 2020, the law aims to establish guidelines and procedures to protect private information for residents of California. The law grants the consumer the right to know what personal information a business has and the business purpose for its collection and monetization, as well as many other things.

The CCPA is a good idea, and many other states will soon follow the lead of California. However, there is a downside to these types of laws. All organizations that are data driven will have to comply with this law or face some steep consequences. And let's face it: most organizations are data driven! I am sure we all will see a reduction in our email inboxes as organizations tighten their belts on the amount of consumer advertising they do. This will also have an impact on traditional marketing. Robocalls will be greatly reduced. Sounds like a dream come true for many people. However: spam! I think you are going to miss it!

Believe it or not, I love getting some spam from advertisers! I want to know what the next best offer is and whether I am able to get a good deal at the pump. I like receiving messages that tell me about movies that are coming out and that I might get 50% off of that pricey yet yummy popcorn. What I fear is that the pendulum will swing and businesses will tighten up their marketing out of fear of violating new privacy laws like CCPA. I won't, however, miss the robocalls!

Are we entering a time when we have a "bigger brother"? One thing I don't like about the CCPA law is that it takes control away from me. I can manage my own spam and robocalls. It is easy enough for me to manage my data! Besides, spam filters work pretty well. I can unsubscribe from emails too.

The new call blocker apps are pretty awesome. I really don't require a big government oversight group looking out for me; I can look out for myself.

In conclusion, I am a data-about-me show-off. But that is me, and that may not be all right with you. We all have a responsibility to protect ourselves and our private data. The CCPA is a well-intentioned set of regulations. It serves to protect private data and consumers. But we all know that the road to hell is paved with good intentions. Sometimes it does seem a bit creepy when I am walking near a store and I receive an email with an offer from that establishment. At the same time, the consumer in me gets a little excited if the offer is right! I would rather keep control and don't mind that there are very smart data scientists constructing my next best offer, even if they use my personal data. After all, data, analytics, marketing, and data monetization are a big part of our economy! I say laissez-faire—"hands off!"

Is It Wrong to Be Right?

Marty Ellingsworth

Senior Analyst, Celent

Better data, better models, and better decision engines get better results. Whether you hand train a model, use automated machine learning systems, or employ any of the newest "x"-learning nets with pretraining, does it really matter why your model performs so well as long as it has great performance? Should not the most accurate model be used everywhere and anywhere in all situations? That's progress, right? Should your model be allowed to learn on its own to further this progress and self-calibrate for better personalization? Practically, if there is no harm, then there is no foul, right?

Academically, many argue it's all about the lift, correct for the data. Professionally, the standards of care are still emerging. There are dozens of fields of practice in which better models and better data appear magically, regularly, and at scale, for better results—no questions asked—resulting in delighted users, inventors, and investors. Privacy rights advocates sound warnings.

Legally, we are in a technological sprint that is far ahead of existing laws and compliance regulations. Many of today's controls emerged back in the 1970s and 1980s around fairness in employment, lending, and housing, and in the 1990s and early 2000s around fraud, theft, collusion, money laundering, and terrorism concerns. Known legal lines are often well defined yet are often not well understood by those closest to the data. Oftentimes there are compound definitions that define something as prohibited or restricted (who, what, when, where, why, how, how much, by what means, in what use case, for what age group, and in which jurisdiction). This can leave more situations undefined than prescribed. If it's not against the law, is it still OK?

Ethically, "what's OK" is often a moving target. Business impact drives the need for better results, and the public can be fickle as well as persuaded and even paid in value for particular information. Who is the ethical gatekeeper, when do they engage, and when do they reengage as situations change? This is an emerging issue in data science.

The rubber on the road usually shows as a variety of skid marks over time. Big skids occur when great predictions don't hold up for subgroups, and when specific protected subgroups get predicted at all. When to predict and when not to predict is an ethical question perhaps broader than "business ethics."

Many bosses kill the messenger. Most ethics departments sprang from a lapse. Many small companies don't even have ethics departments. Non-US companies may have different ethics, as may different companies in the same industries with the same customers in the same geographies. Which ethical framework should be the standard is unclear. Until then, more common will be the cases in which disparate impact on a protected class or infringement of illegal variables occurs. This may be due to bias introduced by underlying data, by poor management of specific types of data, or by distinguishing characteristics of embeddable minutiae (especially when text, image, scan, diagnostic, sound, video, temporal, transaction, biologic, demographic, medical, dental, geographic, sensor, social network, knowledge graph association, past history, current activity, behavior, online activity, purchase, personal interaction, and location data are considered).

Data, analytics, and decision support systems, especially those that can learn post hoc, are all susceptible to risk. They can learn bad behavior, overrepresent unbalanced demographics, "cheat" by mimicking processors in a process, leverage illegal and protected information unwittingly, or find distinguishing characteristics in a data sample that may drift or disappear in a production setting.

Automated machine learning and AI that just needs component assembly with prepackaged data feeds are putting more analytic model building capabilities in the hands of businesspeople and other "citizen data scientists." But making models easy to build does not address the art, craft, and ethics of picking good problems and solving them with ethics at the core.

So many times in an analytics practice, the art of problem definition and the craft of knowing the context of the underlying data before using it in production run up against the delight in a well-performing model and the urgency of a near-term delivery date—not to mention the millions and billions of dollars seemingly raining down on herds of unicorns in the start-up space.

Can the ends justify the means? It's a question that every data scientist—as well as their employer, board of directors, auditors, regulators, and investors —needs to consider.

We're Not Yet Ready for a Trustmark for Technology

Hannah Kitcher and
Laura James

Comms. Manager, Ada Lovelace Institute
Associate, Doteveryone

At Doteveryone, the responsible tech think tank where we worked from 2018 to 2020, we were often asked why we didn't go ahead with an early idea to create a "trustmark" for technology. The short answer is that digital products and services aren't like bananas.

Digital products are complicated and change over time (with software updates, new technologies, new data, etc.)—and our attitudes toward them change too. It's hard to set and evaluate useful common standards in this sort of setting.

At Doteveryone, we looked into what trustmarks for tech would look like, and after research and prototyping, we found a trustmark wasn't the most useful thing we could do to create change.

Trustmarks are common tools to demonstrate business responsibility, whether it's GasSafe for heating technicians, or Fairtrade on food and other products. In 2017, with growing concerns about big tech, algorithms, and more, as well as calls for greater responsibility, a lot of people mentioned trustmarks for digital technology, and it made sense to consider taking an idea common in other sectors into this new one.

After some research, Doteveryone was able to describe the specific challenges of making a trustmark work for digital technologies. We recognized that compulsory marks for a sector are a very long, slow journey to develop —and technology is still working out product categories, too, so it's hard to figure out exactly what products and services would be included.

Some trustmarks use a checklist system. If we were envisaging a mark for a specific product type such as a wrist-worn fitness tracker, it might be possible to come up with a checklist of what responsible fitness trackers would look like. But we'd need an awful lot of checklists to cover all the digital products and services we'd like to have good design, development, and operational practices!

So instead we focused on a values-based approach and on the business and product choices at a higher level. Values are often how people describe their concerns about technologies and are a better frame than details of accessibility of color schemes, or data encryption technologies.

We conceived the "trustworthy tech mark" (*https://oreil.ly/99TtB*)—a trustmark built on values, to help customers identify the products and services that reflected their priorities and concerns. The idea was for this to be a more modern trustmark concept, where the mark on a product or service would be backed by an online resource of live information that justified the mark's use. In this way, as technology changed—such as with software updates—these developments could be accommodated, and the evidence for trustworthy behavior would always be up to date.

The mark would also make it possible to have lightweight accountability and enforcement without the cost and scale of a full standards body or certification authority, and it would be relatively easy to test. If a simple online evidence repository could help demonstrate the value of a trustworthy tech mark system, then it could migrate over time to a formal system later.

Testing this trustworthy tech mark concept—adapting the conventional model of a trustmark for the special case of complex, fast-moving digital technologies—with a small group of organizations (*https://oreil.ly/qncrb*), we found:

- The most significant challenge for the organizations was simply helping them identify ways they could work better. Providing a framework and some tools to support their teams in thinking about responsibility was hugely useful.

- The hardest part to manage for small organizations was the actual evidence, partly because it was about demonstrating things externally that might touch on commercial sensitivities, and partly because it was an extra task—one more thing to do in the already very busy life of a startup or small tech business.

- It was doubtful whether consumers would actually benefit from a mark. Choices are already difficult when you are picking apps and devices, and product offerings are complex, and time (and money) often scarce. Rather than identifying a few "gold standard" products with a trustmark, it seemed more important to enable more businesses to improve their practices in a lightweight and feasible way. (The most ethical digital products today are often fairly easy to find anyway, if you want one! They are still quite scarce, but their unusual business models and brand positioning are generally visible, and there are curated lists of ethical apps available too.)

So while a trustmark, backed by an open repository of evidence, would still be of use and may be a good future direction as the sector evolves and consumer and policy interest in responsible tech develops, we're not yet at the tipping point where there is enough customer demand.

Trustmarks for digital technologies need innovative thinking and prototyping, but they also need an enforcement system that works at scale. This means a big, weighty organization and is much harder and slower to do.

So instead we've been focusing on how we can build on what we've already learned and give organizations tools to help them be more responsible day to day. The results are proving useful (*https://oreil.ly/kkOqR*) and are out there working in practice much more quickly than a trustmark would have been.

PART III

The Ethics of Data

Data is the foundation on which every analytics and data science process is built. This section discusses the ethical issues specific to the collection and usage of the data that underlies those processes.

How to Ask for Customers' Data with Transparency and Trust

Rasmus Wegener

Partner, Bain & Company, Inc.

Most customers know their data is being collected with every online click, like, or purchase, but many wish they had more control over this activity. An ongoing drumbeat of large data breaches in recent years, including at Yahoo, First American Financial, Facebook, Marriott/Starwood, and Equifax, has left many customers feeling helpless against intrusion and theft. Social media giants have also abused their customers' trust by sharing data about them with third parties, who used the information in ways the customers might never have approved.

Breaches like these should make customers more wary about sharing data. But more than ever before, companies rely on customer data to develop new products, tailor online experiences and services, and decide where to invest in new commercial efforts. Companies that have only just begun to develop their analytic muscles aren't likely to walk away from the potential business benefits of customer data.

So how can companies meet their need for data while respecting the concerns of their customers? For most businesses, the problem is finding the right way to articulate their reasons for collecting data and how they will use it.

Research by Bain & Company finds that paying people for their data doesn't work. Customers who are opposed to having their data collected or shared are rarely swayed by offers of money. Trust, it seems, cannot be bought. This is true across many different types of customers. We didn't see a significant connection between, for example, income and willingness to part with data for monetary compensation.

On the other hand, we did find a connection between a company's transparency and customers' willingness to share data. Open, simple communication with customers—about the kinds of data companies would like to collect, why they want it, and the limits of what they would do with it—appears to have an effect. Specifically, people are more willing to share data when they see the rationale for collecting it.

It also matters who is asking. Consumers trust some companies more than others. Grocery and airline companies, for example, are more likely to get a green light from customers to use their personal data than are financial services firms and cell phone providers.

While some companies have made transparency a priority, the European Union has taken steps to enforce uniform standards. Under the EU's General Data Protection Regulation, companies doing business online in Europe must inform customers that their data is being collected. Usually, that takes the form of small banners or pop-ups that inform users that the website they've just landed on uses cookies and may or may not collect personally identifiable information from them if they click to accept. The fact that websites or mobile apps are gathering their data won't come as a surprise to customers. But the GDPR rules don't offer them much control over their data except to decline the cookies or, in some cases, leave the site. It's not clear what the data will be used for, and there are no easily accessible settings allowing customers to select the specific data they are willing to share.

Although a step in the right direction, GDPR remains a rough framework and has drawn criticism for its perceived overreach, lack of flexibility to accommodate the needs of small organizations and businesses, and potentially stifling effect on innovation. Similar to the lengthy (and usually unread) legal agreements that accompany every app download or software upgrade, the initial GDPR rules failed to improve the dialogue between businesses and customers or to explain in clear terms the conditions of data usage. The next revision may be more effective: the EU has announced changes to GDPR that will compel businesses to communicate this information in "clear and plain language."

A better model might be the nonprofit Mozilla Foundation's five succinct data privacy principles (*https://oreil.ly/bCSBc*), first published in early 2011 to guide how Mozilla approaches data privacy. In terms of user data, the three most important tenets are:

No surprises
    Users share data in ways that are transparent to them.

User control
    The customer controls which data is collected and when.

Limited data
> The company collects only what it needs, and it deletes data that it doesn't need anymore.

Together, these principles begin to frame the environment of transparency and trust required to strengthen relationships with customers, upon whose data companies increasingly rely. Open and transparent communication is a good place to start: using clear language up front to ask for permission and letting customers know how their data will be used and protected.

Data Ethics and the Lemming Effect

Bob Gladden

VP, Enterprise Analytics, Highmark Health

Over the past decade, we have witnessed an eruption of individual data being collected and made available for use in the cybersphere. This, coupled with extensive options for burst computing capability, has resulted in analytic algorithms with a voracious appetite for data that may provide unique insights about individuals and/or populations. Seeing data as a playground for data scientists to explore has significant upside, but with it comes a dark underbelly. Of greatest concern is the irresponsible use of very private data to feed algorithms, which can result in unintended consequences, embarrassing public relation challenges, or runaway AI/ML algorithms that can integrate biases.

You may be familiar with the Lemming Effect. It is based on the unsubstantiated tendency of these small rodents to mindlessly kill themselves by jumping off of cliffs, one after the other. It has come to represent unquestioningly following others without consideration of the consequences. So how does the use of expanded personal data equate to the Lemming Effect?

It seems that if one organization is using all the data at its disposal, this behavior acts like an aphrodisiac to other organizations, who feel compelled to do the same thing. They may do this with little or no regard for the consequences. Fear of falling behind and not applying the most advanced analytic techniques to every bit of available data propels analytic teams and companies to unwittingly accept another organization's data ethics (or lack thereof) as the de facto code of conduct. They simply "jump off the cliff" because another organization has done the same thing. However, there are alternatives.

In the development of algorithms, there can be a delicate balance between the ever-increasing demand for individual-specific data and the value that data brings to that algorithm. Certainly, adding more data has the potential to increase lift in the predictive capability of a model, but at what cost? That cost can be one of dollars and cents attached to acquiring the data, but more importantly, it should be considered in terms of ethical impact and the stewardship responsibilities associated with the data entrusted to a company's care.

Categorical data, or data connected to an individual by an association such as street address, is generally less troublesome than individual data that is specific to that person. Models that use categorical data can be almost as effective as those using individual data, depending on the application. That makes categorical data an ideal choice if the individual data needed for a model is considered sensitive. It takes effort to compare output using each of these types of data. However, in doing so the final choice of a model can be focused not just on the variation between the two types of data but also on the ethical concerns of routinely using sensitive personal data.

When considering socioeconomic data that can provide insights into a person's health care needs, publicly available data can provide more than enough veracity for a model to be effective. This isn't to say individual data would not improve the model. For example, when considering the housing vulnerability of a person for health or social needs, knowing how many individual addresses a person has had over a 12-month period, their past evictions and/or foreclosures, or the housing situation of their relatives can certainly better inform a model. However, data input such as current address, and the characteristics of that community/census block/etc.—from income to availability of fresh food and type of housing—can be as effective in guiding a care navigator in their decisions.

All of this isn't intended to disqualify the use of individual data for models. But data stewardship is a critical responsibility, especially when collecting data specific to an individual. The bottom line is that every organization should consider minimizing its sensitive data footprint. Starting with a data code of ethics and establishing rules around what risks an organization is willing to accept will at the very least take this important decision out of the hands of an individual analyst or data scientist and put it back in the hands of the enterprise, where it belongs. Using data for the collective good of others and not for individual gain or profit may seem like an altruistic or perhaps even naive goal, but it is one that should be considered as part of the stewardship responsibility organizations have when contemplating the use of personally identifiable data embedded into a business process.

Perceptions of Personal Data

Irina Raicu

Director, Internet Ethics Program,
Markkula Center for Applied Ethics

Do we own our personal data? If we don't, who does? Or should we ask, rather, whether it's appropriate to think of personal data as a commodity in the first place?

In an article titled "Selling Your Bulk Online Data Really Means Selling Your Autonomy," Evgeny Morozov argues that

> [w]e shouldn't unquestionably accept the argument that personal data is just like any other commodity and that most of our digital problems would disappear if only, instead of gigantic data monopolists like Google and Facebook, we had an army of smaller data entrepreneurs. We don't let people practice their right to autonomy in order to surrender that very right by selling themselves into slavery. Why make an exception for those who want to sell a slice of their intellect and privacy rather than their bodies?[1]

Striking a similar note in a presentation titled "On Personal Data, Forgiveness, and the 'Right to Be Forgotten,'" the philosopher Luciano Floridi reflects that

> [t]here are roughly two ways of looking at personal data. One is in terms of the philosophy of economics. Your data are yours as in "My data, my house, my car: I own it...and if you trespass, you are trespassing the boundaries of my property."...Then there's another way of looking at personal information, that's got to do...with the philosophy of mind—the philosophy of personal identity. My data, or my memories, are more like my hand, my liver, my lungs, my heart. It's not that they are mine because I own them; they are mine because they *constitute* me....Making a copy of my data [is] not taking away

---

1 Evgeny Morozov, "Selling Your Bulk Online Data Really Means Selling Your Autonomy," *New Republic*, May 13, 2014.

that data, but there's something about cloning here, and being intrusive, that's got nothing to do with trespassing, but more like kidnapping.[2]

For a while, it had become common to argue that the provision of various "free" services on the internet represents, in fact, transactions within which users "pay" for those services with their personal data (some still argue this). However, if personal data is not a commodity, but something constitutive of us as human beings, does that make those transactions more akin to organ donations?

If so, these would be "donations" preceded by remarkably inadequate informed consent. Back in 2016, detailing the findings of a study on Americans' attitudes toward privacy and information sharing, the Pew Research Center noted that one "of the most unsettling aspects of privacy issues to many of the focus group participants [was] how hard they feel it is to get information about what is collected and uncertainty about who is collecting the data."[3] By 2019, the same research center was reporting that about "eight-in-ten or more U.S. adults say they have very little or no control over the data that government (84%) or companies (81%) collect about them"; in addition, "81% of Americans think the potential risks of data collection by companies about them outweigh the benefits, and 66% say the same about government data collection about them."[4] In the intervening years, more information about the collection and use of personal data has led to less consent.

Any practitioners working with personal data need to understand and address this reality. Many Americans apparently view personal data not as the "new oil" but as the lifeblood of their autonomy.

---

2 Luciano Floridi, "On Personal Data, Forgiveness, and the 'Right to Be Forgotten,'" Markkula Center for Applied Ethics, March 10, 2015, YouTube video, 7:51, *https://oreil.ly/1PRu5*.

3 Lee Rainie and Maeve Duggan, "Privacy and Information Sharing," Pew Research Center (Internet and Technology), January 14, 2016.

4 Brooke Auxier, Lee Rainie, Monica Anderson, Andre Perrin, Madhu Kumar, and Erica Turner, "Americans and Privacy: Concerned, Confused, and Feeling Lack of Control over Their Personal Information," Pew Research Center (Internet and Technology), November 15, 2019.

Should Data Have Rights?

Jennifer Lewis Priestley

Associate Dean & Dir. of the Analytics and Data Science Institute,
Kennesaw State University

Your DNA has rights. Or at least it is protected under the law. The Genetic Information Nondiscrimination Act of 2008 (GINA) and the Health Information Portability and Accountability Act (HIPAA) both apply information privacy and data security obligations to protect genetic information. By extension, the humans to whom the DNA is attached are protected from discrimination with regard to medical insurance coverage, hiring, termination, or compensation. To clarify, the protection of an individual's DNA under GINA and HIPAA is relevant only when it is connected to that individual.

Millions of people have contributed (actually paid to contribute) their physical DNA to repositories such as Ancestry.com or 23andMe (*https://www. 23andme.com*) and have "clicked" their tacit approval to have the value of their DNA disassociated from their physical person for the purposes of genealogical research, medical research, and even the association and identification of criminals. In 2015, the $20 billion genomics company Helix sequenced about 90% of the world's DNA data, with the expectation of opening it up to consumers in a digital marketplace built on DNA.[1]

Now consider online activity.

Increasingly, our online activity creates a digital DNA that is as unique to each person as their physical DNA. While most people acknowledge that they create "digital exhaust" as a function of daily activities, most may not recognize that they are creating a new form of DNA that may exist and generate monetizable value after they no longer exist physically. This is true of images and likenesses that are captured daily through facial recognition technology.

---

1 Megan Molteni, "Helix's Bold Plan to Be Your One Stop Personal Genomics Shop," *Wired*, July 24, 2017, *https://oreil.ly/7xFBp*.

Consider the fact that the device you use to primarily access the internet (phone, tablet, laptop), the way you input information (case sensitive or all lowercase), the search engine you use, and the time of day that you are most active can be combined to develop a powerful profile of who you are and your likelihood of paying your bills, buying a car, moving, having a baby, or developing cancer.[2] Your image "in the wild" can be used to profile criminals without your consent. Beyond its "source," digital DNA has potential value to society—much like Henrietta's cells.

This narrative creates an ethical dilemma that any analytical professional should then consider. That is, like our physical DNA, should our digital DNA, which is potentially more valuable, have "rights" that are disassociated with the human that generated it?

---

2 Tobias Berg, Valentin Burg, Ana Gombović, and Manju Puri, "On the Rise of the FinTechs—Credit Scoring Using Digital Footprints," FDIC Center for Financial Research Working Paper Series, July 2018, *https://oreil.ly/AfAJs*.

Anonymizing Data Is Really, Really Hard

Damian Gordon

University Lecturer, Technological University of Dublin

Data analytics holds the promise of a more profound and complete understanding of the world around us. Many have claimed that because of the present-day ubiquity of data, it has become possible to finally automate everything from value creation to organizational adaptability. To achieve this, large quantities of data about people (and their behaviors) are required. But there is a balance to be struck between the need for this very detailed data and the rights of individuals to maintain their privacy. One approach to dealing with this challenge is to remove some of the key identifiers from a dataset, sometimes called the "name data," which typically includes fields such as *Name*, *Address*, and *Social Security Number*. Those are the features that would appear to be the key characteristics that uniquely identify an individual. Unfortunately, there is a wide range of techniques that allows others to de-anonymize such data.

Some datasets can be de-anonymized by very rudimentary means; for example, some individuals in a dataset of anonymous movie reviews were identified simply by searching for similarly worded reviews on websites that are not anonymous—IMDB, for example. In another case, AOL released a list of 20 million web search queries it had collected, and two reporters were able to uniquely identify an individual based on clues in their specific searches.

Beyond those simple approaches, a more complex approach is to explore the other fields that remain unchanged, so if the dataset has the name data removed, this could result in problems; for example, if a researcher is looking at the relationship between where someone lives and their level of health, removing the *Address* identifier would prove detrimental to the research. To address this issue, sometimes an *Area Code* parameter is left, and then the research can be successfully completed. However, a hacker can uniquely identify the individual records from a dataset that has the name data removed, but includes *Area Code* and other parameters, by incorporating existing publicly available data into the analysis, as shown by a number of computer scientists, most notably Latanya Sweeney, Director of the Data Privacy Lab at Harvard University.

Anonymizing data in a social media (or networked) context is even more challenging, and it is worth noting that researchers are often more interested in the relationships between people rather than an individual's data. Typically, a social network is represented as a graph, with nodes representing individuals or organizations, and the edges representing connections and communications between the individuals or organizations. So even if the anonymization of the data operates in essentially the same manner as before, by removing common identifiers, specifically the name data, all the hacker has to do is create a number of false individuals and use those to connect to existing individuals within the network (assuming the dataset represents a live system). After connecting to a small number of real individuals, it will be possible to uniquely identify them based on the configuration (shape) of the connections of each individual to others.

The poet Alexander Pope said, "How happy is the blameless vestal's lot! The world forgetting, by the world forgot," meaning that cloistered nuns have forgotten about the outside world, and the world reciprocates; this suggests that perhaps the only way to remain anonymous is to stay away from any services that would record data about you.

Just Because You Could, Should You? Ethically Selecting Data for Analytics

Steve Stone

Founder, NSU Techologies & Former CIO,
Lowe's and Limited Brands

As I am writing, my state is entering week four of a mandatory stay-at-home order because of COVID-19. Like many other Americans, I look to multiple news sources and infographics to better understand the linkage between science and policy, and between data and action. Also, I have found fantastic sources of public data that I pull down daily to analyze using various tools.

A few weeks ago, two companies, X-Mode and Tectonix, joined forces to develop a visualization tracking the cell phone location data from Fort Lauderdale spring breakers who crowded beaches, ignoring social distancing guidelines. This widely seen visualization tracked the immense geographic spread of the spring breakers as they left Fort Lauderdale and returned to their campuses or homes.

It was an amazing demonstration and gave many in the general public their first glimpse of the immense power of analytics and data visualization. However, it also called into question the ethics and legality of tracking cell phone signals for purposes other than the phone owners intended. As we progress through the pandemic, we will face choices on balancing personal privacy against the goals of public safety. This dilemma is not a new one. Data scientists and analysts routinely face similar data ethics decisions.

As an example, in one of my previous roles, my department evaluated video analytics software that worked in conjunction with the video-based traffic counters mounted at the entrance of each of our retail locations. The traffic counters simply counted the number of people leaving and entering our stores. Logic embedded in the counters filtered certain people (employees and children with parents) from tallies. Otherwise, the counters provided numbers in by time and numbers out by time. The analytics software we evaluated could determine the gender and age of those entering the store. We tested this in our lab and found it to be moderately to significantly accurate. However, when we discussed the use of the technology with our general counsel, we unraveled a whole set of ethical and legal concerns. A similar scenario played out when we evaluated "digital fit" technologies that determined the appropriate garment size for a person based on a digital photo.

The COVID-19 and work examples illustrate one of the core ethical challenges for many data scientists and analysts: should I use this data in my analysis? Notice, I used the word "should," not "could." The ethical question of "should" versus "could" is very relevant with the increasing amount of data available in the public domain. How should a data scientist or data engineer go about determining "should"?

Consider the following five criteria for determining the ethical use of data:

- The data must be authentic and trusted. If we do not know or trust the source, we should not use the data.

- Contextual use of the data must match the original intent for which it was collected. If we are using data in a manner that is inconsistent with the purpose for which it was collected, we should not use the data.

- The parties providing the data must give consent for its collection. We verify consent by understanding whether the people who surrendered the data had a choice and clearly understood the ramifications of their choice. If we are unsure of consent, we should not use the data.

- The risk of unintended harm or unwanted exposure for the parties providing the data must be mitigated. If someone provides data under the pretense of anonymity, we must take steps to protect their rights. If we lack adequate measures of protection, we should not use the data.

- Bias in the collection of the data must be identified and mitigated. While this is similar to our first criterion, data can be authentic but biased. Bias in the collection of the data results in bias in ensuing models. If we lack a clear understanding of the methods and practices used in the collection process, we should not use the data.

Data scientists, engineers, and analysts are often the final decision makers on the inclusion of datasets in analytics. Data ethics should play a significant role in this decision. Remember, just because you could doesn't mean that you should.

Limit the Viewing of Customer Information by Use Case and Result Sets

Robert J. Abate

VP & CDO, Global IDs Inc.

One of the challenges of data science today is the availability of many datasets that can be assembled together for a use case (i.e., to provide a 360-degree view of the customer), such that the resulting integrated dataset creates toxic combinations of data, including information that might be misused if in the wrong hands.

Consider that if you combine customer information and shopping history (in the case of a retailer of consumer product goods with direct-to-customer sales) with US Census Bureau information and CDC natality (birth rate) statistics, you can determine a lot about a household—too much, in fact. For example, you can determine the members of the household and their education levels and incomes, the items they've purchased on a regular basis, the age of children in the household, and so on.

We have learned that the right people should see the right data at the right time with the right quality (a standard in data governance programs), but has your organization considered the use cases for information at this level of detail? One way to limit people from viewing Personally Identifiable Information (PII), or to limit the creation of toxic combinations of information (e.g., name, address, age, and phone number), is to "sign data out" from your data lake (or customer information hub) for usage during a given duration or time period. Along with the signed-out data, people would get obfuscated information about name, address, phone number, and other key information that would identify a consumer. If the use case was trying to find out what shoppers are purchasing, this could be identified, and the organization would have to blind consumers' PII.

At a large retailer, we removed the ability of a query to run against these types of fields and simultaneously blinded the data returned. We also limited any query that returned fewer than 10 results—for the reason that if you lived in a very small town (say, a population of 50), you could probably identify the individual(s) if the results were fewer than 10. We could envision that an unethical individual would want to see what their neighbors were purchasing. If a data scientist needed to know more, they would have to justify to an ethics committee their reasoning for the request.

Consider a health care provider who combines many internal and external datasets and can now determine, for example, who has AIDS in a specific community. This would expose the organization to a HIPAA violation, not to mention be highly unethical! To prevent this from happening, we would again allow queries where the result set had to return more than 50 results in order to allow access. The key here is to determine what sensitive data, when combined with other datasets (both internal and external), could result in the exposition or identification of an individual (referred to earlier as toxic combinations of data).

Consider also the case where an employee wants to pull a very large portion of your customer file or data lake—what use case could they have that would require this amount of information? Is it possible that this is an individual who is considering leaving and taking this information with them? Limiting the result set's maximum size is also a consideration in this situation.

This type of blocking and tackling in the data space is now a reality, and organizations have to plan and prepare for securing their information assets as they would their monetary assets. For example, would you allow a single employee to withdraw $1 million in cash without any checks and balances? We all know the answer is no, so why treat datasets any differently?

Rethinking the "Get the Data" Step

Phil Bangayan

Principal Data Scientist, Teradata

My key responsibility as a principal data scientist is creating accurate models, which involves getting appropriate data. This step of getting data occurs early in the data science process that was taught to me and all aspiring data scientists, today and going back to the late 1990s, in the form of CRISP-DM (cross-industry standard process for data mining). After practicing on both the client and vendor sides, I have learned that this step receives insufficient attention, opening up data scientists to traps when they do not understand where the data comes from, misuse data collected for a different purpose, or utilize proxy data in a possibly unethical manner.

The data science process I learned is similar to the one documented by Joe Blitzstein and Hanspeter Pfister at Harvard: (1) ask an interesting question, (2) get the data, (3) explore the data, (4) model the data, and (5) communicate and visualize the results. Going back to 1997, the similar process CRISP-DM, prominent in customer relationship management, includes the following steps: (1) business understanding, (2) data understanding, (3) data preparation, (4) modeling, (5) evaluation, and (6) deployment. In both these frameworks, getting the data is the second step and affects all the following steps. Having the wrong data at the start results in the wrong models.

But what happens when the modeler does not know how the data was generated? A client recently handed me a dataset for building a model. The data appeared to have events leading up to churn. Our solution involved asking the provider three questions: (1) what are all the possible customer journeys? (2) what are the data structures? and (3) what data is collected at each event along all customer journeys? Answering these questions took several hours, as each question led to follow-up topics. Through this investigation, we learned that event collection was inconsistent across groups in that some groups collected more detailed information than others. Building a model with the given dataset would have inappropriately attributed churn more heavily to those groups collecting event-level data.

On the client side, I confronted a related issue of using data collected for a different purpose when building a pricing model. We sought to predict whether consumers would pay a certain amount for a product. Following the model-building process, we asked the interesting question and then found answers to the survey question about what consumers would pay. However, the responses were biased because the hypothesized price was the lowest choice in the survey. Naturally, more respondents picked that price. Without the documentation and guidance of the researcher who ran the study, my model would have produced skewed results. To address the issue, we conducted new research to collect the necessary data even though there was an associated cost.

Along those lines, model builders may be tempted to use proxy data when specific data is unavailable or expensive to collect. In her book *Weapons of Math Destruction* (Crown), Cathy O'Neil brings up an example of using zip code data, which can be used as a proxy for race or wealth. I can understand the temptation to use that data because of its prevalence. After all, consumers are much more likely to provide their mailing address than their income. But multiple issues arise. For example, laws specifically forbid insurance companies from using race as a determining factor for premiums. Moreover, an ethical question arises, as a premium or other rate would be determined by factors outside of the consumer's control, such as the driving records of neighbors. So care must be taken if proxies are to be used at all.

These three examples illustrate the importance of the "getting the data" step in the model-building process. This step is portrayed as going through existing repositories to find appropriate datasets. *Model builders need to go one step further by asking how the data was generated, understanding the purpose of collecting the original data, and understanding the effects of using proxies to determine if the existing data is appropriate.* Sometimes, the proper step is to collect *new* data. Otherwise, the resulting models will be inaccurate as a result of the "garbage in, garbage out" phenomenon.

How to Determine What Data Can Be Used Ethically

Leandre Adifon

VP Engineering & Technology, Ingersoll Rand

Entities such as people, communities, corporations, and so on each have an identity. They have realities, characteristics, and special traits that uniquely qualify them and distinguish them from one another. Such identity defines who they are in the universe of beings. Until recently, before the Big Data revolution that is still unfolding, entities were identified with just a few data points.

For people, it was mainly their first and family names, their place of origin, and maybe their parents' names and tribe. Leonardo da Vinci, who was born in Anchiano near Vinci in Italy, was well known across history and geographies with respect to his place of origin. Companies may have simply assumed the name of their founder. The means of information dissemination were limited; so, too, was what needed to be known about people, communities, or companies. When we were asked a simple question about who we were, our answer was always limited to a few data points that best described us: our name, place of origin, profession and place of work, and so forth.

The 21st century, however, has seen an explosion of information about everyone and everything, amplified by social media. Data has assumed prime importance. It is collected about everyone and everything. More is known about any of us than we can imagine. More and more qualifiers can describe the identity of anyone. Therefore, our freedom is in question. Lives can be instantly destroyed when information is weaponized against them. People's habits are being mapped, and the data collected about them is being used in many ways. Companies that can better capture their customers' buying behaviors can drive them to spend more by anticipating their needs and inviting them to every kind of offering.

Just like any good technology designed to improve people's lives, information in the wrong hands can become poisonous. Instead of helping people receive the right care for a disease, get to the right place at the right time, or minimize their expenditure of time and money, information can essentially empty them of their human content and dignity. It can reveal where they are, what they own, and so on. Therefore, data privacy assumes a vital importance. Unauthorized disclosure of people's concealed information with intrusion in their private life should be prevented.

Now the question is how to determine what data can be ethically utilized. The key word in this question is "ethically." Ethics, in simple terms, is a set of moral principles or values by which particular groups of people live their lives. The rules of the system are defined to guide the conduct of individuals and protect their lives and their community's life. It is therefore crucial that the communities that live by the same ethical rules define themselves, or become involved in defining what constitutes their privacy, to be protected from unauthorized publication. Since such a set of rules can vary between tribes, communities, and nations, the individuals of those groups are best suited to draw the line between public and private, and everyone else that deals with them should respect such demarcation.

When the plethora of data described earlier is not passed through the lenses of a set of rules, every individual's natural life can easily be compromised. This will prevent people from living freely and realizing their potential. The European Union has promulgated the legislation known as GDPR to protect the data and privacy of its citizens as well as control the transfer of their personal information outside of the EU.

To guarantee every person's freedom to control their personal data, a few simple considerations should be made:

- People's well-being and security should be put at the core of any data collection, analysis, and utilization.
- Communities or nations should be involved in drawing the line between public and private data.
- Authorization should be obtained from individuals before the release of their personal data to any third party. The use of fine print (which most people do not read) for privacy notices on paper or online should be discouraged.
- Those involved in criminal investigations and who may have access to people's personal data should collect and manage that data under oath.

- There should be a damage control and repair mechanism or a disaster recovery process to protect victims of privacy violation.
- High school education programs should give instruction on the protection of personal data as well as its handling, to reach individuals at an age when privacy may not be a priority.

Data privacy measures and policies should always be aimed at protecting people's security and lives.

Ethics Is the Antidote to Data Breaches

Damian Gordon

University Lecturer, Technological University of Dublin

In the past few years, you must have noticed depressingly regular reports of data breaches, cloud leaks, and cyberattacks occurring. It would be easy to tell ourselves the problem is that hackers have become so much smarter, or that the systems have become too complex to manage, but the reality is that tech organizations don't take their own security sufficiently seriously, and they don't treat our personal data with the stewardship that we would hope for from them. These organizations think of our personal data as a commodity that can be bought, sold, and traded on the markets. What they don't realize is that our personal data represents fragments of our lives. When a data breach occurs, it is often we as individuals who suffer, as the breach adds to our stress, subtracts from our time, multiplies our fears, and divides us from other people.

This issue is most noticeable in the case of cloud storage, where leaks are constant; the organizations that employ these services appear to have little understanding of how their cloud instances are configured and seem unable to audit and manage them. These misconfigured instances (usually storage buckets or databases left accessible to the general public) have been responsible for many of the largest data leaks in recent years. The issue isn't simply that the IT personnel responsible for managing this relatively new technology don't know how to configure these systems, but rather that they lack the integrity to admit their lack of knowledge, and as a result they misconfigure systems that leave millions of records exposed, with many people's lives inconvenienced.

To solve this problem, we need to start in the third-level institutes, the colleges and universities, and transform the curriculum to make probity, integrity, and, most importantly, ethics central in all computer science degrees. A revolution is needed to imbue these students with a deeply rooted sense of ethics, beyond the legal requirements, beyond the professional guidelines, and toward a sense of kindness and fellowship with others in all their actions. Ethics must be presented and taught in such a way that it will become second nature to students, so that they will never program a computer system without first considering the ethical implications of what they are doing. The content of this new curriculum is being created for us on a daily basis. As we read of more and more examples of organizations that demonstrate carelessness and thoughtlessness in their conduct, we can use these parables to create a new breed of caring and thoughtful students, whose ethical skills we can nurture.

Abraham Lincoln said that "the dogmas of the quiet past, are inadequate to the stormy present. The occasion is piled high with difficulty, and we must rise—with the occasion. As our case is new, so we must think anew, and act anew." Now more than ever, we must act anew to create professionals who consider their actions, who admit their shortcomings, and who reflect on whose lives they can affect.

Ethical Issues Are Front and Center in Today's Data Landscape

Kenneth Viciana

Director, Information Risk Management, Fiserv

Looking back at my data journey, it's really amazing how data management has evolved. I began working in the enterprise data warehouse (EDW) era. We were focused on building a "single source of the truth" that a company could rely on for decision-making, analytics, and reporting capabilities. Lots of money was spent on resources and infrastructure in order to rationalize/organize/store data, and to ensure it was deemed to be fit for use.

Fast-forward, and companies switched gears and began embracing Big Data. The model shifted, as companies wanted to quickly analyze large datasets to determine whether value could be captured prior to spending time, money, and resources to organize and store the data. Companies believed that having huge quantities of data alone was a differentiator. They touted the size of their Hadoop clusters and hired armies of data scientists to find value in Big Data. At this juncture, ethics truly became a game changer in this space!

Data innovation efforts were focused on creating hypotheses and use cases to monetize data. But this presented some key ethical concerns about:

- Data ownership
- Data transparency
- Consumer consent
- Data privacy
- Data security

We've seen Facebook made the poster child for data privacy, with Mark Zuckerberg testifying on Capitol Hill. In essence, many Facebook users simply viewed Facebook as providing a free interface through which they could keep in touch with friends and family. Yes, Facebook does provide that user experience, but it is also a platform that is reposing lots of data about its user base. And it's a highly profitable business, with revenues driven by advertising. Soon we would come to realize the magnitude of ethical concerns that exist here!

Ethical concerns have led to regulations (GDPR and CCPA), and companies could face significant fines if their programs lack compliance and rigor. Storing Big Data (specifically, personally identifiable information [PII] and other sensitive data) is now being viewed as a risk. Great care is taken to partition and/or mask PII and other sensitive data.

To address regulations such as GDPR and CCPA, companies are very focused on providing transparency around data. They are creating data inventories/glossaries that include both business and technical metadata. Documenting data lineage and how the data propagates within the infrastructure is also a key component. Vendor solutions exist to help with this cataloging effort, and this key artifact is leveraged to facilitate audit activities.

Data security has also become a major focus for companies as they work to keep themselves secure and out of the headlines.

A data breach in which PII/sensitive data is leaked has huge ramifications for a company! As such, companies are building out large cybersecurity organizations and equipping them with the latest and greatest shiny objects to keep infrastructures secure. Trust is such an important factor, and the brand reputation can take a big hit if customers' sensitive data is compromised.

In their efforts to stay ahead of the bad guys, cybersecurity organizations are embracing data and analytics to help mitigate risk. They are identifying infrastructure activity baselines and monitoring environments for activities that are outside of normal patterns. Many companies are leveraging AI to perform this analysis, and this bubbles up events that require the attention of security professionals. This filtering activity enables security professionals to focus on actual risks rather than having to mine all event data.

In summation, ethical issues are currently dominating the data landscape. Companies are trying to balance defensive activities (governance/privacy/security) with offensive strategies (data monetization). Risks around customer data are recognized, but companies are still determining their risk appetites in this area. Companies are taking this seriously while paying close attention to the regulations (GDPR and CCPA), and this will play a key role in determining what happens next.

The amounts of data and types of data will certainly continue to grow and evolve. It will be very interesting to see how companies pivot their data strategies, and how they proceed with the management and oversight of data.

Get your popcorn ready...

Silos Create Problems— Perhaps More Than You Think

Bonnie Holub

Practice Lead, Data Science, Americas, Teradata

In our work preparing to write a book focusing on chief data officer (CDO) career success, my coauthor, Dave Mathias, and I have interviewed chief data officers and chief analytics officers from Fortune 500 companies, and one theme has resounded throughout all of our discussions: silos (data silos and perspective silos) create problems. The ethical risk here is that in ignoring best practices and maintaining obsolete data silos, CDOs put their organizations at risk for unethical, and possibly illegal, behaviors.

From a management perspective, data silos are databases, data warehouses, data lakes, and so forth in which data is stored for one purpose and is not integrated with the rest of the data that an organization owns. As consumers, we run into this all the time. Think about the last time you called a customer service phone number. They may have recognized your phone number, and you may have entered your sixteen-digit account number and made five or six selections in the automated menu, but when you finally get to speak to a human being, they still don't know who you are or what you are calling about. That kind of problem happens when the incoming call system is not well integrated with the customer account records. Managers bemoan this situation, because from their perspective, if they are running a report on sales but don't have it correlated to their accounts receivable system, then they may be getting bad data: yes, sales are very high at customer X, but if they are not paying their bills, is it really good business?

Often, isolated silos of data arise in companies as legacy artifacts of mergers and acquisitions that were never fully integrated into the acquiring companies' processes and systems. Sometimes silos exist because specialty software exists to serve one part of the business, but regardless of how they arise, they are the bane of upper management for several reasons. First and foremost, unintegrated data is simply less valuable than integrated, unified, holistically accessible data. Companies have realized that the data they have on clients, products, production runs, logistics, and so on gives them valuable insight into operations, customers, leading economic indicators for their particular industries, demand, and usage patterns, just to name a few things. If a company's data is isolated into data silos, then managers have just a small sliver of a view of the data and can harvest only some of the value that a unified, overall picture can provide. This is a risk to the business because leaders don't have a big-picture view of what is really happening. In effect, executives have a blinkered view of the state of the business and the key interconnections across it. By consciously maintaining this blinkered view, executives are willfully ignoring key data, a dereliction of their duty to serve the business to the best of their ability. This is often described as the "1 + 1 = 3" phenomenon. One set of data gives you certain valuable insights, another gives you other insights, but combined and properly integrated, the two datasets provide more value than the sum of their parts. Now extrapolate that for three, four, or more datasets, and you start to gain perspective on the scale of the problem. Next, silos are bad from an operations perspective—a wider, more specialized workforce is required to support the diverse silos. Silos also create endless headaches for IT leadership, which needs to support couture systems on arcane infrastructures. But I digress.

It is not just silos of data that create problems; perspective silos are another problem. What the CDOs have told us time and again is this: spending time in different job roles, different industries, and different perspectives was essential to each individual's journey to senior leadership. Every senior leader we spoke with credited diversity of education and work experiences in their career as a key characteristic that led to their ultimate success. They see challenges from a variety of stakeholders' perspectives because they have sat in different roles across the organization.

Business leaders are not alone in their appreciation of diverse viewpoints. In her book *Weapons of Math Destruction* (Crown), Cathy O'Neil writes:

> More and more, I worried about the separation between technical models and real people, and about the moral repercussions of that separation. In fact, I saw the same pattern emerging that I'd witnessed in finance: a false sense of security was leading to widespread use of imperfect models, self-serving definitions of success, and growing feedback loops.

This is another way to say that siloed views, lack of perspective, and lack of diverse viewpoints create pernicious outcomes. In some circumstances, these pernicious outcomes cross legal boundaries, putting a CDO's company at risk. In addition, these outcomes may be unethical as well—a further risk in an economy where stakeholders are seeking to align their investment goals with their ethical principles.

In conclusion, silos create problems. Silos can be data silos, where the complete value of the constituent data components is not harvested due to parochial views, or they can be perspective silos, where organizations lack perspective to view opportunities and challenges from diverse enough directions and thus set themselves up for failure.

Securing Your Data Against Breaches Will Help Us Improve Health Care

Fred Nugen

Data Science Instructor, UC Berkeley

When you go to a new health care clinic in the United States, doctors and nurses pull up your patient record based on your name and birthdate. Except sometimes it's not *your* chart they pull up. This is not only a health care problem; it's also a data science problem.

Two things (at least) contribute to this error: a lack of consistent and uniform patient records and public mistrust in protection of data. Both of them hold health care back from data science revolutions.

When patient records are transferred from one major hospital system to another, patient data passes through health information exchanges. The current rate of correctly matching patients between systems is estimated to be around 30%.[1] With considerable effort from data scientists put into data cleaning and better algorithms, we could potentially match as often as 95%. This is an important opportunity for data science to improve health care! It's called "master data management" or "data governance," and while we have a long way to go, we're getting better.

The health care industry works hard to prevent misidentification. It is standard practice to use at least two patient identifiers, such as name and birthdate.[2] Unfortunately, name and birthdate do not uniquely identify a patient; a third identifier should also be used, and there are many options, such as

---

1 RAND Corporation, "Defining and Evaluating Patient-Empowered Approaches to Improving Record Matching," 2018, *https://doi.org/10.7249/RR2275*.

2 World Health Organization, "Patient Identification," Patient Safety Solutions, vol. 1, sol. 2 (May 2007), *https://oreil.ly/sXe-g*.

hospital ID, Social Security number, a wristband with barcodes, photographs, and two-factor authentication devices. However, a third identifier, or even a fourth, won't solve the problem. Humans performing repetitive processes, even under ideal circumstances, are accurate only 99.98% of the time. In high-stress situations such as medical emergencies, accuracy rates fall to about 92%.[3]

Computers supplement health care workers' accuracy. Most of the US health care system uses statistical matching of multiple patient attributes.[4] An alert notifies users that a patient is statistically similar to another patient. Even after decades of improvement, however, medical errors persist.

While excellent master data management can bring us to a 95% correct identification rate in health information exchanges, some have concluded the only way to improve to 99% is by adopting a universal patient ID.[5] Simply put, if society decides to prioritize patient identification, it must be willing to accept a universal patient ID. Master data management, corporate consolidation, Social Security numbers, and national health coverage are all consistent with the use of universal patient IDs.

A universal patient ID may seem inevitable, but it is not. Many organizations have good cause to resist a universal ID or database. As data scientists, we appreciate the American Civil Liberties Union's argument that *any* nationwide ID will lead to surveillance and monitoring of citizens.[6] The ECRI Institute, a health care research organization, identifies understandable cultural and social barriers to patient ID policies.[7] The National Rifle Association has successfully resisted a searchable database of gun owners.[8]

This is where we come in. Before society readily accepts a universal ID, the data science field must demonstrate that users' privacy can and will be maintained. Our challenge is to ensure that people have autonomy over how their data can be used and who can use it. We must prevent catastrophic data breaches like Equifax, or unethical data mining from the likes of Cambridge

---

3 Fred Trotter and David Uhlman, *Hacking Healthcare* (Sebastopol, CA: O'Reilly Media, 2011).

4 RAND Corporation, "Identity Crisis: An Examination of the Costs and Benefits of a Unique Patient Identifier for the U.S. Health Care System," 2008, *https://rand.org/t/MG753*.

5 ECRI Institute, "Patient Identification Errors," June 2016, *https://oreil.ly/3AYr0*.

6 American Civil Liberties Union, "5 Problems with National ID Cards," *https://oreil.ly/vSWN4*.

7 ECRI Institute, "ECRI PSO Deep Dive: Patient Identification," August 2016, *https://oreil.ly/lavcO*.

8 Jeanne Marie Laskas, "Inside the Federal Bureau of Way Too Many Guns," *GQ*, August 30, 2016, *https://oreil.ly/DtejG*.

Analytica and Facebook and Target.[9] We must build something we have not yet earned: trust.

Securing private data against breaches is hard and costly and takes vigilance. The ethical treatment of data *also* comes at a cost—exploitation is often profitable! A universal ID would be a powerful, exploitable tool that invites data breaches. We are not ready for it, but we could be, once we build the public's trust.

Building trust and appropriate data governance—this is how we eliminate medical error.

---

9 Federal Trade Commission, "Equifax Data Breach Settlement," January 2020, *https://oreil.ly/Qhfzl*; Wikipedia, "Facebook–Cambridge Analytica data scandal," last modified May 29, 2020, 21:12, *https://oreil.ly/szpeQ*; Charles Duhigg, "How Companies Learn Your Secrets," *New York Times Magazine*, February 16, 2012, *https://oreil.ly/1jHcf*.

PART IV

Defining Appropriate Targets & Appropriate Usage

It is critical to ensure that any analytics and data science process is targeting an ethical goal. After a process is created, it is then necessary to ensure that the results are applied only in an ethical fashion. This section delves into the issues faced during these two phases of the development and deployment process.

Algorithms Are Used Differently than Human Decision Makers

Rachel Thomas

Cofounder, fast.ai; Director, USF Center for Applied Data Ethics

People often discuss algorithms as though they are plug-and-play, interchangeable with human decision makers—just comparing error rates, for instance, when deciding whether to replace a human decision maker with an algorithmic result. However, in practice, algorithms and human decision makers are used differently, and failure to address those differences can lead to a number of ethical risks and harms.

Here are a few common ways that algorithms and human decision makers are used differently in practice:

- Algorithms are more likely to be implemented with *no recourse process* in place.
- Algorithms are often used *at scale*.
- Algorithmic systems are *cheap*.
- People are more likely to assume algorithms are *objective* or *error-free*.

There is a lot of overlap between these factors. If the main motivation for implementing an algorithm is cost cutting, then adding an appeals process (or even diligently checking for errors) may be considered an "unnecessary" expense.

Consider one case study: after the state of Arkansas implemented software (*https://oreil.ly/m9kHi*) to determine people's health care benefits, many people saw a drastic reduction in the amount of care they received but were given no explanation and no way to appeal. Tammy Dobbs, a woman with cerebral palsy who needs an aide to help her to get out of bed, go to the bathroom, and more, had her hours of help suddenly reduced by 20 hours a week, transforming her life for the worse. Eventually, a lengthy court case uncovered errors in the software implementation, and Tammy's hours were restored (along with those of many others who were impacted by the errors).

Another real-world case study comes from an algorithm that was used to fire public school teachers. Observations of fifth-grade teacher Sarah Wysocki's classroom yielded positive reviews. Her assistant principal wrote (*https://oreil.ly/ALVe-*), "It is a pleasure to visit a classroom in which the elements of sound teaching, motivated students, and a positive learning environment are so effectively combined." Two months later, she was fired by an opaque algorithm, along with more than 200 other teachers. The head of the PTA and a parent of one of Wysocki's students described her as "one of the best teachers I've ever come in contact with. Every time I saw her, she was attentive to the children, went over their schoolwork; she took time with them." That people are losing needed health care or being fired without mechanisms for recourse is truly dystopian!

Mathematician Cathy O'Neil wrote in her 2016 book *Weapons of Math Destruction* (Crown) that many algorithmic systems

> tend to punish the poor. They specialize in bulk, and they're cheap. That's part of their appeal. The wealthy, by contrast, often benefit from personal input. A white-shoe law firm or an exclusive prep school will lean far more on recommendations and face-to-face interviews than will a fast-food chain or a cash-strapped urban school district. The privileged, we'll see time and again, are processed more by people, the masses by machines.

This harm can be compounded by the fact that many people mistakenly believe that computers are objective and error-free. A city official in Lancaster (*https://oreil.ly/mY_If*), California, where an IBM Watson dashboard is being used for predictive policing, said, "With machine learning, with automation, there's a 99% success, so that robot is—will be—99% accurate in telling us what is going to happen next, which is really interesting." This statement is completely false. It is a dangerous yet common misconception that can lead people to overlook harmful errors in computer output.

As roboticist Peter Haas said (*https://oreil.ly/dIvsh*) in a TEDx talk, "In AI, we have Milgram's ultimate authority figure," referring to Stanley Milgram's famous experiments (*https://oreil.ly/yWvhA*) showing that most people will obey orders from authority figures, even to the point of harming or killing other humans. How much more likely will people be to trust algorithms perceived as objective and correct?

Since algorithms are often used at a larger scale, mass-producing identical biases, and are assumed to be error-proof or objective, we can't compare them to human decision makers in an apples-to-apples way. Moreover, it is important that we address these differences when implementing algorithms for decision making. It is essential to implement systems for identifying errors, and mechanisms for recourse, alongside any algorithmic implementation. It is also necessary to make sure that those using the output of the algorithms understand that computers are not error-free, and that they are empowered to raise any issues they spot.

Pay Off Your Fairness Debt, the Shadow Twin of Technical Debt

Arnobio Morelix

Chief Innovation Officer, Startup Genome
Data Scientist-in-Residence, Inc. Magazine

Technical debt is a familiar concept. It is used to describe hacky code created on the fly that does its primary job in the short term but is unwieldy and inefficient to maintain and scale in the long term. It is time we also become familiar with its shadow twin: fairness debt.

Just like its technical counterpart, we incur fairness debt when we build systems that work for our current situation and user base today but that have unintended consequences lurking underneath the surface as we continue to deploy the solutions tomorrow.

One way to incur fairness debt is by optimizing our systems and algorithms for a particular performance metric without constraints. Data scientists and technologists make these types of optimization choices deliberately and often, even if naively.

But optimization often carries a fairness debt when taken to its natural progression. A Google Ventures post (*https://oreil.ly/5fIqQ*), for example, suggests optimizing for the amount of time users spend watching videos on your app. While at first this may seem a perfectly rational way to focus engineering efforts, it can get out of control when usage becomes excessive, to the detriment of the user. As a friend managing AI products at Amazon said, "It is OK when a company is trying to get a user to go from spending seven to eight minutes a day on their app. It is a whole different game when some users are risking going from seven to eight hours a day."

At first, fairness debts are paid not by the company but by users or society. But once they get big enough, they bite our collective asses. The backlash against the companies producing smartphones and apps optimized to capture attention—and the real headwinds these businesses are facing from both a user and a regulatory standpoint—is evidence that debts can be postponed but not forgiven.

Going beyond "attention optimization," imagine a more sinister scenario in which you have a fintech company optimizing only for the profitability of the loans getting approved. It is easy to imagine a situation in which you end up with something like algorithmic redlining, and researchers at UC Berkeley have found evidence of that (*https://oreil.ly/mjawc*). Their research shows fintech lenders costing Latino and African American mortgage refinance borrowers a combined $765 million yearly, partially due to impermissible discrimination.

But just like technical debt, fairness debt can be avoided and paid early. We have one such example with Upstart.

Imagine, as happened with Upstart, that you are a fintech founder or technologist, waking up to a message from the Consumer Financial Protection Bureau (CFPB) that mentions a review of your fair lending practices, only a couple of years after you launched your product.[1] You might have been "moving fast and breaking things" and focused only on improving your tech and growing your business. But you are in a highly regulated industry, and there is growing interest in the unintended consequences of what you do. For instance, Senators Elizabeth Warren and Doug Jones are sending letters to the Federal Reserve, the Federal Deposit Insurance Corporation (FDIC), and the CFPB (*https://oreil.ly/ZkqE2*) asking about their regulatory stance on algorithm-based lending.

Although they did not call it that, the regulators were rightly seeing the possibility of fairness debt occurring. But Upstart took it seriously and did not let the debt happen.

Upstart AI-based models, careful to be fair from the start, have shown fantastic results—so good that the CFPB took the unusual step of widely sharing how well they were performing (*https://oreil.ly/eiyMH*). Upstart was able to approve 23–29% more applicants than the traditional lending model, with 15–17% lower interest rates across every tested race, ethnicity, and gender group. In addition, young adults were 32% more likely to get approved for loans, and people with incomes under $50,000 got approved 13% more.

---

1 For more information, see Upstart's blog post (*https://oreil.ly/hz4PT*) as well as CFPB's No-Action Letter (*https://oreil.ly/4HpAI*) and Fair Lending Report (*https://oreil.ly/926Aq*).

As with technical debt, incurring fairness debt is a choice, not an inevitability. Pay it off early and often, or better yet, do not incur it at all. It is the right choice. AI explainability approaches, like what Upstart used and companies such as Fiddler Labs produce, can help with this process. In a world where our technologies and algorithms will be increasingly under scrutiny, companies that are careful about avoiding fairness debt will get rewarded.

AI Ethics

Cassie Kozyrkov

Chief Decision Scientist, Google Cloud

Why aren't we talking about what makes AI uniquely more dangerous than other technologies?

The topics that come up in connection with AI ethics are vital, timely, and necessary. I just wish we wouldn't use the term "AI ethics" whenever it...isn't even specific to AI. Many so-called AI ethics talking points are about technology in general, and they're nothing new. Take them off the list and you're left with topics that focus on personhood and the singularity. Unfortunately, these distract you from what you really ought to worry about.

Marketing AI as chrome-plated humanoids takes advantage of the public's ignorance. We're a species that sees human traits in everything, from faces in toast to bodies in clouds. If I sew two buttons onto a sock, I might end up talking to it. That sock puppet's not a person, and neither is AI; robots are just another kind of pet rock. The way the term "AI" is used today isn't about developing replacement humanlike entities. Instead, AI is a set of tools for writing software, letting you program with examples (data) instead of explicit instructions. *That's* both the promise of AI and its true peril.

Levels of Distraction

Imagine that you want to automate a task that takes 10,000 steps. In traditional programming, a *person* must sweat over each of those little instructions.

Think of it as 10,000 LEGO pieces that need arranging by human hands. Since developers are blessedly impatient, they'll package up some parts so they don't need to repeat themselves. Instead of working with 10,000 loose bits, you can download those packages so that you only need to put together 50 prebuilt LEGO constructions of 200 little blocks each. If you trust other people's work, you can connect the roof piece to the house piece instead of thinking on the level of tiles and bricks.

But here's the thing: even if *you* didn't have to do all of it yourself (thank goodness), every instruction among those 10,000 steps was agonized over by a human brain...and *that's* the part that goes away with ML/AI.

AI Automates the Ineffable

With AI, instead of coding up "do this, then this, then this, then...," you can say, "try to get a good score on this data."

In other words, AI allows humans to skip handcrafting 10,000 explicit solution steps and instead automatically comes up with those 10,000 lines (or something like them) by making a solution out of patterns in examples a developer gives it. That means you can automate tasks even if no human can think up the explicit instructions for how to do them.

Prepare to have your mind blown if you've never pondered *whose* job ML/AI actually automates:

- A developer automates/accelerates other people's work.
- ML/AI automates/accelerates a developer's work.

Today there's a lot of huffing and puffing in ML/AI engineering, but most of it is about spinning up and wrangling unfriendly tools. You might write 10,000 lines of code in your project, but most of it is in service of coaxing unwieldy tools into accepting your data. As the tools get better and better, you'll eventually see that there are only *two* real instructions in ML/AI:

1. Optimize this goal...
2. ...on this dataset

That's all. Now you can use two lines of human thought to automate your task instead of 10,000. This is beautiful—and scary!

AI Enables Thoughtlessness

Here's the most immediate ML/AI-specific problem: *thoughtlessness enabled.*

Some tasks aren't very important, and it's fabulous that we can get them out of the way without much thought. But when it matters, will whoever's in charge of the project really put 5,000 instructions' worth of thought into each of those two ML/AI lines?

AI is about expressing yourself with examples, but you have the unfortunate option of pointing your system at a dataset without ever verifying that it contains relevant, unbiased, high-quality examples. If you allow yourself to select data thoughtlessly for a mission-critical use case, you could have a disaster on your hands.

AI also won't stop you from picking a flippant goal that sounded good in your head but turns out to be a terrible idea. "Catch as much spam as possible" is something a leader might say to a human developer in expectation of a solid and sensible filter. Express it the same way to an AI algorithm and you'll soon start wondering why no new email is coming in. (Answer: flagging *everything* as spam gets a perfect score on your *stated* objective.)

The scary part of AI is not the robots. It's the people.

Whenever you combine a thoughtlessness enabler with speed and scale, you get a recipe for rapidly amplified negligence.

Am I Afraid of AI?

No.

If you ask me whether I'm scared of AI, what I hear you asking me is whether I am scared of human negligence. That's the only way the question makes sense to me, since I don't believe in robot fairytales or talking to pet rocks.

I'm optimistic about humanity's AI future, but I'm also doing as much as I can not to leave it to chance. I'm convinced that the skills for responsible leadership in the AI era can be taught and that people can build effective systems safely, driving progress and making life better for those around them. That's why I and others like me choose to step up and share what we've learned the hard way, through experience or by ferreting around in previously siloed academic disciplines.

Technology improves our world, frees us from disease, expands our horizons, connects us with loved ones, and gives us longer lives. It can also surprise, destabilize, and redistribute. The more it scales, the more disruptive it can be. It's always more appropriate to think of your tools—including AI—as extending you, rather than being autonomous. When they enlarge you, be sure you've got the skills to avoid stepping on those around you.

That's why it's up to you to reinject the evaporated thoughtfulness back into AI projects you choose to build. By pointing your newfound powers in responsible directions, you'll unlock the best side of technology. Technology can be wonderful if we let it...and I believe we will.

The Ethical Data Storyteller

Brent Dykes

Author and Senior Director, Insights & Data Storytelling,
Blast Analytics

When the topic of data science and ethics is discussed, data privacy and bias in machine learning are often at the forefront of people's concerns. It can be unsettling to think that your personal data could be misused by companies, or that algorithms could perpetuate race-, gender-, or age-based biases. However, if we step back and evaluate the entire data life cycle, we find ethics can influence everything from how we collect data to how we use it to make decisions. A principled approach to analytics is needed at every stage in this data life cycle, including the "last mile" of analytics where key insights are shared or communicated with audiences.

As the need to convey insights to others in an effective manner has grown, many people have shown interest in *data storytelling,* in which key insights are visualized and presented in a compelling narrative format. However, some data professionals are still skeptical and uncomfortable with storytelling's role in communicating findings. Stories are often associated with entertainment, fiction, and fluff—leaving some people to view storytelling as subjective and superficial. Others may recognize the persuasive power of narrative but feel it can compromise the integrity of the facts. For these reasons, some individuals prefer to leave the facts alone and not taint them with any narrative treatments.

Despite the general tendency to believe "facts can speak for themselves," they often don't. Raw logic and reason frequently fail to engage people and inspire them to act. For this reason, many valuable insights are misunderstood, ignored, and forgotten. Interestingly, the human brain has been conditioned to seek out and respond to narrative. As social psychologist Jonathan Haidt states, "The human mind is a story processor, not a logic processor." Neuroscientists such as USC professor Antonio Damasio have also discovered that emotion plays a significant role in decision making. Effective data storytelling can form a bridge between logic and emotion, helping an audience to not only hear your statistics but also feel them as well.

Storytelling with data helps us to share insights more effectively, but it must be done in a responsible, ethical manner. We need not only more data storytellers but also ethical ones who share their data stories with integrity. To be an ethical data storyteller, you'll want to be mindful of the following principles:

Ensure the veracity of your insights.

Data is the foundation of every data story. You want to do everything in your power to verify that the numbers are accurate and can be trusted. While no one can guarantee the exactness of every data point, an ethical data storyteller will be thorough in their pursuit of truth and strive to provide trustworthy, directionally sound insights.

Check your biases and watch for logical fallacies.

Whenever you form a data story, you need to be mindful of potential cognitive biases, such as confirmation bias, that may negatively influence your analysis. You also want to be careful to not let faulty reasoning, such as interpreting correlation as causation, undermine your conclusions. While it may be difficult for fallible human beings to completely avoid biases and fallacies, an ethical data storyteller will seek to be as objective and rigorous as possible with their analyses and reasoning.

Start with data, not with narrative.

When you start with a desired narrative to prove a point or support a decision, you compromise the integrity of your data story. You'll be tempted to select only data points that strengthen your desired narrative and ignore ones that don't. When the destination of a data story is predetermined, the data and narrative will often be constrained and prejudiced. An ethical data storyteller will develop the narrative only after they have analyzed the data—not before—to preserve the integrity of the insights they share. When the data is approached with an open mind, it may take you to unexpected but beneficial places.

Visualize the data in a clear, reliable manner.

The goal of using data visualizations in your data stories is to help the audience clearly understand your insights. Depending on the data you choose to include in a chart or how you decide to visualize it, you can misrepresent or distort your findings—inadvertently or purposefully. For example, valuable contextual data that shows seasonality could be left out, or the size or slope of a trend could be accentuated by adjusting the scale of the y-axis. An ethical data storyteller is disciplined in how they visualize their data so their charts are communicative, not deceptive or manipulative.

When you strive to craft and tell data stories in an ethical manner, you build your credibility as a data storyteller. The care and attention you put into being ethical with your data narratives helps you establish a relationship with your key stakeholders. You become a trusted advisor and guide for them through the numbers and charts. When the goal is to have other people understand, trust, and act on your insights, being ethical with your data stories isn't merely admirable—it's essential to your success as a data storyteller.

Imbalance of Factors Affecting Societal Use of Data Science

Nenad Jukić

Professor of Information Systems, Loyola University Chicago

It is obvious that there is no data science without data. For societal improvements, the most useful data is generated by and/or based on humans. There are many factors that affect the use of such data, such as the need for privacy, the motivation for analysis, and the benefits of shared collective data. For the purpose of this essay, we will assume that the term "shared data" represents the data that combines data entries produced by and/or based on multiple humans, as opposed to data that represents one individual.

Often in contemporary discussions about human-related data, the issue of privacy is perceived as its own issue, more worthy of attention than other relevant issues. This state of affairs, where privacy is considered in isolation from all other issues, is an obstacle to progress in the societally beneficial use of data. There is no doubt that serious improvements in areas such as health care, education, and environmental protection, among others, would be possible if skilled data scientists with good intentions had access to more relevant data.

The issues of privacy and the issues of the use of shared data are treated very differently, depending on the motivation for data analysis as well as the ability to leverage the privilege of ownership. In the case of analysis in the for-profit sector (such as retail, banking, or telecom), where the motivation for analysis is largely the desire to sell more goods and services and maximize profit, the large players (such as Amazon) have access to vast amounts of customer-generated data that belongs to them. These dominant players are more or less free to use this data for the purpose of generating profit as they see fit.

On the other hand, in areas that are traditionally not profit-driven but oriented toward larger societal benefits, and where the data is generated by a large number of stakeholders, such as in education, health care, and public policy, the situation is different. For example, let's take a look at the area of health care.

It is almost certain that numerous health conditions or diseases that are currently untreatable, incurable, or undetected for long periods of time could actually be remedied if data scientists were provided proper data and were allowed to use proper methods with such data. Consider the following scenario: a large health care system collects and stores a large amount of data for each of its hundreds of thousands of patients, with data spanning years and/or decades. The system's patients generate thousands of data points from numerous checkups, blood tests, administered medications, and so on. As a result, this health care system has terabytes of detailed health data about individual patients. Given unimpeded access to this entire dataset, data scientists working together with medical researchers in fields such as epidemiology or oncology would undoubtedly discover previously unknown patterns that could result in new medical discoveries and treatments. Due to many factors, though, this scenario is by and large not likely within US health care systems. One of the main obstacles to this potential achievement is regulation that does not account for the interplay of privacy and other societal benefits.

As a consequence, we find ourselves in a world in which Amazon can easily use your own data, combined with the data of millions of other shoppers, to motivate you to buy more stuff. At the same time, your physician is not allowed/enabled/incentivized to benefit from data science and compare your blood test data with that of millions of other individuals, possibly resulting in the early detection of a medical problem that would otherwise be impossible to detect with existing diagnostic methods. Similar examples exist in other areas such as education, urban planning, and environmental protections.

The time has come to take a look at all the factors affecting the use of personal, individual data and to develop new legal and organizational frameworks that account for how those factors relate to each other. If this development does not happen, progress and discoveries may occur elsewhere, possibly in a place that already has a growing army of highly trained data scientists, more data than anyone, and a center of power that can arbitrarily decide how to use it. Such discoveries would be less likely to be shared with broader humanity than if they originated in free and open societies that understood how to provide societal benefits from data science.

Probability—the Law That Governs Analytical Ethics

Thomas Casey

Executive Director, Teradata

For years, analytics helped us better understand our world and supported our decision making. With the advent of more advanced analytics techniques, we have evolved to a point where nonhumans can autonomously make decisions on our behalf. Much is written about concepts like "machine learning" and "deep learning" as techniques that can drive incredible outcomes. At the end of the day, however, you cannot drive any decisions using these techniques without first understanding probability and its ethical implications for analytically driven decisions.

When Probability and Ethics Collide

If you asked an algorithm whether you should play the lottery, the answer would undoubtedly be "no." It is statistically impossible (based on probability and confidence level) that you will win, and therefore playing is not worth the practical risk. The truth is that even though this decision is appropriate for nearly everyone, given the sheer number of people that play the lottery, someone will eventually win. Making this mistake seems minor in this context (unless you missed out on your millions). What if, however, a decision that was made by an algorithm prohibited you from boarding a plane? What if it misdiagnosed cancer? What if an autonomous vehicle decided to veer right and hit your child because it "predicted" there was a more significant risk in going left? None of these decisions can be certain, and some acceptable level of risk is applied to each based on the likelihood or probability of being right—and the model will not experience a moment of regret if it made the wrong decision.

How Humans Try to Interject Ethics into Algorithms

The marriage of people and machines to augment decisions has a lot of merit. The issue is that each time people try to apply ethical standards to a model, they inherently interject (for good or bad) some level of bias. Examples include:

Injecting the "right" bias
Companies like Google and Facebook have faced significant backlash in studies showing that their algorithms have made recommendations that favor some information providers over others. Whether or not there were nefarious or explicit biases intended, these companies continue to tweak their algorithms to demonstrate that their results better reflect the perceptions of what someone thinks they should represent.

Dumbing down the model
Deep learning has risen to fame in the past few years as a technique used in many high-profile applications (image recognition, speech translation, advanced game play, etc.). The downside of deep learning is that it is difficult, if not impossible, to determine why a particular outcome is reached. In some instances, companies and other agencies are forced to resort to simpler and less effective (some may even say dumber) techniques just so they can explain the rationale behind the decision.

Overriding the decision
There are many instances in which the ability to override an algorithm makes sense. In other instances, though, overriding an algorithm gives us a false sense of security. For instance, some autonomous car services have addressed bad press (due to major accidents) by having an employee sit in the front seat and do nothing, though they are presumably ready to grab the wheel if they must. Although this might give us a feeling of control, one could argue that injecting humans in this way is spurious at best and counterproductive or even dangerous at worst.

The Ethical Implications of Nonhuman Decision Making

The march toward having more autonomous decisions made on our behalf is inevitable. Nevertheless, there undoubtedly will be situations in which a decision is statistically reasonable...but it will be wrong. If you recommend the wrong movie to watch, that is not catastrophic. If, however, an algorithm is making a life-or-death decision thousands or millions of times, the model will be wrong on occasion. Perhaps the benefits far outweigh the potential for errors, and perhaps the algorithm is infinitely better than a human at making that decision. Nevertheless, for someone who is impacted by an emotional outcome made by an unemotional decision maker, this will undoubtedly be insufficient solace. So in the future, as we think about the ethical implications of handing over complex decisions to unemotional algorithms that base their decisions on the laws of probability, we need to ask ourselves: are we sure?

Don't Generalize Until Your Model Does

Michael Hind

Distinguished Research Staff Member, IBM Research AI

The amazing advances in machine learning come from its ability to find patterns in (often large) training datasets. This ability can result in predictions that match, and often exceed, those made by humans on the same task. However, these systems can sometimes be fooled with a prediction task that would not fool a human. One example is an ML system that can correctly identify a street sign, such as a stop sign, but will incorrectly predict that a stop sign defaced by a few black and white stickers is actually a speed limit sign (*https://arxiv.org/pdf/1707.08945.pdf*).

The reason for this surprising deficiency in capability is that machine learning systems make their predictions in a different way than humans. They look for distinguishing patterns of the various outcome groups, such as which loan applicants should be approved or rejected for a loan. Humans, however, apply a combination of pattern recognition and reasoning. The absence of this reasoning step in machine learning systems can lead to surprising results, as with the stop sign example.

The public then gets the following impression of machine learning (AI):

- AI can sometimes "think" better than humans.

- AI can easily be fooled, and thus it is not trustworthy.

The result is a superhuman technology that cannot be trusted. Insert your favorite movie script here.

What can we do about this? Well, as data scientists we have little control over how the media will portray our work, particularly given that technical work will need to be summarized for a nontechnical audience. However, I believe we are not doing enough at the beginning of this communication pipeline to increase trust in AI systems. We need to state more precisely what our systems actually do.

Let's consider an example. Suppose we've developed a model to predict creditworthiness for loan applicants in Brooklyn, New York. The model considers information such as salary, debt, home and car ownership, and so on to predict whether a loan applicant will pay back their loan. The model is tested and deployed in Brooklyn and is shown to be 95% accurate. Based on this success, the company is considering deploying the model to Bismarck, North Dakota. Should we expect it to be as accurate in Bismarck, where other factors, such as home and car ownership, may be quite different than in Brooklyn? I argue that how we describe the Brooklyn experience will greatly affect expectations for the Bismarck rollout. Consider the following two claims:

- The model correctly predicts creditworthiness with 95% accuracy.
- The model correctly predicts creditworthiness for applicants from Brooklyn, New York, with 95% accuracy.

Although the claims differ only in the words "for applicants from Brooklyn, New York," the impact can be significant. The second claim accurately describes the characteristics of the model, whereas the first claim implies that the model works, in general, with 95% accuracy. The second claim makes no explicit or implied claim about applicants from other locations or even applicants from other parts of New York. It encourages an interested party to ask: are loan applicants in Bismarck similar to loan applicants in Brooklyn?

Since it is likely that on average several of the factors will be greatly different between the two cities, one would need to perform extensive testing of the model in Bismarck before having confidence in its effectiveness.

Generalization is the term for whether a model actually works on general inputs (Bismarck or elsewhere) outside the test dataset (Brooklyn). So, data scientists, please describe the results of your model accurately, and do not generalize claims about your model until you know your model generalizes!

Toward Value-Based Machine Learning

Ron Bodkin

Office of the CTO, Google Cloud

Machine learning (ML) has become integral to many aspects of modern life, as digital experiences proliferate and we increasingly rely on automated algorithms for discovery, curation, and guiding our choices in areas as diverse as entertainment content (e.g., Medium and TikTok), communication (Slack and Gmail), navigation (Google Maps), and shopping (Amazon and Stitch Fix).

ML is often viewed as a value-neutral technology and as objective, unaligned with or dependent on values. But the reality is that ML is a tool—and like any tool, its use is based on values, and the consequences it creates impact our values.

I have been responsible for applying ML to real-world problems since 2007 and have repeatedly found that the use of ML leads to unintended consequences. Much like an evil genie, ML models will often grant exactly what you wished for (optimize what you specify) but not what you really intended. Ten years ago, when I was Vice President of Engineering at Quantcast (*http://www.quantcast.com*), we would often be frustrated to see that ML models we created didn't work properly. They would exploit subtle errors in our data or problem setup, and we had to work hard to understand what made them work so we could fix our data and fix our objectives (or *loss functions*) to achieve the results we *intended*.

More recently, there have been important instances of the unintended consequences of ML in areas like biased ML models. Examples include Amazon's hiring algorithms that were biased against hiring female engineers (*https://oreil.ly/UIRbD*) and Alphabet Jigsaw's algorithms for toxic content that were biased against targeted identity groups (*https://oreil.ly/NVLck*). More generally, recommendation systems show a bias toward trashy, inflammatory "clickbait" content (e.g., the impact of recent Facebook algorithmic changes (*https://oreil.ly/ZTC9I*)). There are also value challenges from explicitly harming customer interests—for example, Amazon changing ML-driven search results in favor of its own profitability over what customers want (*https://oreil.ly/1ut8d*).

To date, most schemes to address these problems have been based on the premise that you can optimize for a value-neutral objective function (like maximizing revenue or time spent on an app) while building in various guardrails. Common techniques include filtering out problematic cases, preparing data to avoid bias, devising model explanation tools, and tracking secondary metrics (e.g., tracking for long-term cohort engagement and not short-term response).

I believe this approach is fundamentally insufficient—value-neutral objectives are amoral by definition. Instead, I believe we must do more: we must encode values in the objectives we measure and work on ways to explicitly produce good outcomes with ML, in addition to other ethical AI practices.

An Example of the Importance of Values

Consider content recommendation systems. Tristan Harris (*https://twitter.com/tristanharris*), cofounder of the Center for Humane Technology (*https://humanetech.com*), has a nice way of thinking about this problem. Imagine a spectrum of content ranging from regenerative (i.e., reflective and thoughtful content, such as articles in widely respected publications) to extractive (i.e., inflammatory and extreme content, such as fringe or conspiracy sites), as illustrated in the following figure.

A few years ago, content recommendation systems were often trained to optimize clicks. This resulted in a lot of trashy clickbait content that wasn't engaging for users (or regenerative!). The next evolution was to optimize for aggregate engagement time. This has resulted in more sustained user engagement but has led inevitably to more inflammatory and extreme content (like conspiracy theories, political extremism, and criminal activity). In that spectrum of content, the system is tilted to the right side of the graph—user engagement flows toward the more sensationalist and alarming material (see the following figure).

Regenerative   Extractive

This trend has also increased digital addiction, and in a meaningful way, it has *downgraded* the users of systems and society more broadly. The use of human review, policing of terms of service, and secondary systems to block and/or not recommend and/or not serve ads for inaccurate or other bad content has helped. However, bad actors continuously find ways to probe the boundary and create the worst, most addictive content that will be promoted. You can think of these practices as establishing barriers against the worst content while still keeping the same harmful flow, as illustrated in the following figure.

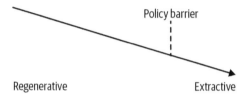

Regenerative   Extractive

Conversely, imagine a system that explicitly optimizes for high-quality engagement by amplifying regenerative content (see the following figure). This should include ideas such as matching resources spent by users to their intentions—for example, "I'd like to enjoy no more than five hours a week of entertaining content," "I don't want to be drawn into watching cat videos until 2 a.m.," or "I'd like to spend at most $50 per month on video entertainment." It should also include impact on society as a whole—for instance, by informing people, provoking meaningful engagement, encouraging deep personal interactions, and allowing political discourse to evolve.

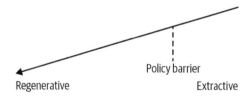

Regenerative   Extractive

Of course, these are hard concepts to represent as a simple mathematical function—and there is a great diversity of perspective on what high-quality engagement means.

How to Proceed?

This shouldn't be viewed as an obstacle to progress but as a grand challenge that the technology community should embrace. How can we better create objective functions that optimize our values? How can we better anticipate and mitigate unintended consequences? How can we incorporate better transparency and visibility into the objectives our systems are encoding?

I believe it will become a critical engineering discipline—blending technical acumen with broader insight into policy goals and ethics. Likewise, François Chollet (the creator of Keras (*https://keras.io*)) views having the right objectives for ML as important, predicting (*https://oreil.ly/WQ4HI*) that "loss function engineer is probably going to be a job title in the future."

There is a lot of opportunity to close the gap between long-term research in AI value alignment (*https://oreil.ly/bTSlx*) (e.g., inverse reinforcement learning (*https://oreil.ly/mKy4_*)) and practical goals in systems today. But the most important step is to take ownership of the ethics of AI systems and incorporate values into their design, especially their objectives![1]

---

[1] Adapted from Ron Bodkin, "Towards Value-Based Machine Learning," Medium, October 12, 2019, *https://oreil.ly/HDlOW*.

The Importance of Building Knowledge in Democratized Data Science Realms

Justin Cochran

Associate Professor of Information Systems,
Kennesaw State University

It is well known that data science tools are becoming more "democratized," or distributed more broadly within organizations to roles that not too long ago had to request analysis rather than perform it themselves. These tools are getting more sophisticated in terms of particular analysis techniques, the ability to connect to data sources of many kinds, and the ability to share data with people inside the organization and beyond. A primary reason that data science tools can be democratized broadly in organizations, even though they are becoming more powerful and sophisticated, is that the developers of the tools are able to successfully hide their complexity from the end users (until a user needs to peel back the layers for specific reasons).

The combination of hidden complexity and sophisticated analyses introduces some risks when the data analysis is driving decision making. In a much-too-simple analogy, we trust users to utilize calculators because they are familiar with and knowledgeable about basic arithmetic. What happens when the analysis capability is available at the click of a button but the end user does not understand the "arithmetic"? It can potentially open the door to analyses using the wrong techniques, violating key assumptions, and presenting results that are misleading—all of which can lead to suboptimal or incorrect decisions. What happens when those incorrect decisions affect employees, customers, or other constituents unfairly?

Generally, this risk is not as high when dealing in the realm of descriptive statistics and data visualization. However, it can become more problematic when the analysis relies more heavily on statistics, algorithms, machine learning, and artificial intelligence. In other words, the level of risk is not uniform when deploying data science tools within the organization. What is the level of responsibility for the analyst and decision makers when they are blind to the methods yielding the results? What are some ways that risk can be mitigated when underlying complexity is high and ease of use is high?

The first avenue is to emphasize continuous education. As generations of tools develop, it is critical for the training and education arms of the organization and universities to cover not only the use and functionality of the tools but also the limitations, assumptions, and pitfalls of various analysis methods. Without continuous education at the end user level, analyses will be wrong—though perhaps only intermittently—and that will undermine the data-driven decision efforts within organizations. If I do not know which analyses I can trust because they are sound fundamentally, use reliable data, and do not violate the assumptions of the techniques, how can I trust any of the analyses?

The second avenue is to use the software to monitor assumptions, make recommendations based on known technique limitations, and notify end users when an analysis may be vulnerable. For instance, does my dataset provide too much statistical power, and do inferences need to be validated in other ways? Does my data violate normality requirements? Embedded warning systems not only have the effect of mitigating risks arising from different kinds of analysis but also serve to let end users know what areas they need more knowledge about.

It is critical for organizations to understand the level of knowledge needed to operate competently, ethically, and responsibly at various levels of sophistication. Without the dedication to knowledge that is appropriate for the types of analyses, the organization will be at risk of undermining faith in decision making, making decisions that impact constituents negatively, or even coming into conflict with organizational values. There may be other techniques to mitigate the risks that come with democratizing data science tools within organizations, but it is clear that the advancing capabilities of these tools require continual knowledge building within analysts, within software, or ideally within both.

The Ethics of Communicating Machine Learning Predictions

Rado Kotorov

CEO, Trendalyze Inc.

People today are fascinated by the amazing computing power that we have. Computers can find information faster than humans, extract insights from data more precisely than many people, answer questions quicker than experts, play chess better than masters, and much more. People have built so much respect for, and trust in, machines that they often communicate machine-generated insights as facts.

In his article "The Median Isn't the Message" (*https://oreil.ly/FhJ5Z*), originally published in *Discover* magazine in 1985, the renowned evolutionary anthropologist Stephen Jay Gould first alerted us to the dangers and moral consequences of presenting statistical and machine learning predictions to ordinary people who do not have mathematical or scientific backgrounds. In the article, he describes his personal experience of being diagnosed with a deadly cancer and the doctor's refusal to tell him his life expectancy. He did the research himself at the medical library at Harvard and learned that the median life expectancy was merely eight months: "So that's why they didn't give me anything to read," he thought. "Then my mind started to work again, thank goodness."

Gould goes on to explain why using the median, the average, or any other statistically derived prediction for communicating life expectancy of incurable diseases is wrong. The positive attitude of terminally ill patients plays a crucial role in increasing the treatment effects. But statistical prognosis is usually a killer of positive attitude because people who are not versed in the science of statistics inevitably misinterpret the message. As he points out:

> What does "median mortality of eight months" signify in our vernacular? I suspect that most people, without training in statistics, would read such a statement as "I will probably be dead in eight months"—the very conclusion

that must be avoided, both because this formulation is false, and because attitude matters so much.

The problem with many measures of statistical tendencies, like the median and the average, is that they are taken as hard facts, while the variation around them is ignored by people not versed in those techniques. But it should be exactly the opposite. Variation is the fact of life, while the median and the average are just artifacts providing an inexact representation of a much more complex reality. After his diagnosis, Gould lived for another 20 years and published many books.

On January 31, 2020, during *The Daily Show with Trevor Noah*, the program's host asked what one would do with the information that life expectancy in the US has grown for the first time in four years, to 74 years. Do we congratulate people who reach this age? Do we set personal goals to reach this age? Do we consider people who do not reach this age losers? All of this points to the importance of how we convey information derived from machine learning.

Imagine an automated decision-making system where a patient is algorithmically diagnosed, and the life expectancy is displayed as a big flashing key performance indicator (KPI). It is not only meaningless; it can also be demoralizing.

As we deploy more machine learning applications, we are likely going to see more such KPIs. We have not developed yet the visualizations that can meaningfully convey to physicians and patients the importance of variation and the interpretation of variation. Data scientists point out that the burden of explanation falls on the doctors. But doctors are not data scientists, and like many other people they are more inclined to accept such projections as facts. The harder it is to explain the meaning of tendencies and the variation around them, the more likely people are to refer to the single number as a fact of life.

This problem is not limited to health care. Imagine if managers in any industry take the central tendencies as hard facts that define the goals they must achieve. There will be many inaccurate plans and even more missed opportunities. Hence, the analytics industry has to focus on fixing the communication problem of machine-generated insights and predictions. We cannot expect ordinary people and professionals to understand all the intricacies of a complex modeling process.

Avoid the Wrong Part of the Creepiness Scale

Hugh Watson

Professor of MIS, Terry College of Business, University of Georgia

Some algorithms that make use of personal data are perceived as helpful, such as movie recommendations on Netflix, recommendations for nearby restaurants from Yelp, and Waze's driving routings. Others are creepy. Remember the first time you viewed an item on the internet and ads from various vendors followed for days? It's also creepy to meet someone for the first time and soon thereafter receive a Facebook friend recommendation for that person. Some uses of personal data are just so wrong, such as Russia's attempts to influence election results through targeted news feeds, or you receiving an ad from a reseller of engagement rings after changing your relationship status from "Engaged" to "Single" on Facebook.

The different reactions to the use of personal data and algorithms can be considered using a creepiness scale, as shown in the following figure, where the degree of creepiness is on the y-axis and the extent of use of personal data and algorithms is on the x-axis.

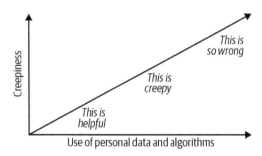

Something is creepy when it differs from the norm and is perceived to be potentially threatening or harmful. To illustrate, an app that reveals your location to others without your knowledge is typically creepy (or just plain wrong), while other app functions, such as Amazon's shopping recommendations, are generally viewed as helpful because they pose no threat.

The timing and content of an ad or a message is also important. For example, receiving an ad for a personal injury attorney while you are in a hospital emergency room doesn't seem right. You also don't want to see ads for hospice care after sending an email to a friend about your newly diagnosed cancer.

What people perceive as creepy differs by individual and can change over time, and people vary in their concerns over privacy and handle it in different ways. For example, millennials are generally thought to be less concerned about privacy than other demographic groups because of their extensive posting of personal information on social media; yet they control their personal information through whom they block (e.g., an ex-boyfriend). After a person experiences for the first time an ad that follows them around the internet, they do not find it as creepy when it occurs again.

An application that heavily uses personal data and advanced algorithms is not always creepy. For example, First Data (recently acquired by Fiserv) uses a considerable amount of personal data and a model based on deep learning to automatically detect and prevent online and in-store credit card fraud. Customers are not bothered by this use (other than the occasional call for a false positive) because they are being protected. It is only the fraudsters who might complain, and no one feels sorry for them.

On the other hand, an application may be heavily criticized even when it uses little personal data. This was the case in the airline industry when some of the airline pricing algorithms sent ticket prices sky-high for people who were trying to flee South Florida before Hurricane Irma hit.

This discussion shows that creepiness is a nuanced concept. Even when a potential application is legal (and this is increasingly a consideration), it does not mean that it is fair and ethical and should be developed. So what should managers, professionals, and companies do to ensure they are not developing and using applications in the "this is creepy" and "this is so wrong" portions of the creepiness scale?

The single most important action is to expand governance (e.g., people, committees, and processes) to include additional people who bring needed perspective for any analytics application. The processes can vary, but business, IT, and analytics managers as well as lawyers, data scientists, and business professionals who interact with customers need to be involved. Business managers and professionals are needed to assess any potential business risk. Lawyers are required to ensure that the way in which personal data is acquired, stored, protected, used, and shared does not violate laws and regulations, such as the European Union's GDPR and the CCPA. IT managers and professionals are responsible for safely collecting, storing, using, and possibly sharing data. Analytics managers and data scientists need to expand their concerns beyond simply developing accurate models to consider the broader issues associated with their work. And people close to the public need to answer the question, is this fair and in the customer's best interests?

Triage and Artificial Intelligence

Peter Bruce

Founder, Institute for Statistics Education at Statistics.com, an Elder Research company

Predictim is a service that scans potential babysitters' social media and other online activity and issues them a score that parents can use in selecting a babysitter. Jeff Chester, the executive director of the Center for Digital Democracy, commented that there is a "mad rush to seize the power of AI to make all kinds of decisions without ensuring it's accountable to human beings. It's like people have drunk the digital Kool-Aid and think this is an appropriate way to govern our lives."[1]

Does/should AI make decisions? In transformative technologies like self-driving cars, the answer is unavoidably "yes." If a human must remain behind the wheel to make or ratify driving decisions, the goal of self-driving technology is largely unattained. But the attention that Predictim attracted has resulted in the loss of its automated access (scraping privileges) to the Facebook platform as a source of data.

The Triage Nurse

In many bread-and-butter applications of statistical and machine learning, the proper role of predictive AI is not that of the robot doctor rendering diagnoses and according treatments but rather that of the triage nurse.

In the 1790s, a French military surgeon established a systematic categorization of military casualties termed *triage* (from the French *trier*, "to separate"). Those for whom immediate treatment was critical and beneficial received priority. Those whose condition was not so urgent, and those whose condi-

---

1 Quoted in Drew Harwell, "Wanted: The 'Perfect Babysitter.' Must Pass AI Scan for Respect and Attitude," *Washington Post*, November 23, 2018, *https://oreil.ly/AWC7q*.

tion was so grave that they were unlikely to benefit from treatment, had lower priority.

President Obama once described the unremitting intensity of presidential decision making thusly: "The only things that land on my desk are tough decisions. Because, if they were easy decisions, somebody down the food chain's already made them."[2]

This is where machine learning and AI should be leading us: not taking all our decision-making jobs away from us, or even the important ones, but just the easy and routine ones.

The Ranking of Records

Just like nurses, predictive models perform triage, ranking records according to their probability of being of interest and allowing humans to make determinations for a very limited set of records. The sorting could happen in two ways. Consider a review of tax returns, where the tax authority has the capacity to audit a certain number of returns per year. A statistical or machine learning predictive algorithm sorts returns according to probability of requiring an audit, and then one of two things happens:

- Humans review all the returns that score high enough and decide whether to refer them for audit.
- The top scoring returns are auto-referred to audit, and then humans review a lower-scoring tier and decide whether to refer those to audit.

The fact that the model's goal is *ranking*, rather than binary *prediction*, has important implications when it comes to assessing predictive models on their performance. Accuracy (the percent of records correctly classified) may not be appropriate—particularly when the percentage of records that are of interest is low. In this "rare case" situation, models can attain high accuracy scores simply by classifying everyone as belonging to the dominant class.

A common metric is "area under the curve," or AUC. The curve in question is the Receiver Operating Characteristics (ROC) curve. The area under this curve is a measure of how well a model discriminates between two classes of records—a "1" indicates perfect discrimination, and a "0.5" indicates no better than random guessing.

---

2 Barack Obama, interview by Steve Kroft, *60 Minutes*, CBS, March 22, 2009, *https://oreil.ly/9wo_e*.

The ROC curve is a measure of the performance of the model with the *entire* dataset that was modeled. Often, one is more interested in how well the model does with a *smaller subset* of records, specifically the top-ranked records. For example, how well did a model do with the top 10% of tax returns judged most likely to be fraudulent?

For this, modelers use the concept of *lift*, the cumulative or segment-wise improvement one gets from the model instead of choosing randomly in search of the records of interest. For example, a lift of 100% in the top decile means that you are twice as likely to find a record of interest in the model's top-ranked decile, compared to choosing randomly. Lift comes from the early days of predictive modeling for direct mail. Direct mailers are usually faced with low response rates and need a tool that allows them to select only the most likely responders.

Ethics in Data Science

AI's role in taking over the routine and repetitive information-based tasks has the potential to enrich working lives by operating via triage, rather than full automated decision making. Jobs will shift toward the more challenging and interesting ones, the supply of which will increase as the economy shifts in response to the unlocking of human creativity. Jeff Bezos, the owner of Amazon, made this case in explaining why he was not worried about AI taking away jobs.

The one potential land mine in this scenario is the one planted by the natural human instinct for making money. Predictim knows that it is imperfect in risk-scoring babysitters. But it also knows that parents aren't able to weigh the nuances of statistical estimates; all they have is a single score. Predictim also knows that the mystery surrounding AI helps it sell the product, which it doesn't even need to overhype.

The *ethical* data scientist would cloak such a product in sufficient warnings that it would not be misused. Or perhaps not sell a product like this at all. The *commercial* data scientist offers up the babysitter score, cloaked in the mystique of artificial intelligence. If the consumer invests it with more meaning than it really has, well,...caveat emptor.

Algorithmic Misclassification— the (Pretty) Good, the Bad, and the Ugly

Arnobio Morelix

Chief Innovation Officer, Startup Genome
Data Scientist-in-Residence, Inc. Magazine

Every day, the systems we build classify the identity and behavior of people nonstop. A credit card transaction is labeled "fraudulent" or not. Political campaigns decide on "likely voters" for their candidate. People constantly claim and are judged on their identity of "not a robot" through captchas. Add to this the classification of emails, face recognition in phones, and targeted ads, and it is easy to imagine thousands of such classification instances per day for even just one person.

For the most part, these classifications are convenient and pretty good for the user and the organizations running them. We mostly forget them, unless they go obviously wrong.

I am a Latino living in the US, and I often get ads in Spanish—which would be pretty good targeting, except that I am a Brazilian Latino, and my native language is Portuguese, not Spanish.

This particular misclassification causes no real harm to me. My online behavior might look similar enough to that of a native Spanish speaker living in the US, and users like me getting mistargeted ads may be nothing more than a "rounding error" by the algorithm. Although it is in no one's interest that I get these ads—I am wasting my time, and the company is wasting money—the targeting is probably "good enough."

This "good enough" mindset is at the heart of a lot of prediction applications in data science. As a field, we constantly put people in boxes to make decisions about them, even though we inevitably know predictions will not be perfect. "Pretty good" is fine most of the time—it generally is for ad targeting.

But these automatic classifications can quickly go from pretty good to bad to ugly—either because of scale of deployment or because of tainted data. As we go to higher-stakes fields beyond those they have arguably been perfected for —such as social media and online ads—we get into problems.

Take psychometric tests, for example. Companies are increasingly using them to weed out job candidates. Some of these companies are reporting good results, with higher performance and lower turnover.[1] The problem is, although these tests can be pretty good, they are far from great. An IQ test, a popular component of psychometric assessments, is a poor predictor of cognitive performance across many different tasks—though it is certainly correlated to performance in some of them.[2]

When a single company weeds out a candidate who would otherwise perform well, it may not be a big problem by itself. But it *can* be a big problem when the tests are used at scale, and a job seeker is consistently excluded from jobs they would perform well in. And while the use of these tests by a single private actor may well be justified on an efficiency-for-hiring basis, it should give us pause to see these tests used at scale for both private and public decision making (e.g., testing students).

Problems with "pretty good" classifications also arise from blind spots in the prediction, as well as tainted data. Several Somali markets in Seattle were unable to accept food stamps because the federal government thought many of their transactions looked fraudulent—with many infrequent, large-dollar transactions, one after the other. But this algorithmically suspicious pattern had a perfectly reasonable explanation: it was driven by the fact that many families in the community the markets serve shopped only once a month, often sharing a car to do so. The USDA later reversed the decision of rejecting those food stamps, although only after four months of trouble for the Somali grocery customers.[3]

---

1 Lauren Weber, "Today's Personality Tests Raise the Bar for Job Seekers," *Wall Street Journal*, April 14, 2015, *https://oreil.ly/3kxOL*.

2 Adam Hampshire, Roger R. Highfield, Beth L. Parkin, and Adrian M. Owen, "Fractionating Human Intelligence," *Neuron* 76, no. 6 (December 2012): 1225–37, *https://oreil.ly/Dd5M1*.

3 Florangela Davila, "USDA Disqualifies Three Somalian Markets from Accepting Federal Food Stamps," *Seattle Times*, April 10, 2002, *https://oreil.ly/MBHwj*; D. Parvaz, "USDA Reverses Itself, to Somali Grocers' Relief," *Seattle Post-Intelligencer*, July 16, 2002, *https://oreil.ly/jOneZ*.

Similarly, African American voters in Florida were disproportionately disenfranchised because their names were more often automatically matched to felons' names. This was simply because African Americans have a disproportionate share of common last names (a legacy of original names being stripped due to slavery).[4] Also in Florida, black criminal defendants were more likely to be algorithmically classified as being of "high risk" for recidivism, and among those defendants who did not reoffend, blacks were over twice as likely as whites to have been labeled risky.[5]

In all of these cases, there is not necessarily evidence of malicious intent. The results can be explained by a mix of "pretty good" predictions and data reflecting previous patterns of discrimination—even if the people designing and applying the algorithms had no intention to discriminate.

While the examples I've mentioned here have a broad range of technical sophistication, there's no strong reason to believe the most sophisticated techniques are getting rid of these problems. Even the newest deep learning techniques excel at identifying relatively superficial correlations, not deep patterns or causal paths.[6]

The key problem with the explosion in algorithmic classification is the fact that we are invariably designing life around a slew of "pretty good" algorithms. "Pretty good" may be a great outcome for ad targeting. But when we deploy classification algorithms at scale on applications from voter registration exclusions to hiring or loan decisions, the final outcomes may well be disastrous.

The road to hell is paved with "pretty good" intentions.

---

4 Guy Stuart, "Databases, Felons, and Voting: Errors and Bias in the Florida Felons Exclusion List in the 2000 Presidential Elections," Harvard University, Faculty Research Working Papers Series.

5 Sam Corbett-Davies, Emma Pierson, Avi Feller, Sharad Goel, and Aziz Huq, "Algorithmic Decision Making and the Cost of Fairness," Computers and Society, Cornell University, last modified June 10, 2017, https://arxiv.org/abs/1701.08230.

6 Gary Marcus, "Deep Learning: A Critical Appraisal," Artificial Intelligence, Cornell University, January 2, 2018, https://arxiv.org/abs/1801.00631.

The Golden Rule of Data Science

Kris Hunt

Partner and Cofounder, Hard Right Solutions

Today, there are infinite data points capturing all our individual purchasing behaviors, browsing histories, driving routes, contact information, fingerprints, scholastic records, legal matters, home/car purchases, medical histories, and so on. People with little to no exposure to analytics or databases may think that there are controls in place to protect this data given the outrage related to recent data breaches. The truth of the matter is that there are very few required safeguards in place.

There are two prominent federal data laws in the United States:

- In the area of financial data compliance, the Sarbanes-Oxley Act (SOX) of 2002 is a federal law that established sweeping auditing and financial regulations for public companies. Lawmakers created the legislation to help protect shareholders, employees, and the public from accounting errors and fraudulent financial practices.

- In the area of medical data confidentiality, the Health Insurance Portability and Accountability Act of 1996 (HIPAA) provides data privacy and security provisions for safeguarding medical information.

When it comes to other sensitive data such as credit card information, there are no federal or state laws that make having this information stored in an office illegal; however, doing so can put you at odds with credit card companies. So how are other types of information about you protected? The answer is that most of the time, the decision is up to the discretion of individual companies and their self-imposed policies. Most companies want to protect their data, prevent malicious attacks, and keep confidential information secure so that they do not get sued; that is, lawsuits are the primary deterrent.

The less obvious or gray area of vulnerability created by so much data and the people who have access to it comprises decisions made that may have unforeseen consequences. We are operating in an era in which most people have the details of their life retained on their computers, in their phones, and in every transactional database that they have *ever* interacted with using their credentials.

The following are some examples of situations that illustrate the types of insight gained from various sources of data/information—some with profound repercussions:

- People looking up the financial or contact information of prospective love interests.
- Credit card companies and retailers comparing data to determine how many of their customers are also shopping at a competitor.
- People reviewing social media to judge a person and make professional and personal decisions.
- Identification of suspects by tracing transaction history at retailers and car rental agencies, camera footage at ATMs, DNA left at crime scenes, and so forth. Many television shows depict this one.
- Comparing a person's prescriptions with their grocery items. This is a tricky one, as it has some HIPAA implications; however, the data is often housed in the same database, and some interesting things could come out of this:
  - Diabetics that buy a lot of sugary products, people on certain medications with food interactions, and pregnant people buying cigarettes and alcohol are potentially going to have some medical complications. Should the grocery clerk or terminal warn them of their bad decisions? What if the insurance company gets this information and starts denying claims?
  - A company is considering some potential new hires. Can the company's hiring manager review an applicant's medical history, lottery ticket purchases, or frequently bought grocery items?
- Refinement of marketing efforts by using a customer's purchasing and shopping data, along with their preferences, to provide a "better" and "more valued" experience for that customer, building loyalty.
- Using data to identify which locations to close, areas that will best support new businesses, employees to lay off, products to discontinue/introduce, the setting of prices for maximum profit, and which customers should receive better offers or amenities.

- Creation of fake accounts or social profiles using readily available information and images to secure loans, steal identities, slander a person, play a prank, spread hate, or catfish lonely people.

Do analysts treat other people's data how they want their own data to be treated? Are data scientists the appropriate people to be given the power of data gatekeeper in an age in which people believe "fake" news/take facts at face value? These are compelling questions given that data breaches of any kind can devastate people's lives and destroy companies.

Ethics in analytics is a sliding scale, as is the level of detail a person is comfortable sharing. Individuals and companies need to be vigilant in protecting the data that they control and access. I wish everyone would follow the Golden Rule of treating data how they want their own data to be treated; however, that is not always realistic.

Causality and Fairness— Awareness in Machine Learning

Scott Radcliffe

Managing Director, MS in Business Analytics Program, Emory University

It has become axiomatic that addressing fairness and bias in machine learning models is not optional. However, the race to deploy learning models has outpaced the development of standards and methods for detecting and systematically avoiding bias. This situation is due in some part to the fact that machine learning practice is typically not concerned with causality but rather is based on observational criteria. The focus is on prediction, classification, and identification. Observational criteria are fundamentally unable to determine whether a predictor exhibits unresolved discrimination.

A long history of data analysis in the social science and medical fields has shown that fairness should be studied from the causal perspective. In order to be fairness-aware, special emphasis is placed on the assumptions that underlie all causal inferences, the languages used in formulating those assumptions, the conditional nature of all causal and counterfactual claims, and the methods that have been developed for the assessment of such claims.

What is a "causal model"? Wikipedia provides a useful definition. A causal model (or structural causal model) is a *conceptual* model that describes the causal mechanisms of a system. Causal models can improve study designs by providing clear rules for deciding which independent variables need to be included/controlled.

They can allow some questions to be answered from existing observational data without the need for an interventional study such as a randomized controlled trial. Some interventional studies are inappropriate for ethical or practical reasons, meaning that without a causal model, some hypotheses cannot be tested.

Causal models are falsifiable—meaning that if they do not match data, they must be rejected as invalid. They must also be credible to those close to the phenomena the model intends to explain.

It is imperative that data science and machine learning practice include understanding and training in causal reasoning. Judea Pearl, a professor of computer science and the director of the Cognitive Systems Laboratory at UCLA, is a pioneer in establishing cause-and-effect relationships as a statistical and mathematical concept. Pearl is the author of the 2018 book *The Book of Why: The New Science of Cause and Effect* (Basic Books).

The central metaphor driving the narrative of *The Book of Why* is three ascending rungs of what the author calls the "ladder of causation." The lowest rung deals simply with observation—basically looking for regularities in past behavior. Pearl places "present-day learning machines squarely on rung one." While it is true that the explosion of computing power and accessible deep datasets have yielded many surprising and important results, the mechanics still operate "in much the same way that a statistician tries to fit a line to a collection of points."

The second rung of the ladder of causation moves from seeing to doing. That is, it goes from asking what happened to asking what would happen based on possible interventions. Pearl notes that "many scientists have been traumatized to learn that none of the methods they learned in statistics is sufficient to articulate, let alone answer, a simple question like 'What happens if we double the price?'" *The Book of Why* provides a detailed explanation and history of how and when a model alone can answer such questions in the absence of live experiments.

The third and top rung of the ladder involves counterfactual questions, such as: what would the world be like if a different path had been taken? Such questions are "the building blocks of moral behavior as well as scientific thought." The ability to look backward and imagine what could have been governs our judgments on success and failure, right and wrong.

Where is machine learning on this ladder? Achievements from state-of-the-art diagnosis in chest radiography to beyond-human-level skill in games such as Go and Dota 2 demonstrate the power and real-world utility of deep learning. Nonetheless, these methods are sometimes condescendingly described as mere "curve-fitting." Suffice it to say that these methods amount to learning highly complex functions defined by the neural network architecture for connecting input X to output Y. For a game-playing agent, X is an observed state of the game (board positions, players' health, etc.), and Y is the subsequent action or plan. As Pearl says, "As long as our system optimizes some property of the observed data, however noble or sophisticated, while making no reference to the world outside the data, we are back to level-1 of the hierarchy with all the limitations that this level entails." Thus we find AI/ML at the first rung of Pearl's causal inference ladder.

So why isn't AI/ML practice moving up the ladder more quickly? One of the challenges facing data scientists and machine learning engineers interested in learning about causality is that most resources on the topic are geared toward the needs of statisticians or economists, versus those of data scientists and machine learning engineers. Closing this gap represents a major opportunity to advance fairness-awareness in tandem with the rapid advances in AI/ML technology.

Facial Recognition on the Street and in Shopping Malls

Brendan Tierney

Principal Consultant, Oralytics

Over the past couple of years, most of the examples of using deep learning have involved image or object recognition. Typical examples include examining pictures to identify a cat or a dog, some famous person, and so on.

But what if this same technology was used to monitor people going about their daily lives? What if pictures or video captured you walking down the street or around a shopping mall, or on your way to work or to a meeting? These pictures and videos are already being taken of you without you knowing.

This raises a wide range of ethical concerns. There are the ethics of deploying such solutions in the public domain, but there are also ethical concerns for the data scientists and other people working on these projects. Remember: just because we can doesn't mean we should. People need to decide, if they are working on one of these projects, whether they *should* be working on it—and if not, what they can do.

Ethics are principles of behavior based on ideas of right and wrong. Ethical principles often focus on ideas such as fairness, respect, responsibility, integrity, quality, transparency, and trust. A lot of ideas are there, but we all need to consider what is right and what is wrong. But what about the gray-area, borderline scenarios in which an interesting project in an experimental environment, once deployed, leads to ethical concerns?

Here are some examples that might fall into the gray space between right and wrong. (Why they might fall more toward the wrong is because most people are not aware their image is being captured and used, and not just for a particular purpose at capture time: their images are stored longer term to allow for better machine learning models to be built.)

Imagine walking down the street with a digital display in front of you. That display is monitoring you and other people around you. The digital display then presents personalized advertisements aimed specifically at you. A classic example of this is in the film *Minority Report*. Only this is no longer science fiction; it is happening at shopping centers across Europe. These digital advertising screens are monitoring people, identifying their personal characteristics, and then customizing the ads to match the profiles of the people walking past. The companies behind these technologies are using deep learning to profile individuals based on gender, age, facial hair, eyewear, perceived mood, engagement, attention time, group size, and so forth. They then use this information to:

Optimize
Deliver the appropriate advertisement to the right audience at the right time

Visualize
Use gaze recognition to trigger a creative or interactive experience

Enable augmented reality
Use HD cameras to create an augmented reality mirror or window effect, creating deep consumer engagement via the latest technology

Analyze
Understand a brand's audience and undertake post-campaign analysis and creative testing.

Many companies have developed solutions that monitor people walking down the street. Some have taken this to another level, where they can identify what brands of clothing you are wearing. Imagine if you could combine this personal monitoring with location-based services. For example, you are walking down a street, and people approach you and try to entice you into a particular store by offering certain discounts. But you are with a friend, and the store is not interested in them. The store is using video monitoring, capturing details of every person walking down the street and about to pass the store. The video is using deep learning to analyze your profile and what brands you are wearing. The store has deployed a team of people to stop and engage with certain individuals, just because they match the brands or interests of the store. Depending on what brands you are wearing, they may offer customized discounts specific to you.

How comfortable would you be with this? How comfortable are you about going shopping now?

This can be an ethical dilemma for a data scientist. You may have worked on an interesting project in a lab or an experimental environment. The real challenge comes when this work is taken out of the lab and deployed for commercial gain. Your ethical responsibility involves looking at all aspects of how the project is deployed and its implications. It is easy to understand why retail outlets are interested in these technologies, but as data scientists we need to consider the ethics of applying technologies to these types of projects, and whether we as humans are OK with our work being used in this manner.

Ensuring Proper Transparency & Monitoring

Few topics are as hotly debated as transparency. Specifically, what level of transparency is required when building and deploying analytics and data science processes? Even once such processes are deployed, ongoing monitoring is required to ensure that they are acting as anticipated. This section provides views on how to approach these critical issues.

Responsible Design and Use of AI: Managing Safety, Risk, and Transparency

Pamela Passman

Vice Chair, Ethisphere
CEO, Center for Responsible Enterprise And Trade (CREATe.org)

AI is having a growing impact on markets and business practices around the world. And its potential is even greater. The IDC found in September 2019 (*https://oreil.ly/sMAiL*) that "spending on AI systems will reach $97.9 billion in 2023, more than two and one half times the $37.5 billion that will be spent in 2019." According to the McKinsey Global Institute, AI could deliver additional global economic output (*https://oreil.ly/hJ1d5*) of $13 trillion per year by 2030.

Yet even as it unleashes business potential and broader societal benefits, the use of AI can also result in a host of unwanted and sometimes serious consequences (*https://oreil.ly/lz_zR*). These considerations have given rise to no fewer than 32 different industry, NGO, and government AI ethics codes (*https://oreil.ly/TetYv*), which outline steps that organizations should take to develop, implement, and use AI in ways that support societal values and manage risks.

Many forward-thinking companies—some with firsthand experience in dealing with unintended consequences of AI—have also developed their own codes of ethical AI. While these codes can vary quite a bit, nine common responsibilities have been identified (*https://oreil.ly/PIYYz*). These responsibilities can be divided into three groups: responsible design and use, lawful use, and ethical use. Here we take a focused look into the first group, *responsible design and use,* which encompasses AI security, safety, risk management, and transparency.

Security and Safety

From time to time, the media will highlight a dramatic AI incident, such as an accident involving a self-driving car. This type of coverage reflects the widespread concern of consumers and businesses, thus solidifying the need for AI to be developed, implemented, and used in a safe and secure way.

For companies, this means taking a comprehensive approach to managing the security and safety implications of AI, engaging all relevant parts of the organization beyond technology. This cross-functional institutional approach would allow companies to embrace the power and responsibility of AI in an efficient, effective way while also avoiding unintended risks of harm.

For example, Microsoft, as one of the early adopters of AI, directly addresses safety and security considerations in its principles for responsible AI (*https:// oreil.ly/iBUvd*). By requiring that "AI systems should perform reliably and safely" under both normal and unexpected conditions, Microsoft commits to having AI systems that operate as they were originally designed to do, respond safely to unanticipated conditions, and resist harmful manipulation. Initial and ongoing testing, maintenance, and protection of AI systems are thus vital. And human judgment remains key to identifying potential blind spots and biases in AI systems, and to determining how, when, and for how long an AI system should be used.

Ongoing Risk Management

Given the relatively recent appearance and use of AI technologies, it appears that not many companies have taken a close, institutional look at AI risks and risk management. Thus, it is critical for companies to recognize that while the potential risks posed by AI cannot be eliminated entirely, they can and should be anticipated, assessed, and managed to an extent commensurate with their expected impact.

"Few leaders have had the opportunity to hone their intuition about the full scope of societal, organizational, and individual risks [of AI]," notes the McKinsey analysis *Confronting the Risks of Artificial Intelligence* (*https:// oreil.ly/RCggZ*). "As a result, executives often overlook potential perils ('We're not using AI in anything that could "blow up," like self-driving cars') or overestimate an organization's risk-mitigation capabilities ('We've been doing analytics for a long time, so we already have the right controls in place, and our practices are in line with those of our industry peers'). It's also common for leaders to lump in AI risks with others owned by specialists in the IT and analytics organizations ('I trust my technical team; they're doing everything possible to protect our customers and our company')."

Many companies already use the enterprise risk management (ERM) approach of *Identify > Assess > Manage* to address other kinds of risks across their organizations. So it would be logical to assess and manage newly arising AI risks within the overall ERM framework.

As our networks grow more and more interconnected, it would also be logical to extend AI risk management practices to a company's third parties. Whether they are suppliers, customers, or other business partners, the management of key AI risks that may arise among such third parties should not be neglected. Telefónica illustrates this principle by contractually reserving the right (*https://oreil.ly/zzQ0D*) to verify with its third parties on an ongoing basis that their disclosures on the logic and data use of the suppliers' AI-based products are true.

Transparency

As AI systems expand and grow, and as more risks resulting from the use of AI appear, consumers and companies are starting to demand more transparency about the AI-based products and services that they use. Research reveals (*https://oreil.ly/rIpRv*) that consumers are split on their feelings about AI: only 35% say they are comfortable with a business using AI to interact with them, while 28% say they are not comfortable with this, and the biggest group—37%—say they just do not know yet.

This helps to explain why most of the industry, NGO, government, and company AI ethics codes include a requirement of transparency for various aspects of the development, implementation, and use of AI. For example, IBM's Principles for Trust and Transparency of AI (*https://oreil.ly/G9ykX*) mandate that if AI is used to make important decisions, it must be explainable: "Technology companies must be clear about who trains their AI systems, what data was used in that training, and, most importantly, what went into their algorithm's recommendations."

As part of its particular AI transparency principle, IBM has undertaken to make clear when and for what purposes AI is being applied, the data and training methods used in its AI systems, its commitment to ongoing testing and improvement, its protection of client data, and its support for ensuring that people can understand how an AI system came to a conclusion or recommendation.

Conclusion

The further expansion of AI is inevitable. With many consumers still harboring fears about AI, the emerging requirements for responsible AI present a major opportunity for businesses to develop and explain their AI initiatives in a way that is consistent with customers' expectations.

By focusing on safety and security, managing the risks, and maintaining transparency and responsible disclosure of AI, companies are in a position to not only earn the trust of their customers but also improve business and society in unimaginable ways.

Blatantly Discriminatory Algorithms

Eric Siegel

Founder, Predictive Analytics World

Imagine sitting across from a person being evaluated for a job, a loan, or even parole. When they ask how the decision process works, you inform them, "For one thing, our algorithm penalized your score by seven points because you're black."

We are headed in that direction. Distinguished experts are now campaigning for discriminatory algorithms in law enforcement and beyond. They argue that computers should be authorized to make life-altering decisions based directly on race and other protected classes. This would mean that computers could explicitly penalize black defendants for being black.

In most cases, data scientists intentionally design algorithms to be blind to protected classes. This is accomplished by prohibiting predictive models from inputting such factors. Doing so does not eliminate *machine bias*, the well-known phenomenon wherein models falsely flag one group more than another via "surrogate" variables (discussed in my article in Part VII of this book, "*To Fight Bias in Predictive Policing, Justice Can't Be Color-Blind*, page 243"). But suppressing such model inputs is a fundamental first step, without which models are *discriminatory*.

I use the term "discriminatory" for decisions that are based in part on a protected class, such as when profiling by race or religion to determine police searches. An exception holds when decisions are intended to benefit a protected group, such as for affirmative action, or when determining whether someone qualifies for a grant designated for a minority group.

Discriminatory algorithms meet the very definition of inequality. For example, for informing pretrial release, parole, and sentencing decisions, models calculate the probability of future criminal convictions. If the data links race to convictions—showing that black defendants have more convictions than white defendants—then the resulting model would penalize the score of each black defendant just for being black. There couldn't be a more blatant case of criminalizing blackness.

Support for discriminatory policies and decision making paves the way for discriminatory algorithms. Thirty-six percent of Americans would support a religion-based policy to ban Muslims from entering the US. The US bans transgender individuals from serving in the military. Three-fourths of Americans support increased airport security checks based in part on ethnicity, and 25% of Americans support the use of racial profiling by police. Résumés with "white sounding names" receive 50% more responses than those with "African American sounding names."[1]

Expert support for discriminatory algorithms signals an emerging threat. A paper cowritten by Stanford University assistant professor Sharad Goel criticizes the standard that algorithms not be discriminatory. The paper recommends discriminatory models "when…protected traits add predictive value." In one lecture, this professor said, "We can pretend like we don't have the information, but it's there….It's actually good to include race in your algorithm."

University of Pennsylvania criminology professor Richard Berk—who has been commissioned by parole departments to build predictive models—also calls for race-based prediction, in a paper on the application of machine learning to predict which convicts will kill or be killed. Berk writes, "One can employ the best model, which for these data happens to include race as a predictor. This is the most technically defensible position."

Data compels these experts to endorse discriminatory algorithms. To them, it serves as a rationale for prejudice. It's as if the data is saying, "Be racist."

But "obeying" the data and generating discriminatory algorithms violates the most essential notions of fairness and civil rights. Even if it's true that my group commits more crime, it would violate my rights to be held accountable for others, to have my classification count against me.

Discriminatory computers wreak more havoc than humans enacting discriminatory policies. Once it is crystallized as an algorithm, a discriminatory process executes automatically, coldly, and on a more significant scale, affecting greater numbers of people. Formalized and deployed mechanically, it

---

1 References for many specifics in this article can be found in Eric Siegel, "When Machines and Data Promote Blatant Discrimination," *San Francisco Chronicle*, September 21, 2018, *https://oreil.ly/8YzGp*.

takes on a concrete, accepted status. It becomes the system. More than any human, the computer is "the Man."

So get more data. Just as we human decision makers would strive to see as much beyond race as we can when considering a job candidate or criminal suspect, making an analogous effort—on a larger scale—to widen the database would enable our computer to transcend discrimination as well. Resistance to investing in this effort would reveal a willingness to compromise this nation's freedoms, the very freedoms we were trying to protect with law enforcement and immigration policies in the first place.

Ethics and Figs: Why Data Scientists Cannot Take Shortcuts

Jennifer Lewis Priestley

Associate Dean & Dir. of the Analytics and Data Science Institute, Kennesaw State University

> *I would not give a fig for the simplicity this side of complexity, but I would give my life for the simplicity on the other side of complexity.*
> —Supreme Court justice Oliver Wendell Holmes Jr.

Data scientists should take a minute to reflect on the preceding quote.

Simplifying the complex is hard. Calculators, computers, and downloadable packages are all mediums of expediency of calculation rather than substitutions for computational ability.

In the rush to become a "data scientist," many individuals are shortcutting the process—stopping at the near side of complexity. While the concept of the "citizen data scientist" has its place, too many individuals who represent themselves as data scientists have no formal training in data science beyond a weekend boot camp. The consequence is greater than just confusion related to the definition of "data scientist"—it's a major source of the myriad ethical issues that are emerging relative to algorithmically biased outcomes.

Note that "algorithms" themselves are not biased; deep learning is no more "biased" than addition. However, both are subject to two sources of bias—human biases inherent to model specification and the data we select to build an algorithm.

To that end, ethical data scientists should consider three basic questions in the context of algorithm development.

What problem am I trying to solve?
> Too many individuals shortcut the logic and go straight to the methods without understanding the data. Worse, many analytical platforms simply allow the dumping of data into a "black box," with multiple machine

learning approaches happening simultaneously, followed by an automated sorting by classification rate. These platforms—on the near side of complexity—require no model specification consideration for the original question. In other words, the approach could be computationally optimized—but for a different question.

Is the data that I am using to train the algorithm representative of the population that will be subject to the outputs?

If the data selected to develop and train the algorithm comes from a homogenous subset of the population, but the results are intended to be applied to a diverse population, classification accuracy for groups not included in the original training set will always be worse. If they are responsible for primary data collection, data scientists need to understand the principles of experimental design and sampling to ensure representation. If the data were collected previously (more likely), data scientists still have a responsibility to ensure the training dataset does not exhibit meaningful differences across the population to which the algorithm will be applied.

Can I explain the effects of the inputs/features (or if not, can I prove that the outcomes are not biased)?

The "right to explanation" means that individuals have a right to understand how decisions that have a direct impact on their lives were made. The common example is the requirement that lenders be able to explain credit decisions. In mathematical terms: what is the effect of x on y?

While most supervised statistical modeling techniques are directly interpretable, many machine learning techniques are not. Data scientists need to thoughtfully consider whether it is acceptable if they cannot explain how inputs used to develop an algorithm impact people's lives (and almost all algorithms do so in some way). Alternatively, if the algorithm is correctly specified and the input data has been tested for bias, is it acceptable to forgo interpretability in favor of post hoc interpretations and explanation by example?

As a community, most data scientists have ethical intentions. However, intentions are insufficient, and shortcuts have consequences. As a community, data scientists have a responsibility to work through to the simplicity on the far side of the complexity to ensure the development and application of socially responsible algorithms, which are prone to falter on the near side of complexity.

What Decisions Are You Making?

James Taylor

CEO, Decision Management Solutions

Data science is a means to an end—specifically, a means to improve decision making. If data science does not improve decision making, it has no value. As Goethe said, "Knowing is not enough; we must apply. Willing is not enough; we must do." It is not enough that we use data science to know something; we must act on what it tells us.

When it comes to ethics, this leads to the conclusion that it is not enough that data science is ethical; it must be used ethically also. The decisions we make with data science must be ethical. We must be clear about the moral principles that govern how we conduct our decision making.

Ensuring decisions are made ethically with data science has two elements. We must design our decision-making approaches to be ethical, and we must be able to demonstrate that any specific decision we have made was ethical.

Designing Ethical Decision-Making Systems

Most decisions that use data science are made repeatedly. Data science relies on having data about how decisions were made in the past, and this focuses it on high-volume, repeatable decisions about transactions or consumers. Should we pay this claim? Can this person have credit? What's the right treatment for this patient? Is this person who they say they are? These day-to-day decisions are the prime use case for data science.

Because these decisions are made more than once, we can define a decision-making approach to follow each time. This might have been done in the past with a policy and procedure manual or checklist. Today it's more likely to be defined using a more rigorous model of decision making, such as the Decision Model and Notation (DMN) standard.

You can clearly show the role of data science in such a defined decision-making approach. You can show, for instance, that the data science does not impact eligibility but that it is used only to identify a risk of fraud, or that the prediction of credit risk is not used in the calculation of a discount. You can define when the data science makes a difference to the decision making and when it does not. Was a decision to refer someone for manual review made because of a data science result or to reject them out of hand, for instance?

Only if you can clearly define the decisions impacted by your data science can you be sure you have defined an ethical approach to your decision making.

Demonstrating Ethical Decision Making

Being able to show that you are proactive in designing an ethical approach to decision making must be complemented by an ability to demonstrate that you applied such an approach in the decisions you made. It's all very well to show that a prediction of fraud is not enough to have someone rejected out of hand, but when someone *is* rejected, they may demand proof—or a regulator may.

Those elements of the decision that are automated must create a record of how the decision was made, the business rules or decision logic that was executed. Manual decisions must be recorded by the user. These logs must be combined with the data science results—and ideally with an explanation of those results. Especially when significant elements of the decisions are automated, creating and storing these logs can be a side effect of making the decision.

Keeping these logs allows any decision to be reviewed to ensure an ethical decision was made. This information also supports continual improvement and review of the decision-making process/system/approach. How might the decision-making approach be refined to make better decisions? Are there circumstances in which the data science should have been consulted or where its usage was unhelpful? Only data about how the decision was made can support this kind of analysis and turn machine learning into business learning.

An ethical approach to data science is necessary but not sufficient. We must also have an ethical approach to our data science–enabled decision making.

Ethics, Trading, and Artificial Intelligence

John Power

Professor, Mercy College School of Business

The US stock market conjures an image of adrenaline-fueled traders yelling out orders on a trading floor. That image is a memory. Now computers do most of the trading, silently—and very, very quickly. This trend is likely to accelerate with the inclusion of machine learning and artificial intelligence replacing ever more direct human interaction with the marketplace. The question that immediately comes to mind is: since the marketplace, and all its rules and regulations, has been structured primarily to protect investors, does this trend constitute a problematic ethical environment for the average investor?

The market structure was designed primarily to protect investors from corporate behavior and not from other investors. Since the formation of the Securities and Exchange Commission (SEC), there have been traders who were faster than others, and the SEC does not seem to be making a distinction about why that is the case. Technology-enabled investments are not a focus for them. Rather, the regulators are focused on the fact that these algorithmic trading practices provide incremental liquidity that benefits the overall market. The current approach seems to be to take no action. This is likely true for the foreseeable future.[1]

The average investor buying or selling shares is adversely impacted. Most investors will place an order to buy or sell at the prevailing market price, thereby making them susceptible to market dynamics and providing an opportunity to take advantage of them. For example, a person will place an order to buy 1,000 shares of stock when the current market offer price is $9.81. The number of shares available at $9.81 is typically 100. Once this market order hits, the algorithms will pick up on the fact that there is an

---

1 "5 Ways AI Is Transforming the Finance Industry," Marutitech, December 25, 2018, *https://oreil.ly/A8DVK*.

order to buy at market and will increase their offer prices in one-cent increments for the remaining 900 shares. This will result in the investor paying an average price between one and three cents higher per share for the 1,000 shares. The total impact may seem small—$10 to $30 on a transaction of nearly $10,000—but when multiplied by hundreds of thousands of trades every day, the total impact is very significant. The negative impact is fully born by the average investor, while the total positive impact accrues to the machine-driven trading organization. And this is just one simple example.

Or think about the case of the recently opened New York Stock Exchange data center, which allowed high-frequency traders to colocate their servers in the data center for faster data access. Initially, only the racks closest to the NYSE servers were in demand. It was the fiber optic cable length that made the other racks less appealing. Think about that—the time it took data to travel along 20 extra feet of fiber at near the speed of light produced a competitive disadvantage. The NYSE solved it by using the same length of fiber to every server no matter its location.

What creates this need for speed? Trading methodologies. Simply put, computer algorithms continually test the market by issuing orders looking for inefficiencies. They post the order (buy or sell or both) near the current market. If they get a trade, it is because the market moved toward them, and it usually reverts, giving them a profit. If not, they cancel the order. This gives a false impression of robust market depth and can result in price manipulation or front-running orders (both of which are illegal but remarkably hard to police).[2]

What if we could harness the power of artificial intelligence to solve this problem of asymmetry? The real ethical dilemma is that when humans interact with machines, they are incapable of competing. Suppose we evolve to a market where all the transactions are conducted by machines that are capacitated by artificial intelligence techniques. In this scenario, the artificial intelligence machine will look at all the information at its disposal to make decisions. In this scenario, the degree of rationality in the market is increased because the irrational agent, the human, is not participating. In this situation,

---

2 Sam Stanton-Cook, Ryan Sparks, Dan O'Riordan, and Rob Hodgkinson, *Technical Whitepaper: Surveillance Techniques to Effectively Monitor Algo and High Frequency Trading (Edition 18)*, Kx.com, February 8, 2014, *https://oreil.ly/jQGs3*.

the degree of information asymmetry in the markets will be greatly reduced, almost to no asymmetry.[3]

The hurdle is that humans don't know how the AI systems make decisions. This hurdle is starting to be cleared with the advent of explainable AI (see the following figure comparing today's AI with explainable AI[4]), empowering investors to utilize (probably for the first time in their lives) an investment strategy that reflects their own values, contributing to an ethically more robust marketplace, and eliminating most of the opportunity for bad actors. Help the machine understand you, your goals, and your constraints, and allow it to direct your interactions with financial markets.

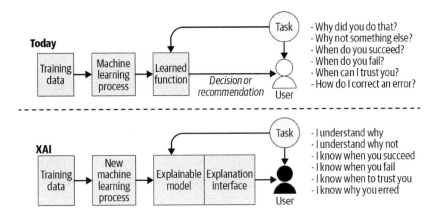

3 Viktor Ivanitskiy and Vasily Tatyannikov, "Information Asymmetry in Financial Markets: Challenges and Threats," Economy of Region (Centre for Economic Security, Institute of Economics of Ural Branch of Russian Academy of Sciences), vol. 1, no. 4 (2018): 1156–67.

4 Matt Turek, "Explainable Artificial Intelligence (XAI)," Defense Advanced Research Projects Agency (DARPA), retrieved September 10, 2019, from *https://oreil.ly/--C81*.

The Before, Now, and After of Ethical Systems

Evan Stubbs

Partner and Associate Director, Boston Consulting Group

Closed-loop systems that use data to fuel artificial intelligence have the ability to change the world. Such systems are already saving lives, allocating capital, executing contracts, and making increasing numbers of decisions on behalf of their human overlords. As an architect of the future, wielding this power to make the world a better rather than a lesser place demands respect and consideration. Much like privacy or security, ethics in these systems can't be treated as an aside. It needs to be treated as an integral part of design right from inception through to execution and beyond.

In a very practical sense, there are three points in every engineer's journey at which poor choices can lead to perverse outcomes: the before, the now, and the after.

All of the following examples are real, albeit with the names withheld to protect the guilty.

During the *before* point, the firmament has yet to be built. Here, the biggest risk is unintentionally causing personal or social harm despite the best of intentions; algorithms are trained on data, and if that data reflects institutionalized disadvantage, the future will be forced to mirror the present.

Consider a firm that's interested in using AI to identify and accelerate high performers within its staff. To train its algorithms, it pulls HR data and trains a model to discriminate between people who succeed and those who don't. However, by doing so it has unintentionally created a monster that runs the risk of institutionalizing sexism into the firm's operating model.

Let's assume the firm isn't sexist, nor is it operating with a deliberately sexist governance framework; how did we get here?

Even if the firm's management team has always tried to promote based on merit, historically male-dominated research fields have created a generational bias toward hiring male graduates for decades. The data that the algorithm uses is fundamentally contaminated; even if the model doesn't explicitly include gender as a predictor, gender is likely to be historically correlated with male behaviors such as a lower likelihood of taking parental leave.

The perverse outcome is that an accurate model may have an inherent bias toward accelerating males, not because men are better candidates, but simply because they outnumber women and therefore have historically been more likely to have been promoted in absolute terms.

In the before, you need to think about how your choices might unintentionally undermine the very problem you're trying to solve. Even the best intentions can go unintentionally awry given the wrong data.

In the *now* point, we have to make a choice. We know we can do it, but should we?

Consider a bank interested in maximizing profits. Credit cards drive margins, but only if they're used in a particular way. Spend too much and the customer can't cover their debts, forcing a default and costing the bank money. Carry over too little and the bank is probably breaking even on card fees but making minimal profit. The ideal customer is a "revolver," one who carries a debt from month to month and pays off the minimum balance, maximizing interest revenue for the bank.

With the right data, it's trivial to build a model that identifies how best to encourage people to spend more. There are infinite ways to nudge behavior, including loyalty rewards, badges, and indiscriminate use of dark patterns. Doing so can have a material impact on the bank's bottom line. However, what subset of people will end up trapped in a cycle of debt if the bank chooses to do so?

In the now, you need to be comfortable with the consequences of your algorithms. Your work reflects your power to change the world, for better or worse.

In the *after* point, everything is working and hopefully working well. It's tempting to think that the need for oversight is over. That belief is false.

Consider a media company interested in tailoring content. Its algorithms excel at matching content to interest. Over time, though, these same algorithms create highly insulated echo chambers. Dopamine-driven information consumption drives entire cohorts to see only the content that agrees with their worldview. Views become polarized and increasingly extremist in the absence of countervailing viewpoints. What might have started as a relatively harmless method to increase viewer stickiness can easily end up as a hotbed for societal unrest, due almost entirely and yet unintentionally to the underlying algorithms.

In the after, you need to actively keep an eye on things you've built to make sure you're not creating a world you wouldn't want to live in. Your algorithms are your children, and their actions are your responsibility.

Business Realities Will Defeat Your Analytics

Richard Hackathorn

Industry Analyst, Bolder Technology

The next generation of data analytics (casually called *AI*) is rapidly evolving and achieving impressive feats of reasoning at increasing scale. For a few high-tech companies, it has globally transformed their ecommerce interactions and the entire market dynamics.[1]

Most executives of typical corporations assume that enterprise systems will be the next to benefit. Although next-gen analytics is here for some, the skills and practices for using next-gen analytics properly are not evenly distributed. Unfortunately, this gap steadily widens.[2]

In the past, analytics was limited to self-contained projects to generate visual insights into specific business situations, which managers then used to set policies and procedures. Next-gen analytics is shifting to operational modules embedded throughout enterprise systems, directly exposing analytics to the complexities of live business realities. Analytic-savvy executives are likely to be unjustifiably comfortable that next-gen analytic tools will triumph over those nasty realities.

Will these next-gen analytic solutions survive the wilds of your business realities? The following key areas of the *data-to-action value chain* should be of special concern to all executives.[3]

---

1 Amy Webb, *The Big Nine* (New York: PublicAffairs, 2019). This book takes an in-depth look at the global AI corporations that dominate the commercialization of this technology.

2 Richard Hackathorn, "Confronting Deep Learning Systems: How Much Things Have Changed and How Much We Do Not Know," Towards Data Science, March 28, 2019, *https://oreil.ly/eLDkQ*. This summary of recent Strata surveys about the adoption of AI in corporations highlights key implications about the haves and have-nots of next-gen analytics.

3 Richard Hackathorn, "Finding Value in Analytics," Eckerson Group (blog), 2019–2020, *https://oreil.ly/P_ekV*. This is a six-part blog series that develops the economic principle of analytic value and describes the analytic value strategy for organizations to realize that value.

Conceiving

Business use cases for next-gen analytics are tricky to define adequately for new infrastructures like Google's TensorFlow Enterprise. Instead of supervised learning frameworks that train and validate models with curated data, we are entering an era of real-time data streams of images, speech, and other strange Internet of Things (IoT) data that no longer stagnates in data lakes. Analytics will continuously transform this data, generating image categories, speech-to-text segments, and other business-relevant objects consumable by various system modules. Defining these use cases requires new skills and methodologies, along with new performance metrics. Upgrading the role of business/data analysts as coordinating partners will be critical.[4]

Developing

Options for developing analytic models have exploded one hundredfold. Neural networks are like LEGO sets for data scientists. Neural architectures such as transfer learning, reinforcement learning, generative adversarial networks, and style transfer are expanding daily. Just tracking these technology developments requires one's full-time attention. Data scientists educated more than five years ago are now obsolete unless they have constantly updated their skills. DataOps infrastructures, so carefully architected during the data warehousing decades, now must be reengineered to constantly monitor training and test datasets to ensure unbiased sampling.

Deploying

The transition from applications of manually crafted logic to systems of constantly learning logic is a major conceptual shift. Managing constant contests of the challenger (the new analytic model) versus the champion (the production analytic model) will take the current A/B testing schemes to new levels. Traditional system phase-over procedures are inadequate with next-gen analytics. The shift in the roles of DevOps professionals is similar to hunters becoming farmers. Stop thinking about bagging that deer for dinner tonight. Start thinking about seeding a crop for this fall, along with the seasons to come.

---

4 Richard Hackathorn, "Shifts & Twists in Business Analytics: Reflections from Qlik Qonnections and Alteryx Inspire," Towards Data Science, August 2019, *https://oreil.ly/0yxya*. This article offers reflections from recent tech conferences on strategies for utilizing next-gen analytics properly.

Governing

Your next-gen analytics system is now in production, so now what? The deep challenges will begin. Paco Nathan states it concisely: "[Analytic] models degrade once exposed to live customer data."[5] Your carefully trained models degrade because the training data is now out of sync with the live data. Business realities today are not the same as they were yesterday. How do you know when the degradation is significant? How do you correct the degradation? How do you prevent security exploits from spoofing your system? How do you explain the system's behavior, whether to customers on the phone or to jurors in a courtroom? And who is accountable when the analytics results in significant libel damages?

Governing analytic systems requires a clear lineage from data to action, implying each analytic-generated action can be associated to its underlying data. Further, the proper role for human intuition and judgment should be woven into the analytic system to minimize *AI stupidity* and its unintended consequences.

Conclusion

There are significant ethical implications to next-gen analytics, as outlined here. Any executive involved with these systems should be humble about the abilities of these analytics to comprehend changing complexities of their business reality. A healthy dose of anxiety is warranted.

---

5 Hackathorn, "Confronting Deep Learning Systems." Note the later section "Take-Away: One Other Thing," where Nathan concludes his thoughts on the future of business analytics. Sobering...

How Can I Know You're Right?

Majken Sander

Chief Analytics Officer

Of course you strive to be neutral. You more than anyone know that it is essential to avoid skewing results, to stay away from applying any bias, and you find that it is important to let the numbers do the talking.

As a professional on a quest to solve a task, you try to choose the most suitable model and use the best tool available.

Once in a while, someone asks a question like, "How do I choose the best regression model?"

You're in luck. Years of experience have taught you things such as how to choose the best confidence levels, how to know which values provide the highest success rate in predictive modeling, how to do data cleansing most efficiently, and which records to leave out altogether because of poor data quality.

Data Literacy for Data Users

The people on the receiving end of analytics are seldom aware of what lies behind the data they are looking at. Nor do they have a huge interest in gaining more in-depth knowledge of math, algorithms, and data. Often they find themselves more than happy to trust your craftsmanship and skills. Every once in a while, someone will question the results, but seldom will they question the method.

They need us to take them by the hand and show them the way, maybe even challenge them a bit. Nowadays, a certain amount of data literacy is required for the users of any analysis, visualization, white paper, or report to understand what they are looking at.

Declare Your Work

How we, the data professionals, choose to put data to use begins by allowing others to gain insights into how we decide to solve the task at hand.

I offer this suggestion: add an extra page at the end of every analysis—a declaration of content. Imagine a plaque similar to the one placed on the back of every piece of electronic equipment stating the manufacturer, voltage, and so forth.

Suggested content:

- Which datasets are included, from which sources
- Deliberately excluded parts of the dataset
- The data cleansing rules applied
- The analytical models used, and preferably also a short note explaining why these were considered to be the best and mentioning alternative roads not taken
- Depending on the model, a description of the relevant settings being parameters, values, etc.
- Software/tools used, including versions
- ...

Consider how you can document the framework around your analysis to help others understand the premises and quality of your work and the results you put forward as answers.

Enlighten your audience to a degree that enables them to feel informed and knowledgeable enough to ask questions and show their interest in the findings of your analysis.

Over time, people might become familiar with your style and preferences, and who knows? A pattern might even surface around how you approach the different tasks. This in return offers insights for you to use to sharpen your analytical edge.

And on a more personal note: you might find it very valuable if someone asks you questions about that particular piece of work months or even years from now. How did you in fact choose which model to use and which records to exclude?

A Framework for Managing Ethics in Data Science: Model Risk Management

Doug Hague

Executive Director, School of Data Science at UNC Charlotte

As data scientists work to understand the ethics and implications of their models, a management framework is needed. Fortunately, the model risk management (MRM) framework emerging from the financial services industry may be expanded to include ethics. Models from various industries, including résumé screeners, recidivism models, and health care payment models, may be biased against various users or protected groups and have resulted in poor publicity for any corporation found to be using them. As data scientists develop methods to manage bias, MRM may be useful for documenting and ensuring best practices are followed. My focus here is on applying MRM processes to mathematical biases of a model; however, the MRM framework is also applicable when broadening to fairness and the overall ethical implications of data science.

In simple terms, MRM is a process that reviews and monitors model development and operations. It consists of examining data quality, mathematical soundness, quality of predictions, appropriate use, and ongoing monitoring, all through independent review and validation. In each of these areas, bias may creep into a model's prediction.

Data

If data is biased at the start (as most data is), MRM has checks and balances to ensure that as much bias is removed as possible through management of input data via selective sampling, ensuring representative data, and other methods. Older methods of removing protected variables are still necessary but are no longer enough, as other correlated variables will bring bias back into the predictions.

Math

It is important to understand the implications of the mathematical techniques utilized while developing models. For example, it may be important for the mathematics to show why a particular result was produced. Explainability (especially for models once considered to be "black boxes," such as neural networks) becomes critical to enabling some use cases and is therefore required during validation and in production.

Performance

When examining the quality of model predictions, MRM can ensure not only that the full dataset is examined but also that the outcomes for protected subgroups are as similar as possible. This may result in a detuning of the overall performance to achieve a more unbiased outcome. MRM should require debate and internal transparency around these choices. One item of note: while protected variables should not be used during development, they should be available during validation to determine whether bias exists in the performance.

Appropriate Use

Appropriate use is where MRM limits the reuse of models outside of the data and assumptions made during development. The reuse of models makes data scientists much more efficient; MRM ensures that this reuse does not cause ethical considerations. For example, does a model developed in Asia apply in the US, where different protected variables are important? Sometimes the questions and checks posed by MRM are easy, while other times they are not. Ensuring that the questions are asked and answered goes a long way toward establishing more ethical models.

Monitoring

One of the more important process checks in MRM is the monitoring of model performance, as model performance will drift. This is true for both static models and those auto-tuned frequently, although *performance* drifts in the former and *parameters* drift in the latter. As models drift, bias tends to creep back into the performance as well. Adding a bias check as well as a performance check during model monitoring will enable redevelopment at appropriate times.

Validation

Independent validation and monitoring of a model is a great way to ensure different stakeholders and viewpoints are considered. This can be done through a separate reporting chain, as is common in financial service companies, or, at a minimum, through peer review. Having an outside perspective prevents tunnel vision and provides some initial diversity of understanding. Best practice is to include validators that have different and relevant life experiences.

Summary

Applying the MRM framework to its model development practices can help a company better understand and reduce the risk of operating models that may have challenging ethical outcomes. Adding bias checks and assurances throughout the MRM process is one step that can help data science practitioners develop and manage the bias and ethical considerations in their work.

The Ethical Dilemma of Model Interpretability

Grant Fleming

Data Scientist, Elder Research Inc.

Progress in data science is largely driven by the ever-improving predictive performance of increasingly complex "black-box" models. However, these predictive gains have come at the expense of losing the ability to interpret the relationships derived between the predictors and target(s) of a model, leading to misapplication and public controversy. These drawbacks reveal that *interpretability is actually an ethical issue*; data scientists should strive to implement additional interpretability methods that maintain predictive performance (model complexity) while also minimizing its harms.

Any examination of the scholarly or popular literature on "AI" or "data science" makes apparent the profound importance placed on maximizing predictive performance. After all, recent breakthroughs in model design and the resulting improvements to predictive performance have led to models exceeding doctors' performance at detecting multiple medical issues (*https:// oreil.ly/yK67h*) and surpassing human reading comprehension (*https:// oreil.ly/PynnL*). These breakthroughs have been made possible by transitioning from linear models to black-box models like Deep Neural Networks (DNN) and gradient-boosted trees (e.g., XGBoost). Instead of using linear transformations of features to generate predictions, these black-box models employ complex, nonlinear feature transformations to produce higher-fidelity predictions.

Because of the complex mathematics underlying them, these black-box models assume the role of oracle, producing predictions without providing human-interpretable explanations for their outputs. While these predictions are often more accurate than linear models, moving away from the built-in interpretability of linear models can pose challenges. For example, the inability to interpret the decision rules of the model can make it harder to gain the trust of users, clients, and regulators, even for models that are otherwise well designed and effective.

Forgoing model interpretability also presents an ethical dilemma for the sciences. In improving our ability to predict the state of the world, black-box models have traded away part of their ability to help us *understand* the reasoning motivating those predictions. Entire subfields of economics, medicine, and psychology have predicated their existence on successfully translating linear model interpretations into policy prescriptions. For these tasks, predictive performance is often secondary to exploring the relationships created by the model between its predictors and targets. Focusing solely on predictive performance would have neutered our understanding in these fields and may prevent future discoveries that would have otherwise been drawn out of more transparent models.

Outside of public policy and science, forgoing model interpretability has posed more direct challenges. Misapplied black-box models within health care (*https://oreil.ly/OLcSU*), the legal system (*https://oreil.ly/Mi7MW*), and corporate hiring processes (*https://oreil.ly/HFLet*) have unintentionally harmed both the people and the organizations that they were built to serve. In these cases, the predictions of the black boxes were clearly inaccurate; however, debugging and detecting potential issues prior to deployment was either difficult or impossible given the nature of the models. Such cases have understandably led to public controversy about the ethics of data science as well as calls for stronger regulation (*https://oreil.ly/OzS46*) around algorithmic data collection, transparency, and fairness.

Balancing complexity and model interpretability is clearly a challenge. Fortunately, there are several *interpretability methods* that allow data scientists to understand, to an extent, the inner workings of complex black-box models that are otherwise unknowable. Applying these methods can allow for maintaining the improved predictive performance of arbitrary black-box models while gaining back much of the interpretability lost by moving away from linear models.

Individual interpretability methods can serve a wide variety of functions. For example, global interpretability methods such as partial dependence plots (PDPs) can provide diagnostic visualizations for the average impact of features on predictions. The plots depict quantitative relationships between the input and output features of black-box models and allow for human interpretations similar to how coefficients from a linear model might be used. Local methods like Shapley values can produce explanations for the impacts of specific feature values on individual predictions, increasing user trust by showing how the model relies on specific features. Model debugging efforts are also made simpler by the increased insight that these methods allow, indicating opportunities for increasing the performance even of black-box models that may already perform well.

Ethical data science surely encompasses more than just being able to interpret the inner functioning and outputs of a model. However, the case for why model interpretability should be a part of ethical best practices is compelling. Data scientists integrating interpretability methods into their black-box models are improving the ethical due diligence of their work; it is how one can maintain model interpretability while still leveraging the great potential of black-box models.

Use Model-Agnostic Explanations for Finding Bias in Black-Box Models

Yiannis Kanellopoulos and Andreas Messalas

Founder, Code4Thought
Data Scientist, Code4Thought

The need to shed light on the opacity of "black-box" models is evident: Articles 15 and 22 of the EU's General Data Protection Regulation (2018), the OECD Principles on Artificial Intelligence (2019), and the US Senate's proposed Algorithmic Accountability Act (*https://oreil.ly/2Xgzm*) are some examples indicating that machine learning interpretability, along with machine learning accountability and fairness, has already (or should) become an integral characteristic for any application that makes automated decisions.

Since many organizations will be obliged to provide explanations about the decisions of their automated models, there will be a huge need for third-party organizations to assess interpretability, as this provides an additional level of integrity and objectivity to the whole audit process. Moreover, some organizations (especially start-ups) won't have the resources to deal with interpretability issues, rendering third-party auditors necessary.

In this manner, however, intellectual property issues arise, since organizations will not want to disclose any information about the details of their models. Therefore, among the wide range of interpretability methods, model-agnostic approaches (i.e., methods that are oblivious to a model's details) are deemed to be appropriate for this purpose.

Besides explaining the predictions of a black-box model, interpretability can also provide us with insight into erroneous behavior of our models, which may be caused by undesired patterns in our data. In this article, we will examine an example in which interpretability helps us identify gender bias in our data, using a model-agnostic method that utilizes surrogate models and Shapley values.

We use the Default of Credit Card Clients Dataset, which contains information (demographic factors, credit data, history of payment, and bill statements) about 30,000 credit card clients, with the target label being if they defaulted on their next payment (i.e., in October 2005). The following figure breaks out the defaulting and nondefaulting bank customers by gender; the left and middle bars in each group represent the original distributions of female and male customers, while the right bar in each group depicts the newly constructed biased distribution of male customers.

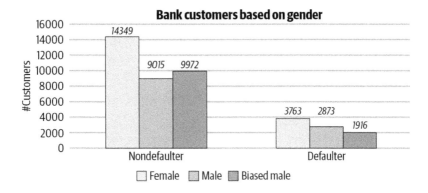

We distort the dataset by randomly selecting 957 male defaulters (i.e., one-third of the overall number of male defaulters), and we alter their label. This creates a new biased dataset with 34% male and 66% female defaulters and 41% male and 59% female nondefaulters.

We then remove the gender feature from the dataset and take the predictions of a black-box model trained on this biased dataset (whose structure we are indifferent about). We then train a surrogate (*https://oreil.ly/hpq8U*) XGBoost model, from which we extract the Shapley values that help us explain the predictions of the original model. More precisely, we use the Shapley values to pinpoint the most important features and then use them in the explanations through simple sentences in natural language.

We examine the explanations for a false negative prediction for a male customer (i.e., falsely predicted as a nondefaulter) and a false positive prediction for a female customer (i.e., falsely predicted as a defaulter). They are both unmarried university graduates with similar credit limits. However, the male customer delayed the last four payments, while the female delayed only the most recent one—see the following table.

ID	Credit Limit	Education	Marital Status	Payment Status (months delayed)					
				Sept.	Aug.	July	June	May	April
26664 (*male*)	80,000	university	single	5	4	3	2	paid duly	U.R.C.
599 (*female*)	60,000	university	single	2	U.R.C.[a]	U.R.C.	U.R.C.	U.R.C.	U.R.C.

[a] Use of revolving credit.

For the male customer, the delay for the September payment had a negative impact of 33% (i.e., contributing toward "Default"), as the following explanation indicates. However, counterintuitively, the delay for the August payment had a positive impact.

```
1  dcc2.print_ReasonCode(26664, 6)
```

Factors contributing that the customer (ID: 26664) will not default the next payment:

1) **5 month(s) delay** for the payment of **September, 2005** (Impact: 33.26%)

2) **4 month(s) delay** for the payment of **August, 2005** (Impact: 16.14%)

3) **Amount of previous Payment** (16000 NT dollars) for May, 2005. The Bill Statement for this month was 51722 NT dollars (Impact: 12.28%)

4) **Amount of previous Payment** (1100 NT dollars) for April, 2005. The Bill Statement for this month was 44956 NT dollars (Impact: 5.64%)

5) The customer is single (Impact: 4.94%)

6) Customer's **age** is 27 (Impact: 3.88%)

For the female customer, the two-month delay for September also contributed negatively, but at a much greater percentage (47%) compared to the five-month delay of the male customer (33%); see the following figure for more details.

```
1  dcc2.print_ReasonCode(599, 6)
```

Factors contributing that the customer (ID: 599) will default the next payment:

1) **2 month(s) delay** for the payment of **September, 2005** (Impact: 47.34%)

2) **Amount of given credit** (80000 NT dollars) (Impact: 10.89%)

3) Customer's **age** is 24 (Impact: 7.42%)

4) The customer is single (Impact: 5.88%)

5) **Amount of Bill Statement** (58683 NT dollars) for July, 2005. Customer paid 5000 NT dollars (Impact: 3.65%)

6) **Amount of Bill Statement** (58886 NT dollars) for June, 2005. Customer paid 2500 NT dollars (Impact: 3.61%)

Although the gender feature was not included in the training of the model, we observed with the help of the explanations that the gender bias was encoded into other features (e.g., positive contribution for the delay of payment for the male customer). Moreover, in observing the percentages of the impact in the explanations, we detected harsher treatment of the female customer by the model (e.g., greater negative impact for a lesser delay of payment). This strange behavior should alarm us and motivate us to get a better sample of the defaulters.

In summary, in cases where the dataset contains real people, it is important to ensure that the model does not discriminate against one group over others. Explanations allow us to detect bias even if it is hidden, pinpoint unintended decision patterns of our black-box model, and motivate us to fix our data.

Automatically Checking for Ethics Violations

Jesse Anderson

Managing Director, Big Data Institute

Data science likes to be quite meta sometimes. There is a push to use machine learning models to check the actions of data scientists or other machine learning models for ethics violations. The watchers are being watched by the machine learning model.

I'm often asked whether it's really possible for a machine learning model to automatically check for ethics violations. This question usually comes from companies that are worried about the sheer number of queries and overall discovery that a data scientist needs to run. With data democratization, even more people will have access to the data, which means even more possible ethics violations. It will be virtually impossible for the management team or general counsel to review every single query.

In my opinion, it isn't possible to rely on a machine learning model to find ethics violations. The people who write the machine learning model are the same ones the machine would be watching for potential violations. If they aren't the ones who wrote it, they will have enough of a background to know how not to have their query be flagged as an ethics violation. The data scientists especially will be able to make educated guesses as to which algorithms are being used and will know what the weakness of each algorithm is.

Despite all of this, the company's exposure to ethics violations remains the same. Something has to be done. What can the company do?

Before a company can even attempt a manual or automatic check for ethics violations, it will need to centralize the code and queries so that they are logged in a single place. This is something that the data engineering team would need to put in place. Without a single place to log all queries and code execution, there will be too many one-off locations for checks to be run. That would enable the easy circumventing of logging when someone is really dead set on behaving unethically.

Once all the queries and code execution are centralized, the management team and general counsel can start to look for violations. With SQL queries, the intent and results will be relatively straightforward to review.

With code, the review process may be far more difficult and time consuming. This is because the management team and general counsel may not know how to read code. Even if they know how to code, the intent and results of the code may not be readily apparent—the code could even be obfuscated to hide the intent behind it. Also, the code itself may not be accessible or checked into source control so that the exact code that was run can be read.

I think the only viable solution is to hire good people, give them training on what is and isn't acceptable to do with the company's data, and do spot checks of their code and queries. Checking every piece of code simply isn't a realistic approach. The two alternatives that avoid code checks are both untenable. One option is to never put the data into people's hands for fear of ethics violations—at that point, why even have a data strategy? The other option is to implicitly trust everything that your people do and hope for the best. I think the best option lies somewhere in the middle.

Should Chatbots Be Held to a Higher Ethical Standard than Humans?

Naomi Arcadia Kaduwela

Head of Kavi Labs, Kavi Global

We have seen an explosion of chatbots in the market. AI has become ingrained into the daily fabric of our lives. Service industries have turned to AI-driven chatbots to manage customer interactions, increasing speed and quality of resolution while decreasing cost. Millennials increasingly prefer to interact with chatbots rather than humans. As we embrace chatbots in our lives, it is paramount to evaluate the role they play in reinforcing and perpetuating societal biases and stereotypes. With the proliferation of chatbots creating a new paradigm of human and machine collaboration, an interesting ethical question emerges: should we hold chatbots to a higher ethical standard than we hold ourselves?

Underlying chatbots are natural language processing (NLP) models made up of deep learning algorithms called neural networks. Deep learning models have the ability to accurately map complex relationships from messy data—in text as well as images. So what are popular NLP models like convolutional neural networks (CNNs), recurrent neural networks (RNNs), and long short-term memory networks (LSTMs) doing in chatbots? They are mathematically defining relationships between words, as explicitly or implicitly defined in the training corpus.

Examples of Chatbots Inheriting Human Biases

There have been several disconcerting NLP algorithm mishaps. Amazon's secret AI recruiting tool showed bias against women. Microsoft's now-infamous chatbot Tay14, a machine learning experiment in social interaction, had to be decommissioned when it picked up a series of racial slurs.

These stories shock and outrage us. We are quick to blame the company or the AI developer. Yet it is human-generated data that these NLP models are trained on. NLP models are only exposing the existing human bias learned from the training data. NLP mishaps are a reflection of humanity's dark side.

How Chatbots Perpetuate Human Biases

Just as a child's code of ethics is shaped by its parents and environment, machine learning models learn from human-generated training data specified by their creators. Just as humans grow wiser with experience, machine learning models require large training corpuses to learn robust and generalizable relationships. And just as children grow up and pass on their code of ethics, as well as their biases, machines too will perpetuate their code of ethics and their biases through interactions with future generations. The difference is that these machines are immortal and will transcend generations in time. Thus our chatbots must be held to the highest ethical standard and must correct for the biases in training data generated by fallible humans.

Ways to Correct Biases in Chatbots

In continuous pursuit of excellence, we must admit our fallibility and look to correct it in generations to come. From an NLP modeling perspective, three bias correction methods exist to help chatbots overcome human biases in their training data.

One option is to completely remove the biased concept from the NLP model. For example, in preparation for an NLP model, words and phrases in a training corpus are mapped to a vector of real numbers called word embeddings. Mathematically, gender can be subtracted from these vectors. However, completely removing the concept of gender might not prove practical in applications where it is a key predictor or segmentation variable. An alternative for removing gender stereotypes, while still keeping the concept of gender, is to simply remove gender stereotypes we don't want (e.g., receptionist) and keep those we do (e.g., CEO). Finally, additional data can be synthetically generated by flipping pronouns (i.e., "he" and "she") so that the model does not learn any unintended bias due to lack of representation in the training data.

Why Continuous Learning Is Required for Chatbots

We see that our code of ethics has continually evolved over thousands of years. Recent progress has been made with civil rights, women's rights, and the LGBT movement. Though the core principles of ethics have not fundamentally changed since the time of Socrates, the practical application of ethics is fluid and is constantly evolving alongside society. If we hardcode today's biases into immortal machines, we will pollute the minds of future generations with the biases of generations past, slowing the ethical evolution of the human race. Instead, we can leverage techniques to help chatbots overcome today's human biases, so they can in turn make the human race better, ethically speaking!

"All Models Are Wrong." What Do We Do About It?

Miroslava Walekova

Senior Manager, Transformation Platform Ltd.

Machine learning will continue to transform every aspect of our lives: the way we interact with each other, the way we learn and develop, and the way we interact with society. Yet these systems will inadvertently break down every so often.

> All models are approximations. Essentially, all models are wrong, but some are useful.
>
> —George E. P. Box

In other words: no model, machine learning, or artificial intelligence solution can be right all the time. If we agree that failures cannot be avoided, then our main concern is to focus on the processes and controls that can effectively and efficiently minimize any adverse impact on individuals.

A machine learning governance framework has to cover solutions from idea inception to solution decommissioning, and it needs to:

1. Prevent solution problems by design
2. Rectify any issues in an expedited, transparent, and responsible manner
3. Improve the governance framework continuously

Let's walk through each of these requirements.

1. Prevent

The effort to minimize adverse impacts starts with an internal assurance that a solution will adhere to principles of fairness.

Defining fairness, however, poses a number of challenges. Not only do individuals have different perceptions of what is fair, but there is also a great variety of views across geography. There is a need to establish professional bodies that will actively develop a unified vision of what fairness means. With appropriate definition and clarity around what constitutes a fair solution, "fairness" may become a core element of the machine learning solution design. And if instead of embedding our own bias we incorporate "diversity by design," we may find the ultimate impact of machine learning to be positive.

Every principle or rule that a professional body or internal governance framework may stipulate is still, however, subject to individual interpretation. Segregation of duties and a formal compliance process with these principles are the key to success.

2. Rectify

As we are unable to completely eliminate adverse impacts with prevention by design, it is important that the process to rectify any failures in a transparent and expedited way is defined and that it is at the core of any product or service deployment.

A core component of any organization's culture should be ART— accountability, responsibility, and transparency. ART should be translated into the objectives of all individuals involved in the development and maintenance of machine learning solutions. Raising ethical issues related to any internal or external application of machine learning should be encouraged, and the same protections given to whistleblowers should apply.

In fact, the responsibility to raise ethical concerns should reside not only with internal staff but also with external stakeholders—that is, customers, suppliers, the government, and so forth. Both the organizations who develop machine learning solutions and professional bodies need to enable all stakeholders to raise their concerns.

The process could be similar to the EU's GDPR process, where individuals have the right to request information from companies to understand what personal information they hold. The organizations in turn are obligated to respond to such requests within a month. This period is sufficient to carry out an "ethical principle" assessment and enable the organization to prevent any further adverse impact on individuals.

3. Improve

Machine learning applications, as well as society, will continue to evolve. As a result, the fairness definition and governance framework will need to evolve simultaneously. All organizations should therefore allow for flexibility to enable continuous review and improvement of machine learning solutions.

Data Transparency: What You Don't Know Can Hurt You

Janella Thomas

Data Scientist, Cox Enterprises Inc.

Transparency in data is one of the most important aspects of the ethical data science conversation. Transparency in data science primarily means effectively informing others of the data that is collected and how it will be used. Lack of transparency can result in unintended consequences for the business and can have a lasting impact on your customers. Whether you are developing analytics for internal customers or providing capabilities to external customers, data transparency has to be an integral part of the conversation.

Predictive analytics capabilities are extremely valuable and can play a strategic role in attaining the next level of an organization's growth. When providing capabilities that will only be used internally, one of your primary responsibilities is to inform stakeholders of what data you're using and how it will be used. However, informing others of the data collection and intended usage is not enough. It is important to go a step further and analyze potential outcomes of the tools we provide. There are applications of predictive analytics that require ethical analysis.

For example, Target Corporation used a predictive model to score the likelihood of pregnancy for marketing purposes. The consequences of Target's predictive model resulted in a father finding out his teenage daughter was pregnant before she informed him.[1] While these types of models are widely used in marketing analytics, the subject matter of the Target use case was particularly sensitive to consumers and caused unintended scrutiny of the company. This has quickly become a classic example of the ethical analysis required before actions are applied to the insights gained.

---

1 Charles Duhigg, "How Companies Learn Your Secrets," *New York Times Magazine*, February 16, 2012, *https://oreil.ly/RtRZL*.

The importance of data transparency for externally facing customers has become one of the field's most significant ethical concerns. The average consumer is steadily becoming more aware of the access they are giving companies to their personal data. For many, this awareness brings worry and diminishes trust. In some instances, consumers are content with the cost–benefit analysis of allowing companies to use their data. Alternatively, many consumers find that the cost of using applications like FaceApp, which uses facial recognition to allow users to view themselves differently, does not justify the benefit. FaceApp is one of the more highly publicized examples of how the average consumer is not aware of how their data is used.[2]

It is important to gain the trust of your customer. This is necessary to sustain their continued use of your products or services. Practicing effective data transparency allows the consumer to consciously consent to the collection and usage of their data. This can mitigate potential future scrutiny. Analyzing the best method of communication for data transparency must be a significant part of the development process. There is not a "one size fits all" method of how to effectively communicate data transparency; every industry is different. It's important to have an effective data communication strategy in place.

Data science is rapidly being used in areas where it was not traditionally applied. This means that the new information and insight obtained may need to be used differently than before—or in some cases, not at all. Target and FaceApp have shown us that internal and external data transparency are equally as important. Lack of either can be harmful, not only to your business but also to individuals. Strategy and analysis around effective data transparency communication needs to be a priority as we continue to embark upon the digital evolution.

---

2 Geoffrey A. Fowler, "You Downloaded FaceApp. Here's What You've Just Done to Your Privacy," *Washington Post*, July 17, 2019, *https://oreil.ly/1UmFN*.

Toward Algorithmic Humility

Marc Faddoul

Research Associate, School of Information, UC Berkeley

Defendant #3172 is an unmarried 22-year-old female. She previously served two months in prison for marijuana trafficking and has just been arrested for engaging in a violent public altercation with her partner. Is the defendant going to commit a violent crime in the three-month period before the trial? To answer such a question, many American jurisdictions use algorithmic systems known as pretrial risk assessment tools. Let's consider one of the most common of these tools, the Public Safety Assessment (PSA).[1]

When the PSA sees a high risk, it raises a red flag, and this automatically sends the defendant into detention, without further consideration from the judge to challenge the machine's prediction. The stakes are high, as pretrial detention often comes with devastating consequences for the job and housing security of defendants, including those who are later proven innocent at trial. *Tragically, 97% of these life-wrecking algorithmic red flags are in fact false alarms.*[2] In other words, 3% of flagged defendants would have actually committed a violent crime had they been released, while the other 97% were detained unnecessarily. This is a strikingly poor performance, but it is somewhat unsurprising.

Foreseeing a crime in the near future is hard, and machines are not oracles. They could, however, contribute valuable predictive clues, but only with the intellectual humility required for this task. Deplorably, the PSA was designed as an arrogant algorithm.

---

1 The PSA is used as an illustrative example, but the shortcomings depicted in this essay also apply to the other pretrial risk assessment tools used in American jurisdictions. The PSA is arguably one of the more ethically designed tools.

2 Marc Faddoul, Henriette Ruhrmann, and Joyce Lee, "A Risk Assessment of a Pretrial Risk Assessment Tool: Tussles, Mitigation Strategies, and Inherent Limits," Computers and Society, Cornell University, submitted May 14, 2020, *https://arxiv.org/abs/2005.07299*.

If defendants were systematically released before their trial, about 1% of them would commit a violent crime. By comparing the profiles of those offenders and that of a given defendant, the PSA does three times better than a random guess: it puts *only* 33 defendants in jail for every offender it detects.

Indeed, the limited demographic and judicial data available is vastly insufficient to predict a crime. Information about mental health or housing stability would be more predictive, but also hard to collect in a fair and systematic way. Even then, some randomness would remain. Two people who look identical to the algorithm can end up in different situations and react with different decisions.

Moreover, the algorithm cannot learn from its mistakes. When a particular defendant is detained, there is no way to know whether they actually would have committed a crime had they been released. Inherently, the predictive signal is weak. Therefore, the algorithm could never predict crimes with high accuracy.

Errors are inevitable, but that is not a problem per se. Like other empirical sciences, data science can deal with uncertainty by making probabilistic predictions and including confidence intervals. The PSA, however, makes predictions on an arbitrary scale, with no indication of confidence or error rates. Some justify this design by claiming that it is simpler for judges to read, that they can't make sense of probabilities. This is arrogant thinking. The current system is not simple; it is simplistic, which makes it deceiving. The algorithm misleads judges in its raising of prescriptive red flags. If it gave actual probabilities instead, judges would know that a "high risk flag" actually means "a chance of about 3%."

This design also understates a judge's ability to gain additional contextual information. For instance, a humble algorithm might point out that domestic violence is a likely risk scenario for a particular defendant, encouraging the judge to investigate that defendant's current partnership. For certain profiles, the algorithm's training records may be limited or inconsistent. If the statistical signal is not strong enough to make a decent prediction, a humble algorithm would withdraw to completely defer the decision to the judge.

Algorithms and humans are the same in that their expertise is never complete or uniform. As such, they should acknowledge their limits. The point of using algorithms in court is to remove human biases. This is a legitimate concern, as judges can be laden with bias regarding race, gender, social classes, and even what they had for lunch.[3]

Algorithms are sometimes thought of as being purely objective, but aside from the lunch menu, they are not immune to bias. As with humans, their biases stem from inaccurate generalizations based on their limited and non-representative experience of the world. When an algorithm is presented with American judicial records, it instantly induces that African Americans are more likely to commit crimes. America's lingering legacy of racial discrimination, and the fact that the judicial system is structurally biased against African Americans, is irrelevant to the machine. Even if a defendant's ethnicity is not provided, it can still be inferred from the defendant's zip code or from the number of juvenile misdemeanors in the defendant's record.

To balance for this effect, algorithms can be designed to enforce a certain fairness proposition. For instance, error rates can be constrained to be equal across different ethnic groups. Concretely, this constraint defines an affirmative action policy: *How much more tolerant should the algorithm be when considering black defendants to offset for racial discriminations?* Algorithms are scattered with such parameters, which can tweak crucial trade-offs behind the curtains. Arrogant algorithms can be intentionally opaque to conceal policy decisions. The most fundamental parameter is this one: *How many innocents are we willing to put in jail in order to prevent one person from committing a violent crime?* The answer—"33 innocents in jail for every offender" —is hidden inside the code. Indeed, who could legitimately argue out loud that a 1:33 ratio is fair? That number was picked so that the algorithm would reproduce the incarceration rates of the current system. But this is the wrong approach: instead of discreetly automating preposterous judicial standards, algorithms should expose and challenge their assumptions.

In the digital age, computer programs have become preeminent regulators of our liberties—hence the dictum "Code is Law."[4] Algorithmic designs, training sets, error rates, and fairness propositions therefore should all be transparent, for opacity can be tyranny. Data science can provide precious insights to guide complex and consequential decisions. However, data science can be detrimental to decision making when it conceals the complexity of the underlying problem.

---

3 Shai Danziger, Jonathan Levav, and Liora Avnaim-Pesso, "Extraneous Factors in Judicial Decisions," *Proceedings of the National Academy of Sciences* 108, no. 17 (2011): 6889–92, *https://doi.org/ 10.1073/pnas.1018033108.*

4 Lawrence Lessig, *Code and Other Laws of Cyberspace* (New York: Basic Books, 1999).

The popular mythology around artificial intelligence overstates the power of prediction tools. If algorithms are to replace or support human expertise, they should behave not like mysterious referees with almighty veto power but more like wise advisors. The same diligence should be expected of both machines and human experts: justifying decisions, acknowledging blind spots, and being intellectually humble. In turn, humans should engage with algorithms critically, by employing that essential part of their cognition that artificial intelligence will forever lack: common sense.

PART VI

Policy Guidelines

To make ethics a cornerstone of an organization's analytics and data science practices, a necessary component is a set of policies to guide people's actions. This section provides perspectives on how ethical policies might best be defined.

Equally Distributing Ethical Outcomes in a Digital Age

Keyur Desai

Chief Data Officer, TD Ameritrade

Data is an incorruptible raw material that is analyzed to reveal and prove the Truth—essentially, "Data is Truth." This is a notion that has erroneously permeated society ever since data was first used for scientific understanding in the mid-17th century. What is closer to reality is that, when used incorrectly, data is a corruptible raw material that can be physically manipulated to derive a truth/insight that suits an originator's own interests or to derive a truth/insight that fits an originator's conscious or subconscious bias. I like how author Stephen Jay Gould succinctly and poignantly phrased this in his book *The Mismeasure of Man* (W. W. Norton): "Expectation is a powerful guide to action." Recent and distant history is littered with examples of individuals and communities who have been wrongly affected by actions justified by the biased analysis of data or algorithms. Data can impact the dynamics of power, human life, health, knowledge, beliefs, and welfare. Algorithms can reinforce oppression and inequality and can tie into surveillance capitalism. What I like to think is that "Data is Truth only when used with ethics and integrity."

To reveal its truth, data must be used with integrity and ethics throughout its entire supply chain. That is, data must be used with integrity and ethics from the point where a human being creates it, defines it, finds it, inspects it, procures it, prepares it for analysis, analyzes it, and shares insights from it or builds artificial intelligence systems with it. What can we do to assure ourselves that this entire analytics supply chain has operated with ethics and integrity so we can then fully trust the truth/insights we are subjected to? There are three things.

First, we need an ethics framework to ensure all participants enabling the analytics supply chain understand the common set of operating expectations placed upon them. To build this framework, we need to ensure that these expectations can be easily and quickly understood and are flexible enough for community members to apply to many different situations. A set of guiding principles rather than a rigid set of rules is what is called for. Furthermore, we need to realize that this entire analytics supply chain has been created by human beings, is operated by human beings, and will affect other human beings. Therefore, when we define an ethical framework, we need to do so with a sociological view and not a technical one. It so happens that the medical research community grappled with a similar set of integrity and ethical issues in the 1970s as a result of egregious lapses in ethics by human originators during the Tuskegee Syphilis Study. A commission created by the National Research Act of 1974 was charged with identifying the basic ethical principles that should underlie the conduct of biomedical and behavioral research involving human subjects and with developing guidelines to assure that such research is conducted in accordance with those principles. The result was the Belmont Report. This report outlined three principles:

Respect for persons
> Protecting the autonomy of all people and treating them with courtesy and respect and allowing for informed consent. Researchers must be truthful and conduct no deception.

Beneficence
> Honoring the philosophy of "do no harm" while maximizing benefits for the research project and minimizing risks to the research subjects.

Justice
> Ensuring that reasonable, nonexploitative, and well-considered procedures are administered fairly—through the fair distribution of costs and benefits to potential research participants—and equally.[1]

Adapting these principles to the analytics world, we can restate them as: (1) autonomy—people should be given the ability to make autonomous decisions about the collection and use of their data; (2) do no harm; and (3) empathy and transparency—would you be equally happy being the person creating the data truth/insights or the person who is affected by the actions the truth/insights create, and can you explain to the affected the lineage of data and analysis that led to the action?

---

1 Wikipedia, s.v., "Belmont Report," last modified May 17, 2020, 07:41, *https://oreil.ly/jkUv-*.

Second, we need independent oversight of the analytics supply chain, with diversity of thought in the overseers. A set of ethics principles is a good starting point and will align human beings participating in the analytics supply chain, most of whom are thankfully well intentioned. But principles alone cannot prevent that one bad originator who deliberately wants to distort the truth being revealed by the data, or an originator who has no ill intent but has unconscious biases. The consequences of either can be catastrophic to a person or group of humans. To protect against such consequences, we need a mechanism for independent oversight for the entire analytics supply chain. But independent oversight alone cannot eliminate biases. For that we need to also ensure multiple diverse perspectives among the overseers. The perspectives of social scientists working collaboratively with data science and artificial intelligence experts can surface consequences that the latter two types of experts may have been blind to, as can the perspectives of those who are or could be affected by the actions that come from the data/systems.

Third, independent oversight needs to be adapted to a fast-moving digital world. The nondigital construct of every decision having to gain committee approval would hamper the speed and agility the digital world needs to maintain. A compelling and modern solution to this is to create a digital capability that allows data and analytics experts the ability to independently perform their work at each point in the analytics supply chain. And as they perform their work, in much the same way that Amazon can see your browsing activity and purchases without your having to explicitly deliver this data to Amazon, the oversight committee has the ability to examine information about sources of data used; how data in the sources is created, updated, and deleted; the data quality of these sources; specific calculations performed on the sources; and reports using the calculations and conclusions being made to actions being proposed. This is made possible by the capture of end-to-end lineage for the entire analytics supply chain, and by technologies that include data lakes, data catalogs, and data preparation coupled with modern data governance. Data science and artificial intelligence can be used on top of such a technology system to digitally flag suspect behavior for the oversight committee, in much the same way that potential fraud may be flagged for further review by a bank.

With an easy-to-understand and flexible ethics framework, independent oversight of the entire analytics supply chain, diversity of perspectives within the oversight process, and a digital oversight system, we can ensure the insights and actions resulting from our artificial intelligence systems are ethical.

Data Ethics—Three Key Actions for the Analytics Leader

John F. Carter

Former SVP, Data & Insights, Charles Schwab

The topics of data privacy and data ethics have grown significantly in importance over the past few years. This development has been driven in part by new legislation such as the EU's GDPR and the CCPA, laws that are intended to provide more control, transparency, and ownership of data to individuals. These new laws, in addition to more new legislation on the horizon, could significantly limit the use of data, which could thwart innovation and impact our ability to provide valuable data-driven services to customers such as preventing fraud, providing relevant personalized products, and improving customer service. We should be very worried about these trends, especially as we are now seeing how massive amounts of unstructured data combined with artificial intelligence can provide tremendous improvements in client experiences as well as create new business opportunities.

It is critically important that companies get ahead of the curve and take proactive steps to drive data ethics guidelines and best practices into their businesses. Many companies have appointed an individual to oversee the use of corporate data, giving them a title such as chief privacy officer, chief data officer, or chief compliance officer. These individuals have focused mostly on the legal aspects of data and on ensuring their company stays in compliance with the laws. That is understandable, as a violation of the law will result in severe consequences. We must, however, take data legality and privacy to the next level, and that is where data ethics comes in.

Customers trust us to respect their privacy and use their data securely and ethically. We have seen many instances in which poor data ethics has resulted in a tarnished brand, loss of customers, and a drop in company profits. Data ethics goes beyond what is required by law and is about the proper collection, management, and use of data within an organization. A company may, for example, leverage a wide set of data for highly targeted marketing offers through programmatic ad buying, but if the offer is intrusive and out of context and leverages sensitive confidential information, then the "creepy factor" may set in and create concerns for the consumer. The short-term impact of increased sales could be miniscule compared to the long-term loss of trust and brand consideration. Smart organizations recognize the importance of building trust with their customers and prospects and are incorporating data ethics guidelines and practices into their operations.

Analytics leaders are in a unique position to contribute to this effort, as they and their teams generally have the deepest knowledge of how data is collected, organized, and used in their firms. It is time for analytics leaders to step up and play a key leadership role in advancing the data privacy and ethics practices within their organizations. Here are some immediate suggestions on how to play that leadership role:

Join the company's enterprise data council.

If such an entity doesn't exist, then influence the company to start one. This council should be cross-functional and should perform a number of functions, including establishing data ethics guidelines, ensuring those guidelines are well understood across the company, and reviewing and approving new uses of data. The approval for a new data use should consider the business value, consumer privacy, and the value the application brings to the consumer, as well as brand and operational risk. Different people will no doubt have different opinions, but through the cross-functional discussion a consensus decision can usually be reached or the data use appropriately modified. As the analytics leader on the council, you will be able to explain how data is used to support different use cases; this will be valuable in educating the council and providing important new areas to discuss and resolve.

Create a strategy to measure data ethics.

Metrics can be created to measure internal processes, but more importantly, the strategy should include metrics to understand how you are perceived by customers. Many companies have ongoing surveys to measure brand health, customer sentiment, trust, and so on. By adding a few questions about data ethics and privacy, you will establish a benchmark that can be tracked and measured over time. Another source of insight will be found by mining unstructured data using AI/machine learning algorithms. Voice/text data from call centers and emails, social posts and blogs (Twitter, Reddit, etc.), and internal customer complaint databases are important sources to analyze daily for trends and for providing immediate indicators of any data ethics issues. Opt-out rates can also be tracked for trending purposes, as well as for identifying the reason behind the opt-outs so that adjustments in marketing content and frequency can be made when necessary.

Educate the data science team on data privacy and ethics.

Data scientists are great at finding and integrating data for the models, but just because the data exists in your enterprise data warehouse or can be scraped from an external website doesn't mean that data can be used ethically. Strong analytical teams have up-front planning processes in place before algorithms are created, and each use case should also be reviewed from a data ethics perspective. Does your company have authority to use the proposed data? Does the application violate any laws or privacy policies? Does the use case provide value to the customer as well as the company? Will there be a "creepy factor" that could tarnish the company's brand? These questions are all areas that data scientists need to review and escalate to the enterprise data council when in doubt.

In summary, analytics leaders can play a big leadership role in establishing and implementing robust data ethics practices for their company. This will lead to better management and use of data, greater data protection for customers, and lower risk to a company's brand equity.

Ethics: The Next Big Wave for Data Science Careers?

Linda Burtch

Managing Director, Burtch Works

With the spotlight on data privacy and ethics concerns in the wake of regulations like the European Union's GDPR, data breaches at high-profile companies, illegal use of data, and more, all organizations will need to examine the ethics of their own approaches to data collection, analysis, and monetization. The power and scope that our data collection capability now offers is increasingly introducing a multitude of ethics questions on a wide range of applications that have never needed to be addressed in the past.

One consequence of this heightened awareness of data ethics may be the impact of negative publicity on an organization's ability to recruit in a very tight labor market. It's important that senior level analytics leaders be aware of how ethical dilemmas in data science can impact their organization's appeal to potential talent. Data scientists have an increasing number of career options, and as the data movement continues to mature, we're seeing many data scientists making career decisions based on what a firm does, or its "mission." In many cases, data scientists are even willing to trade off higher salaries in favor of "mission-driven" roles. Not only can high-profile ethics snafus and controversies create a public relations crisis, but they can also impede a firm's ability to attract top-tier talent, who may think twice about joining a firm with a business model that does not match their values.

The organization's position on data-related ethics and privacy should be reflected in the attitudes and behaviors of analytics staff, as well as being one of the criteria used to evaluate new additions to the quantitative team. Data scientists and analytics professionals are naturally screened based on their skills and tool proficiencies. Identifying professionals who are also a strong cultural fit is dependent on many factors, and going forward one of these factors should be whether or not a candidate's attitudes toward ethical and privacy concerns match those of the organization.

Given the importance and complexity of these issues, I ask the question: is a dedicated ethics lead required to drive the conversation around these increasingly prevalent ethical quandaries on data science teams? This could be a leader specifically responsible for developing the organizational road-map and guardrails when it comes to how ethics and privacy guidelines are observed by the organization. Similar to data governance, which is concerned with who has access to which information, and data protection, as well as other related functions, the role of an ethics lead would be to gather consensus to develop ethical guidelines and ensure organizational compliance.

A few short years ago, data scientist "unicorns" were expected to have the skills to tackle everything from data acquisition to cleaning, modeling, and evangelism, and with the rapid maturation of the discipline, we're now seeing other roles splinter off to tackle different aspects of this process. By now everybody's heard about data engineering, and roles like the data storyteller are also on the rise—will data ethics roles be the next big wave for data science talent?

Organizations have a responsibility to consider how their data is being used and monetized, and if analytics leaders do not take a proactive approach to establishing their team's values on privacy and ethics dilemmas, or if the firm does not appoint someone to manage this task, it may leave the organization vulnerable. We've seen ethics roles scattered among some organizations in industries like financial services and health care, where customer or patient privacy regulations are paramount, but as more industries expand their use of data, it may be prudent for all companies to prioritize this type of role.

Framework for Designing Ethics into Enterprise Data

Keri McConnell

Executive Director, Northwestern Mutual Data Science Institute,
Northwestern Mutual

If you are leading any enterprise effort to deploy data and predictive models, it's critical that you design ethics into the process early on. You want your team to be confident that the ethical aspects of their deployment are addressed in a way that contributes to an amazing customer experience, and being proactive can help your project teams plan for the necessary steps and costs to achieve just that. Not sure where to start? Here are four strategic steps to take to enable your enterprise to design ethics into your technology and data science efforts from the start.

Take a Tiered Approach

Institutionalizing ethics may seem like something that should be second nature—after all, you likely have gone to great effort to ensure that you hire employees with a strong ethic. However, to avoid any unintentional interference with that ethic, your teams need to understand why having the principles articulated is critical. You can start by taking a tiered approach to designing the ethical principles, beginning with why you need them. The why is addressed with an aspirational statement and commitment and through articulation of the alignment between the enterprise's core values and how data and analytics efforts can support those values. Policies discuss what needs to be done and what needs to be avoided to support the principles. There likely are multiple policies that support each principle. Data and analytics professionals will need to know how to implement the policies—guidelines, standards, and procedures will help articulate the operational components of the policies.

Do Your Research

Many of the best and brightest minds in the data and analytics industry have already gone through efforts to implement data and analytics ethical principles. Identify those organizations and seek to learn about their sets of principles. Sources can include company websites and research firms (e.g., Gartner and Forrester). Talk to your peers and anyone in your network whom you consider to be an expert in data and analytics—chances are good that they have some form of principles already in place. Get input from scholars of ethics who may have developed principles that have not yet been dispersed to the industry. Look to fields other than your own for innovative ideas. For example, an insurance company may look to biomedical research for useful principles and guidelines, while an online retailer can evaluate digital native companies.

Identify and Engage Your Stakeholders

At an enterprise level, assess the various departments/areas of the company that will need to help shape and implement the organization's data and analytics ethical principles. Consider subject matter expertise in, and decision-making authority for, institutionalizing the ethical principles. Establish a cross-functional team that includes all key players in these spaces. Define a team charter, roles, and responsibilities. The charter should outline the business drivers, objectives of the team, strategic alignment, scope, and interdependencies. Evaluate current governance structures and identify intersections. Don't reinvent the wheel—doing so will only confuse people who know how to use the existing policies.

Be Agile

Approach all engagement activities with an agile mindset—seeking to gain consensus from all parties will create an unending chain of approvals and delay the ability to implement actionable principles. Implement the ethical principles iteratively and gain approval from the top levels of the organization in phases. Once the first version is agreed on, use a series of case studies on what it would look like to implement the principles. The case studies should consider the various personas, or stakeholders, that the principles will impact and allow the organization to test the principles for feasibility, cost, and scope before implementing organizational changes. Review the principles, case study outcomes, and implementation progress in a regular cadence while working to understand key gaps and risks to the implementation of the principles. Regular updates to industry and regulatory standards, research, and strategy are necessary to sustain the impact of the ethical principles and ensure an effective balance of advancing strategy while honoring the original charter set forth for the project team.

By leveraging this design framework, an organization can deploy data and predictive models with ethics designed into the development. This will help all organizations define a tailored approach to implementing ethical practices for data and analytics, while also safeguarding privacy and creating a positive customer experience. Ethics and superior customer experience will then be synergistic!

Data Science Does Not Need a Code of Ethics

Dave Cherry

Executive Strategy Advisor, Cherry Advisory LLC

This may seem like an odd title for an essay in a book about ethics and data science. But it's true. Data science does not need a code of ethics. It needs something else (which I'll reveal shortly).

Ethics is defined as a set of "moral principles that govern a person's behavior or the conducting of an activity." Building on that definition, morals are defined as "a lesson, especially concerning what is right or prudent, derived from a story, a piece of information, or an experience."

Let's dig into these definitions through the following components of data science: data, models/tools, and people.

Data is not a person. It is not alive in the sense that it can make decisions or exhibit behavior on its own. Therefore, one can conclude that data can be neither ethical nor unethical. It is just numbers, facts, attributes, and so on. Data can have biases within it. However, those biases are typically created by people, and the resulting data is still an accurate representation of what happened. Ethics should not be confused with bias.

Data science models and algorithms follow the same logic. Developed by humans, models have the ability to introduce bias into data. But again, the model itself is not capable of being ethical or unethical.

That leaves us with people. Data scientists. Business partners, technology partners. And more. Through their beliefs and actions, people can be ethical or unethical—sometimes both. People are the biggest wild card, because every one of us has a completely unique set of life experiences that inform and influence our behavior. We also unfortunately have the capacity to behave irrationally and erratically.

So if this is true, then why wouldn't data science need a code of ethics to guide and govern people? If other professions have one, then why not data science?

It is because data science simply needs heavy and repeated doses of common sense. Common sense is defined as "sound practical judgment concerning everyday matters, or a basic ability to perceive, understand, and judge that is shared by nearly all people."

Common sense is contextual. For example, I think that we'd all agree that it would not be good common sense for me to break my neighbor's front window. But in the right context—for example, if my neighbor's home is on fire and my intention is to save their pet—then breaking the window is perfect common sense based on my ability to perceive what nearly all people would do in a similar situation.

Ethics and common sense can be confused, but there is an important difference. Ethics typically is not as contextual as common sense. Looking again at the definition of ethics stated earlier, we can see that "context" is not mentioned. Most of us would agree that lying is unethical. But we've all done it at some point and likely don't beat ourselves up about it. That's because we've applied context. Sometimes common sense dictates that the unethical is acceptable and is even the recommended course of action.

It's the same with data science. Better decision making, which is the ultimate goal of data science and analytics, depends on two things: insight and intuition. Insights are the easier part to discuss—the patterns and anomalies in the data. Intuition is a little more tricky, encompassing experience, gut feel, and, most importantly, context.

Let's not move forward with creating a code of ethics for data science as yet another element of governance or standardization that cannot flex as rapidly or as dynamically to account for context as today's changing environments necessitate. Let's not spend time defining or debating what those ethical standards should be, recognizing that we likely have different views and the exercise could last forever—or worse, result in multiple, different, potentially confusing and conflicting sets of ethical standards for data science.

Let's instead demand that we all simply employ regular and repeated doses of common sense. Let's do it when we define the problem to be solved. Let's do it when we are gathering and cleansing the data. Let's do it when we are building our models and identifying our insights. Let's do it when we are evaluating our options and making our decisions.

Let's keep it simple. Let's perceive, understand, and judge everyday matters as nearly all people would. And most importantly, let's do it again, and double-check ourselves, before we act.

How to Innovate Responsibly

Carole Piovesan

Partner and Cofounder, INQ Data Law

The phrase "responsible innovation" used to be oxymoronic. Rewind 15 years or so and you would have been mocked for using those two words together. The accepted ethos of innovation in the early 2000s was to "move fast and break things." This ethos prioritized experimentation and exploration over caution and diligence. Boundless curiosity was embraced, fueled by an investment frenzy to fund the next big idea.

Fast-forward to the 2010s, however, and the consequences of that boundless curiosity could no longer be ignored. As we now collect all aspects of human behavior and analyze that data using sophisticated, predictive technologies such as AI, the fundamental implications of innovation are being scrutinized and tested.

Concerns over "responsible" innovation have invited a robust and sincere debate about technology in society (not new, mind you, but reinvigorated). Everything from the could, should, and would to the how, why, who, and then what is being asked about big data and AI. The very real social, political, economic, human rights, and legal implications of AI are legitimately being questioned, and demands for guardrails to protect society from unintended harms are proliferating.

But listen closely to those debates. Policymakers, civil society leaders, academics, entrepreneurs, ethicists, lawyers, and others are not debating algorithms per se. We are debating the impact of technology on our values— values that underpin our democratic societies—to ensure our creations augment the kinds of societies we want to live in, not subvert them. Scandals such as Cambridge Analytica or the recent exposé on law enforcement's use of Clearview AI's facial recognition system are not only (or at all) about the technology but also about the intentions behind their use.

Responsible innovation—words that can and should be used together—is governed by thoughtful, diligent, and defensible processes for development, operationalization, and oversight of these complex technological systems. Diligence can coexist with innovation. I propose a four-point framework to plan for responsible innovation in any organization:

Start with the human factor

Think about the user and align user interests and expectations with the organization's innovation plans. As well, identify organizational values and align those values with the organization's innovation agenda. In short, get people on board and align your organization's narrative in advance.

Ensure good data practices

Compliance with data protection laws is just the beginning. A thoughtful and contextual assessment of data practices for AI systems is valuable, particularly for those systems that are used in higher-risk activities—for example, in concert with certain medical devices. Map and document the process undertaken to assess and evaluate the training data and ongoing data exposure for those higher-risk systems. Document appropriate mitigation activities to help reduce risk.

Assess the AI system in context

Review and document the level of risk reasonably attributed to an organization's more advanced AI projects. Not all AI systems are created equal. Some pose very little risk to human well-being and/or society. Those systems do not require the same level of scrutiny as systems that are being used in more sensitive or transient contexts, such as health care or security.

Establish reasonable and thoughtful actions for higher-risk AI systems

Diligence and accountability are crucial and, frankly, good legal defenses for when an unintended consequence arises. Demonstrating a considered, well-informed, and proactive approach to managing risk is important for trust building, risk mitigation, organizational narrative, and, the most important part of all, doing the right thing.

This risk-based framework is being proposed as a reasonable guardrail until or in lieu of relevant regulation. We will see regulation of some AI uses in some contexts (e.g., facial recognition by law enforcement and governments). In the meantime, organizations must continue to innovate but, unlike the philosophy of the past, must do so responsibly.

Implementing AI Ethics Governance and Control

Steve Stone

Founder, NSU Techologies & Former CIO,
Lowe's and Limited Brands

The release of the movie *War Games* coincided with the start of my career in technology. For many, *War Games* introduced the notion of AI and the potential impact it could have on our lives.

Fast-forward 36 years, and we see intelligent algorithms playing prominent roles in everything from how we purchase products to how we defend our borders. Major advances in computing power and data storage, coupled with the increased digitization of formerly analog processes, have fueled unprecedented growth in computer intelligence solutions.

While most would argue these advances have greatly benefited society, many others are concerned over the ethical implications of machine-driven decision making. Just as we saw in *War Games*, machines will do what they are trained to do, even if that training is detrimental to large segments of society. Ensuring the safe and ethical operation of computer intelligence solutions is a significant concern both for corporations using these solutions and for society in general. I want to focus this discussion on developing the necessary governance and control environment for AI solutions to ensure a safe and ethical state for all constituents.

As with any form of software development, outcomes of AI projects are impacted by the development ecosystem, the processes needed to migrate to a production state of operation, and the continuous audit of the end solution. However, ensuring the ethical state of an AI solution requires additional controls at various steps of the solution's life cycle.

Adopt an AI Code of Ethical Conduct

Maintaining the proper development ecosystem for AI solutions begins with an AI code of ethical conduct. This code of conduct should outline the steps all AI developers must follow to eliminate bias, promote transparency, and be socially responsible. The AI code of ethical conduct should contain standards and practices to guide developers on such topics as auditability, accessibility, data management, delegation of rights, and ethical/moral responsibilities. The code of conduct would be reinforced with mandatory training for all developers to ensure they understand the organization's ethical responsibility.

Stress Diversity in Hiring and Recruiting

In addition to adopting an AI code of ethical conduct, organizations should focus on the recruitment and hiring of a diverse set of developers to help eliminate "groupthink" and to reinforce a culture of inclusive thought in the development ecosystem.

Finally, in cases where the outcomes of AI efforts have the potential to impact large segments of society, organizations should hire ethicists. Ethicists are specialists who educate and work with developers on ethical development practices.

Ensure Compliance with an Ethical Review Board

With a proper development ecosystem in place, the next area of focus is the process of migrating AI solutions to production. In IT, the concept of a Quality Review Board (QRB) or an Architecture Review Board (ARB) is commonplace. For AI solutions, a new governing body, the Ethical Review Board (ERB), is required. While establishing the governance framework to ensure ethical practices in the development and use of AI, the ERB also acts as the gatekeeper for new AI solutions moving to a production state. New solutions that do not pass ERB review are not allowed to move into production.

Establish Audit and Feedback Loops

Once AI applications are in production, results must be continually audited to ensure compliance. These audits would review not only the algorithms but also the data feeding the algorithms. As AI algorithms learn through iteration, biases in the data would lead to biased "learning" by the algorithms.

While auditing and continuous testing to understand unexpected results is critical, it isn't enough. In addition, feedback loops should be provided to users who operate outside the AI controls of the system. Feedback loops could be built into applications or accomplished using survey instruments.

In summary, establishing an operational AI ecosystem with the appropriate level of independence and transparency is mandatory for organizations building and operating intelligent solutions that have societal impacts.

AI ethics controls aren't sexy or exciting. But let's face it: had these controls been in place, *War Games* would have been a much more boring movie.

Artificial Intelligence: Legal Liabilities amid Emerging Ethics

Pamela Passman

Vice Chair, Ethisphere
CEO, Center for Responsible Enterprise And Trade (CREATe.org)

Enthusiasm is growing around the use of AI, with 30% of a surveyed sample (*https://oreil.ly/5brAF*) of top Global 500 companies in 2019 reporting that they are already using AI in selective business functions. AI can be useful in a broad spectrum of applications and activities, from product design and testing to all kinds of data analysis, marketing functions, machine learning, medical testing, virtual assistance, and other tasks.

Concerns about the reliability and potential misuses of AI are also front-of-mind among businesses, investors (*https://oreil.ly/JxvO-*), governments, and consumers. The wide range of new opportunities and risks presented by AI have led to the development of at least 32 different AI ethics codes (*https://oreil.ly/4PwWR*) put together by industry, NGOs, and governments to provide guidance on developing, implementing, and using AI in ways that support societal values and manage risks.

By and large, AI codes deal with three high-level issues (*https://oreil.ly/FMsMO*): the responsible design and use of AI, the ethical use of AI, and the issue that we will delve into a bit more here—the lawful use of AI. Lawful use of AI involves compliance with a company's legal requirements and responsibilities in areas relevant to AI, including *data privacy* and *cybersecurity*. It also involves using AI for *lawful purposes*, and not for activities that are themselves illegal, that are dangerous, or that could otherwise attract liability for the company.

Data Privacy

Many AI functions involve analyzing large amounts of data in order to predict behavior or outcomes and to make better-informed decisions. In practical terms, this means, for example, that AI systems can analyze and synthesize millions of medical reports, patient records, clinical trials, scientific studies, and other data points to help provide faster and more accurate medical diagnoses and treatment recommendations.

The Memorial Sloan Kettering Cancer Center in New York and other oncology hospitals and clinics have been using IBM Watson AI (*https://oreil.ly/oPdji*) to do just this sort of large-scale data analysis to help doctors make diagnoses and create management plans for cancer patients.

When individuals' medical data or other personal information is collected and used in these and other ways, one obvious compliance issue is protecting and maintaining the privacy of such personally identifiable information. In the US, the specific federal HIPAA law and regulations (*https://oreil.ly/YjY0d*) require those who collect and handle "protected health information" (*https://oreil.ly/-hu7x*), including patients' medical and personal data, not to use or disclose such information except in compliance with HIPAA.

Broader data protection laws—such as the EU's General Data Protection Regulation (*https://oreil.ly/29sdy*) and the California Consumer Privacy Act of 2018 (*https://oreil.ly/l_qPQ*), which regulate the collection, processing, use, and transfer of all types of personally identifiable information—are establishing new regulatory paradigms. Data protection authorities have expressed concerns publicly (*https://oreil.ly/loP0h*) that "personal data [has] increasingly become both the source and the target of AI applications," and that the use of AI should not undermine users' rights to data protection.

Many companies are invested in addressing these challenges. In large part, emerging AI ethics codes are very specific that the development, implementation, and use of AI should protect individuals' personal data. IBM's own AI principles (*https://oreil.ly/f5q-n*) are clear that "IBM complies with the data privacy laws in all countries and territories in which we operate [and] is fully committed to protecting the privacy of our clients' data, which is fundamental in a data-driven society."

Companies that develop, implement, or use AI in ways that collect and process personally identifiable data would be well advised to ensure that their own company policies and procedures likewise protect personal data in accordance with applicable laws and regulation.

Cybersecurity

Emerging legal requirements and ethics codes related to AI are also highlighting the related need for the use of AI to be accompanied by effective security—cybersecurity in particular—to mitigate the risk of hacking and data theft.

Cybersecurity risks have generated significant government, industry, and popular attention in recent years, resulting in a "rising tide of cybersecurity regulation." There are specific cybersecurity requirements for data protection, government contracting, health care, and other areas, and also general securities laws and due-care requirements that impose cybersecurity duties and liabilities that are enforceable by governments and private party litigants.

The development, implementation, and use of AI can involve a variety of cyber risks—not only risks that the data analyzed and used by the AI system might be lost or stolen, but also risks to the accuracy and reliability of the AI system itself. In one famous experiment (*https://oreil.ly/mdwjS*), hackers were able to fool an AI-based image recognition system into interpreting the image of a cat as that of a dog—or even a stealth fighter—by changing just a few pixels.

AI ethics codes, such as the OECD Recommendations on Artificial Intelligence (*https://oreil.ly/sItzf*), call for AI systems to be "robust, secure, and safe throughout their entire lifecycle," and for AI actors to apply systematic and continuous risk management to each phase of an AI system's life cycle to address risks related to AI systems, including digital security.

It is vital that the security of a company's AI-related activities be examined and incorporated into the company's overall cybersecurity and other security policies and management systems.

Use for Lawful Purposes

It should come as no surprise that technologies like AI, which help facilitate a whole range of beneficial uses, can also be used in activities that are harmful or downright illegal. In early 2019, for example, cybercriminals used AI-powered voice technology to mimic a European company executive's voice (*https://oreil.ly/ID2yU*) and successfully tricked his UK CEO by phone into sending $243,000 to the fraudsters' bank account in Hungary.

Beyond fraud, some company officials and various NGOs have expressed concerns about the potential use of AI in autonomous weapons and even "killer robots." Google, for example, has made specific commitments in its AI

Principles (*https://oreil.ly/HHBAM*) that it will not design or deploy AI in technologies that cause or are likely to cause overall harm, and that it will not develop AI for use in weapons. The company also will not use AI in "technologies whose purpose contravenes widely accepted principles of international law and human rights." In a similar vein, Microsoft's president has called for a new "digital Geneva Convention" (*https://oreil.ly/6xUqn*) to address the potentially harmful uses of AI and other technologies worldwide.

The legal considerations and potential harm that can arise from the development, implementation, or use of AI technologies can vary quite a bit from company to company. But it is important for companies dealing with AI to consider commitments not to use AI for illegal or dangerous purposes when developing their own specific AI policies or implementing a broader group's AI ethics principles.

Make Accountability a Priority

Yiannis Kanellopoulos

Founder, Code4Thought

There is little doubt that algorithmic systems are making decisions that have a great impact on our daily lives. As Yuval Noah Harari notes in his book *21 Lessons for the 21st Century* (Random House), "Already today, 'truth' is defined by the top results of the Google search." So transparency about the function of these systems matters not as an end in itself but merely as a means toward accountability.

According to assistant professor Nicholas Diakopoulos, director of the Computational Journalism Lab (CJL) at Northwestern University, *accountability* in this context means the degree to which one decides when and how an algorithmic system should be guided (or restrained) in the risk of crucial or expensive errors, discrimination, unfair denials, or censorship.

Simply put, holding a system accountable means we should control it at a technical as well as an organizational level. This is important, especially if we consider (a bit simplistically) that an algorithmic system is nothing more than a piece of software that:

- Solves a business problem set by the organization that procures it (the system)
- Receives data as input that has been selected and most likely preprocessed either by a human or an automated process
- Utilizes a model (e.g., support vector machine, deep learning, random forest, and others) that processes the selected data and ultimately makes a decision or suggests an answer/solution to the question/problem set by the organization

To be able to control this software, then, we need to gain insight into (or make informed decisions about) every aspect just mentioned.

The organization that creates the system needs to cater to and design for the system's accountability even before it starts the system's development. More specifically, the organization should:

- Establish visible ways of redress for adverse individual or societal effects caused by its system.

- Follow the human-in-the-loop principle and assign the proper persons for making the right decisions if problems appear.

- Be able to explain the decisions of its system to end users and other stakeholders in nontechnical terms.

- Know the potential sources of error for its algorithms and how their effect is mitigated.

- Enable interested third parties to probe, understand, and review the behavior of its algorithms.

- Ensure that algorithmic decisions do not create discriminatory or unjust impacts when considering different demographics (e.g., race, sex, education level, etc.).

Regarding the input data of the system, the so-called "new oil" of the modern economy, we primarily need to care about its:

- Quality, which involves accuracy, completeness, and uncertainty, as well as timeliness, representativeness of a sample for a specific population, and assumptions or other limitations

- Handling, which includes data definitions, ways of collection, vetting, and editing (manually or automated)

Regarding the model itself, the most important things to consider are:

- Whether it is fit for the problem at hand. It may seem strange, but we have seen models that never get operationalized simply because they weren't fit for purpose.

- The process followed for the model's construction, i.e., identifying its input and the selected features or variables, along with their weights (in case they are weighted).

- The way this model will be evaluated, i.e., identifying the evaluation metrics to be used, the reasoning behind their selection, and, most importantly, how these are being utilized and interpreted.

- The model's accuracy or error margin, and the ability of a data scientist to benchmark it against standard datasets and standard measures of accuracy.

An organization that considers accountability and designs its system with accountability in mind can gain the following benefits:

- Trust between the organization using the system and those affected by its output (be they clients, citizens, or simple users), since the results can be explained
- Improvement in the system's output, since identified weighting factors and thresholds can be calibrated/fine-tuned if needed
- Rendering the system more persuasive, since its reasoning will be easier to explain

Presently, the public discourse is full of examples of how automated decision making can go seriously wrong, from crucial (e.g., Amazon's HR system favoring male candidates) to even life-and-death mistakes (e.g., the fatal accident caused by Uber's self-driving car). It is obvious that we humans need to be in control of the technology we create. Establishing evaluation processes before we even start developing an autonomous decision-making system and having humans in the loop should be a prerequisite for organizations to deploy any system that will make decisions for us but without us.

Ethical Data Science: Both Art and Science

Polly Mitchell-Guthrie

VP, Industry Outreach and Thought Leadership, Kinaxis

> *I will remember that there is art to* data science ~~medicine~~ *as well as science, and that warmth, sympathy, and understanding may outweigh the* area under the curve ~~surgeon's knife~~ *or* R-squared ~~the chemist's drug~~.
> —excerpt from the Hippocratic oath (edits mine)

The Hippocratic oath (*https://oreil.ly/W6Kwf*) is considered one of the earliest examples of a professional code of ethics, dating back to approximately 500 BCE. The world of medicine at the time was experiencing rapid changes, with many physicians selling their services primarily to profit from their skills and capture the growing interest in what we now think of as Western medicine. The oath was a radical reorientation toward prioritizing the interests of patients instead of profit.

Since the creation of the Hippocratic oath, many other professions employing highly specialized skills have adopted codes of ethics, recognizing that there's a responsibility that comes with their expertise. In addition to medicine, there are codes of ethics for professions ranging from dieticians and accountants to stockbrokers and lawyers. If the factors contributing to the creation of the Hippocratic oath sound familiar (big changes in the field, growing interest, proliferation of those seeking to profit from new demand), then you may be glad to know that since 2013 there has been a code of ethics for analytics professionals. I was part of the founding task force that led to the creation of the Certified Analytics Professional (CAP) (*https://certifieda nalytics.org*) program, which includes signing a code of ethics (*https://certifie danalytics.org/ethics.php*) as a requirement to achieve certification.

Ethics is critical to the practice of analytics and data science given the breadth of application in our world today. As the CAP code of ethics states, "Analytics professionals participate in analysis that aids decision makers in business, industry, academia, government, military, i.e., all facets of society; therefore, it is imperative to establish and project an ethical basis to perform their work responsibly. Furthermore, practitioners are encouraged to exercise 'good professional citizenship' in order to improve the public climate for, understanding of, and respect for the use of analytics across its range of applications."

We live in an era of seemingly insatiable demand (and hype) around artificial intelligence and machine learning (AI/ML), a prospect that excites me, given the great good I believe it can do for our society. The McKinsey Global Institute (*https://oreil.ly/mWnXH*) has compiled a library of 160 use cases, but a few of my favorites are using AI/ML to achieve greater accuracy in cancer diagnosis (with fewer false positives), using natural language processing to track human rights violations in supply chains, automating analysis of satellite images to combat illegal logging, and creating adaptive learning tools for everything and everyone.

AI/ML also powers tools your average modern consumer uses daily with delight—calling out to Siri or Alexa, hailing an Uber or a Lyft, finding a movie on Netflix, or shopping on Amazon. In spite of the good it can do, I regularly encounter people who fear the impact of AI/ML on our world, imagining at best robots taking our jobs, and at worst, robots taking over entirely.

For these reasons I believe we must hold the application of AI/ML accountable, which is why I support a code of ethics for its practice. While I don't share the fear of the singularity or other apocalyptic scenarios, I do recognize that AI/ML models can repeat the biases of humans and be used to perpetuate inequities. A great example is facial recognition technology: if a model is fed images that are mostly white and male, it will show great accuracy identifying white men (99%) and perform poorly when identifying women of color (65%), as the Gender Shades project (*http://gendershades.org*) has shown. This kind of bias has major implications when it is built into law enforcement, for example, where facial recognition technology is deployed to identify perpetrators. At the same time, AI/ML may be able to prevent bias, which has prompted many start-ups to apply math to fields such as recruiting and retention.

Preventing the negative ramifications of AI/ML requires accountability in the form of a code of ethics, which itself calls on our higher, better selves. Humans at their best, employing the high touch of empathy and expert judgment, combined with the high tech of machine learning models, which at their best can correct human bias, are a powerful combination.

Algorithmic Impact Assessments

Randy Guse

Director Optum Enterprise Analytics, United Health Group

Automated decision systems are being used in every industry. The systems vary in transparency and effectiveness, oftentimes resulting in unintended consequences. An Algorithmic Impact Assessment (AIA) can surface issues with the solution functionality and provide the opportunity to undertake corrective actions before serious harm is inflicted.

The AI Now Institute (*https://ainowinstitute.org*) has multiple publications to address the potential ethical issues and biases within analytic algorithms and automated decision systems. One of its reports, *Algorithmic Impact Assessments: A Practical Framework for Public Agency Accountability*, establishes protocols for evaluating adverse effects of automated decision systems.[1]

While the report is written for government agencies, industry should be held to the same standards. The key elements of the AIA are:

- Agencies should conduct a self-assessment of existing and proposed automated decision systems, evaluating potential impacts on fairness, justice, bias, or other concerns across affected communities.

- Agencies should develop meaningful external researcher review processes to discover, measure, or track impacts over time.

- Agencies should provide notice to the public disclosing their definition of "automated decision system," existing and proposed systems, and any related self-assessments and researcher review processes before the system has been acquired.

- Agencies should solicit public comments to clarify concerns and answer outstanding questions.

---

1 AI Now's report (*https://ainowinstitute.org/aiareport2018.pdf*) is available under a Creative Commons license.

- Governments should provide enhanced due process mechanisms for affected individuals or communities to challenge inadequate assessments or unfair, biased, or otherwise harmful system uses that agencies have failed to mitigate or correct.

The report goes on to highlight that AIAs will help achieve four goals:

- Respect the public's right to know which systems impact their lives by publicly listing and describing automated decision systems that significantly affect individuals and communities.

- Increase public agencies' internal expertise and capacity to evaluate the systems they build or procure, so they can anticipate issues that might raise concerns, such as disparate impacts or due process violations.

- Ensure greater accountability of automated decision systems by providing a meaningful and ongoing opportunity for external researchers to review, audit, and assess these systems using methods that allow them to identify and detect problems.

- Ensure that the public has a meaningful opportunity to respond to and, if necessary, dispute the use of a given system or an agency's approach to algorithmic accountability.

Corporate entities may be reluctant to comply with the level of disclosure outlined for AIAs. However, they should adhere to the accountability standards while still maintaining proprietary knowledge. For example, the report specifically addresses the challenges of trade secrecy in Section II.

Section II also covers the challenge of securing the required funding and resources to implement AIAs. For government entities, this can be a challenge with the suggested independent oversight body. However, for industry, if the guidelines are incorporated into existing product development frameworks, incremental costs should be minimal. In fact, highlighting potential flaws in the algorithms prior to implementation should result in more efficient product development and the reduction of unintended consequences.

Ethics and Reflection at the Core of Successful Data Science

Mike McGuirk

Faculty Member, Babson College

I often think back to some very sound advice I received from my mentor early in my analytics career, when I did not yet have a significant client-facing role. His advice to me as I worked on analytic projects was that I make sure I could always explain, justify, and defend each and every decision and recommendation I made as I progressed through the analysis. I should put myself in the *shoes of the client* and fully anticipate and understand their needs, and then exceed their expectations. That left a lasting impression on me and conditioned me to always be thoughtful and thorough across all stages of the analytics process: the analysis design, the use of consumer data, the recommended insight-driven business actions, and the measures of success. That approach worked extremely well in a *business-centric* operating model.

Fast-forward to today's business environment, where *customer-centric* operating principles rule the day, and it becomes clear that business-centric analytic and data science processes are no longer sufficient. Companies have become obsessed with using consumer data to find a competitive advantage. In fact, Forrester Research explains in its *Predictions 2020: Customer Insights* (*https://oreil.ly/ggp8F*) report that 56% of the businesses surveyed will be launching initiatives and appointing "data hunters" to identify new sources of data. Personally, as a consumer, I find that a bit disturbing! This increased emphasis on data collection requires a new set of analytics and data science operating procedures to ensure this information is not misused or abused.

That great advice that taught me to anticipate my clients' needs must now be extended to include another key constituent: the *consumer*! That is, all of us in the analytics community could benefit from adopting work habits and processes that encourage analysts to step into the *shoes of the consumer* to help inform and govern our data management and data science practices. To pledge to be transparent and act in the best interest of consumers. To be comfortable explaining to consumers how we use their consumer interaction, transaction, and demographic data to generate insights, and how those insights influence our business decision making and actions. Using this approach, we can not only satisfy *business needs* but also build *consumer trust*.

The notion of adopting customer-centric business practices is certainly not a new concept. Thought leaders such as Don Peppers and Martha Rogers have been highlighting the benefits of these principles for many years. In fact, the overarching theme in Peppers and Rogers's book *Extreme Trust: Honesty as a Competitive Advantage* (Portfolio) is to "treat the customer the way you'd want to be treated if you were the customer."

Unfortunately, companies have not always followed these principles. Even more alarming is that several recent corporate transgressions have been linked to the inappropriate use of consumer data. In 2018, Facebook enabled Cambridge Analytica to use millions of members' personal data without their consent for targeted political advertising. In early 2019, YouTube's recommendation engine was facing major criticism for making it easier for pedophiles to find and share content related to young children. Even more recently, Goldman Sachs has been under fire for having blatant gender bias in algorithms used to establish credit limits for Apple Card customers.

So how do we change the underlying practices that are enabling intentional and unintentional misuse of consumer data before state and federal government data protection regulators step in to do it for us? I believe it starts by creating greater awareness of the damaging consequences of poor data stewardship and reckless analytics practices. This should begin in higher education and be reinforced through recursive training programs in the corporate environment.

After spending 25 years in the analytics industry, and working now as a full-time educator, I think it is critical that educational institutions commit to the development and integration of student learning objectives that focus on inspiring and empowering students to use ethical and socially responsible data collection and analytic practices. We must:

- Teach students how to implement safeguards that reduce the risk of deploying unintentionally biased predictive and ML algorithms.
- Explain how cross-functional data governance teams can be created to ensure diverse perspectives are considered when deciding what data is

appropriate to be collected, analyzed, and used to drive business decision making and AI solutions.

- Illustrate how many traditional approaches to consumer segmentation using gender, ethnicity, and socioeconomic status often perpetuate the exclusion of consumers.
- Challenge students to reflect on the appropriate and inappropriate use of consumer data.

These learning objectives should be a core and fundamental element of every data science and business analytics program.

In 2017, the *Economist* published the article "The World's Most Valuable Resource Is No Longer Oil, but Data" (*https://oreil.ly/yeDqg*). I posit that we will soon lose access to this incredible resource if we don't prove to the resource providers—the consumers—that we can be trusted to use their data in a responsible and value-added manner.

Using Social Feedback Loops to Navigate Ethical Questions

Nick Hamlin

Data Scientist, GlobalGiving

Technological change *is* social change. As data-centric technology proliferates, product questions must be asked alongside social impact questions if companies hope to succeed in either area. These blurring lines also mean that data scientists must emphasize the ethical implications of their expanding impact. While oaths, checklists, and communities of practice for ethical data science are critical,[1] these constructs omit a key component: the social feedback loops that allow the voices of affected communities to inform product decisions.

"Mechanistic" feedback loops, like the results of a reinforcement learning algorithm informing future training iterations, are common in data science. They're technical constructs that amplify a dataset's signals in service of better predictions. In contrast, we're focused here on "social" feedback loops—the processes that emphasize voices in a community of users whose ideas, concerns, and input are key to effective navigation of ethical challenges.[2]

But social feedback loops are hard! Their nuance makes them time consuming to analyze, and they often include contradictory ideas. When users' feedback clashes with the company's bottom-line goals, financial incentives frequently win out. Organizations without a culture of listening and openness to pivots will struggle to solve ethical problems with social feedback loops. Social feedback loops may also exclude the voices of people who don't

---

1 The first edition of *Ethics and Data Science* by Mike Loukides, Hilary Mason, and DJ Patil (O'Reilly) describes several examples of the progress made to establish manifestos, working groups, and other ethical frameworks for the field.

2 Thanks to Marc Maxmeister (*https://chewychunks.wordpress.com*) for his integral help in distinguishing the two categories of feedback loops in this way.

have the time, resources, words, or freedom to speak openly about their challenges.[3]

Still, organizations can take steps to streamline their adoption of social feedback loops to help answer ethical questions in their data products. The rest of this article touches on some of these steps.

Establish a values-based approach to inclusion and feedback

Mantras like "don't be evil" or "move fast and break things" can help provide a framework for decision making,[4] but they don't place enough emphasis on openness and inclusion to ensure that social feedback loops will flourish. To make these priorities explicit, use alternative values like "Always Open: We believe in the power of great ideas and that these ideas can come from anyone at any time" and "Listen, Act, Learn. Repeat: We continually experiment and use data and feedback to guide our course."[5] Companies setting the cultural context for feedback at the core of their ethos are more likely to succeed.

Build concrete goals for representation into your product's success criteria

Most data scientists know that "what gets measured, gets managed" (*https://oreil.ly/sjw9p*). Inclusion of otherwise unheard voices in the product development process is no exception to this rule. Committing to key performance indicators (KPIs) like "X% of new data ethics policies are based on inputs of our community" helps ensure that social feedback stays prioritized. Catherine D'Ignazio and Lauren Klein present a sterling example of this approach in the values and metrics they set for (*https://oreil.ly/Yy_Pc*) the writing of their new book, *Data Feminism*.[6] They call out areas of structural inequality they seek to avoid and establish concrete goals for ensuring the voices they amplify remain in the lead of the decision-making processes surrounding their product.

---

3 This is challenging to implement effectively, but tools such as pluto.life (*https://pluto.life*) are now being created to specifically help address diversity, equity, and inclusion issues in surveys by restructuring how this data is collected.

4 Chad Storlie, "Manage Uncertainty with Commander's Intent," *Harvard Business Review*, November 3, 2010, *https://oreil.ly/4DgeF*.

5 These are two of the four core values of GlobalGiving (*https://www.globalgiving.org*), the first and largest crowdfunding community for nonprofits (and this author's current employer).

6 Catherine D'Ignazio and Lauren F. Klein, *Data Feminism* (Cambridge, MA: MIT Press, 2020), *https://oreil.ly/bE9aB*.

Close the loop

Data ethicist Anna Lauren Hoffman points out that researchers "should not draw on the lives and experiences of their subjects without contributing something in return."[7] In that spirit, organizations should close feedback loops by clearly reporting back to the community what they said, what was heard, and what changes will follow as a result.[8] Importantly, this doesn't mean that every individual request will be fulfilled. Rather, it highlights that users' voices have been heard, confirmed to represent their actual opinions, and, after thoughtful conversation and collaboration, added to the product where appropriate. Good social feedback loops take the same approach as random forest algorithms and use a wide and often noisy range of distinct components to converge on an underlying answer.

The role of social feedback loops in navigating ethical challenges in data science is clear. The alternative is akin to strip mining. A company can optimize its product for profit and ignore its community, at least temporarily. Eventually though, the backlash will build as users' voices remain unheard. At this stage, responding to such feedback, even if well intentioned, can seem disingenuous.[9] Instead, organizations should embrace the modern connection between technology and society and establish the social feedback loops needed to navigate it sustainably and ethically. Our communities deserve nothing less.

---

7 Anna Lauren Hoffmann, "Data Violence and How Bad Engineering Choices Can Damage Society," Medium, April 30, 2018, *https://oreil.ly/vrNz6*.

8 "LabStorm: Relationship Based Feedback," Feedback Labs, October 20, 2017, *https://oreil.ly/ZnxcJ*.

9 One famous example of this is the criticism that Facebook faced (*https://oreil.ly/Xx9po*) for its experimentation with the manipulation of users' news feeds to spark emotional responses.

Ethical CRISP-DM: A Framework for Ethical Data Science Development

Collin Cunningham

Data Scientist, Amazon Web Services

Good data science creates the illusion of something human; something beyond a cold, colorless process that disallows empathy. The goal of a model, however, is singular: make decisions that have previously minimized loss functions (or something equally mechanical). Therefore, we must systematically enforce empathy and ethics where there is none.

The *cross-industry standard process for data mining*, more commonly referred to as CRISP-DM, is a widely used methodology in analytics development. The steps of CRISP-DM are:

- Business understanding
- Data understanding
- Data preparation
- Modeling
- Evaluation
- Deployment

Although CRISP-DM was developed for data mining, successful data science projects knowingly or unknowingly follow these procedures in some way. To make more ethical decisions in handling data, we can augment this process by considering a question at each step. By doing so, we create a concrete ethical framework for doing data science.

Business Understanding

What are potential externalities of this solution? Every successful data science project must start with an understanding of the problem as well as of the environment within which it exists. This is the foundational step in positioning a project for success in terms of both effective modeling and ethics—because the model does not exist in a vacuum. It may have users, but other people are affected by its results. Allocating time to consider the consequences of the solution can not only save time but also prevent catastrophe. It is critical to engage relevant stakeholders to explicitly discuss these potential repercussions.

Data Understanding

Does my data reflect unethical bias? Hidden in human data are the conscious and subconscious biases of the sample population. These explicit and implicit biases deserve a paper of their own, but an example of each type of bias follows:

- Tay, a Microsoft Twitter chatbot, began spewing anti-Semitic tweets after ingesting slurs intentionally directed at it.
- A recruitment model is trained on previous hiring patterns where positions have been held by a particular demographic.

As data scientists, we understand the value of an intimate knowledge of the content and patterns in data, but it is also crucial to evaluate how data could corrupt a model.

Data Preparation

How do I cleanse data of bias? The integrity of data is inviolate. However, it is possible (and important) to cleanse data of problematic content without compromising its integrity. Before the statisticians riot, let me explain.

Assume developers are creating an application to predict check fraud. The natural imbalance between fraudulent and authentic checks may prompt a need to balance the dataset. An ethical next step would be to balance the data across, say, demographic groups to avoid a possible imbalance in the enforcement of the system. Otherwise, this implicit bias may generate more instances of check fraud within a given demographic, which will again be ingested by the model, perpetuating a cycle of exaggerated bias. This is not always easy, as in the example of gender bias in word embeddings.[1] Explicit bias should be filtered directly.

Modeling

Is my model prone to outside influence? Online design patterns are growing in popularity. There is great value in giving models the freedom to adapt on the fly, but doing so invites back in hazards eliminated in the previous step. Under high-risk circumstances, vigilance in monitoring and cleansing incoming data prior to ingestion is critical. In the Microsoft example, developers failed to foresee potential biases in the dataset—becoming aware of the offending content Tay ingested only after the damage was done.

Evaluation and Deployment

How can I quantify an unethical consequence? Responsible deployment of a model requires metrics that monitor and evaluate its performance in the wild. We can add metrics that track unethical externalities. For example, a law enforcement crime prediction system should track whether it is overpolicing a particular neighborhood, enforcing a balance across demographic areas where officers are deployed. The full effects of a model may be impossible to predict, so it is important to periodically reevaluate models by, among other things, gathering feedback from those who interact with them. Ethical metrics should be presented prominently alongside efficacy metrics.

Empathy cannot be quantified; it lacks rigor and rigidity. We must find ways to imprint our own moral compasses in solutions we deliver. Ultimately, we are responsible for the product we deliver, along with its consequences. Thus, by holding ourselves to a strict regime of reflection throughout the development life cycle, we can assure delivery of ethical models that minimize harmful impacts.

---

1 Emerging Technology from the arXiv, "How Vector Space Mathematics Reveals the Hidden Sexism in Language," *MIT Technology Review*, July 27, 2016.

Ethics Rules in Applied Econometrics and Data Science

Steven C. Myers

Associate Processor of Economics, University of Akron

I have taught ethics in applied econometrics and data analysis for more than 20 years. But I rarely have used the word "ethics," resorting to phrases such as "data skepticism" and other attitudes that suggest acting ethically.

Nothing in the past 20 years has had as much impact on me, my classroom teaching, and my ethics of data analysis as Peter Kennedy's "Sinning in the Basement: What Are the Rules? The Ten Commandments of Applied Econometrics."[1] This essay also appears in his *Guide to Econometrics* (Blackwell).[2]

From the moment I read this paper, I was completely transformed and forever a disciple of Kennedy. I was fortunate to host him on my campus, where he spoke of the misuse of econometrics and the failure of research to make it past his editor's desk at the *Journal of Economic Education.* In one example, a paper was rejected because the author(s) did not acknowledge a problem in their analysis, ignored it, and probably hoped the editor would not notice. Being honest and transparent enough to acknowledge a problem of which the authors were aware but which they were unable to solve is sometimes enough, Peter would point out. Hiding one transgression suggests other ethical abuses of data.

I used the word "ethical," but Kennedy did not, preferring the oft-used words "sin" and "sinning." But the point is made. When I got my PhD at Ohio State in 1980, I had taken nine separate statistics and econometrics courses over the five years that I was there. I learned classical estimation and inference

---

1 Peter E. Kennedy, "Sinning in the Basement: What Are the Rules? The Ten Commandments of Applied Econometrics," *Journal of Economic Surveys* 16, no. 4 (2002): 569–89, *https://doi.org/10.1111/1467-6419.00179.*

2 Peter E. Kennedy, *A Guide to Econometrics*, 6th ed. (Malden, MA: Blackwell, 2008).

---

from some of the best professors, but there was scarcely a day's instruction on how to use the computer, much less how to conduct what Kennedy would call the moral obligation of applied econometrics 20 years later.

Kennedy says, "My opinion is that regardless of teachability, we have a moral obligation to inform students of these rules, and, through suitable assignments, socialize them to incorporate them into the standard operating procedures they follow when doing empirical work....[I] believe that these rules are far more important than instructors believe, and that students at all levels do not accord them the respect they deserve."[3] I could not agree more and have tried to follow these rules faithfully and to teach my students and colleagues to do likewise.

Failing to follow Kennedy's rules for applied econometrics brings about ethical implications, if not direct unethical behavior. To knowingly violate the rules is to be, or at least to risk being, unethical in your handling of data. To unknowingly violate the rules would nevertheless lead to the unintended consequences of poor outcomes that could be avoided.

The rules of applied econometrics	
Rule 1	Use common sense and economic reasoning in the articulation of the problem.
Rule 2	Avoid a Type III error—getting the right answer to the wrong question.
Rule 3	Know the context.
Rule 4	Inspect the data.
Rule 5	Keep it sensibly simple.
Rule 6	Use the interocular trauma test—do people roll their eyes when you explain what you are doing?
Rule 7	Understand the costs and benefits of data mining.
Rule 8	Be prepared to compromise.
Rule 9	Do not confuse statistical significance with meaningful magnitude.
Rule 10	Report a sensitive analysis.

Failing to fully articulate the problem in Rule 1 is so critical that to not spend time on the problem, the common sense, and the economic theoretical solution can lead to serious flaws in the study from the very first step. It might lead to a violation of Rule 2, where the right answer to the wrong question is discovered. What if you fail to inspect the data (Rule 4), fail to clean the data and provide for necessary transforms, or fail to control for selection bias?

---

3 Kennedy, "Sinning," 571–72.

Then you will have results based on assumptions that are not realistic and produce results that are unduly influenced by the dirty data.

Zvi Griliches once said that if it weren't for dirty data, economists wouldn't have jobs. What if you violate Rule 7 and, knowingly or not, allow the data to lie to you? In the words of Nobel Prize–winning economist Ronald Coase, "If you torture the data long enough, it will confess."[4] A violation of Rule 9 might lead you to worship R2 or participate in p-hacking. It might cause you to ignore a huge economic implication (large magnitude) only because it has a large p-value. Violations of Rule 10 may be the most critical of all. Suppose you believe your model is from God (as suggested by Susan Athey). Then why would you look at alternative specifications or validate the robustness of your findings?

As Jennifer Lewis Priestley wrote in a 2019 LinkedIn post, "Many data scientists make bad decisions—with ethical implications—not because they are intentionally trying to do harm, but because they do not have an understanding of how the algorithms they are taking responsibility for actually work."[5] Likewise, many in the field who ignore Kennedy's rules for applied econometrics risk doing real harm, not out of intentionality but out of ignorance or neglect. This latter lack of motive is just as real and likely more widespread than the intentional harm.

The American Economic Association (AEA) has adopted ethical code of conduct guidelines that state the following: "Integrity demands honesty, care, and transparency in conducting and presenting research; disinterested assessment of ideas; acknowledgement of limits of expertise; and disclosure of real and perceived conflicts of interest."[6]

The AEA statement does not go directly to data ethics, but it is suggestive, since little economic research—and *no* applied economic research—can be conducted without data. The AEA statement is a beginning, but I suggest that those who do applied economic research would do well to hold to the rules for sinning in the basement. This is so important now that going to the basement is no longer the norm, and many more analysts should be trying to avoid sinning wherever and whenever they have their hands on their laptop.

---

4 Ronald Coase, *Essays on Economics and Economists* (Chicago: University of Chicago Press, 1995).

5 See also Jennifer Lewis Priestley, "The Good, The Bad, and the Creepy: Why Data Scientists Need to Understand Ethics" (presentation, SAS Global Forum, Dallas, TX, April 28–May 1, 2019).

6 American Economic Association, "AEA Code of Professional Conduct," adopted April 20, 2018, *https://oreil.ly/_m4x-*.

Are Ethics Nothing More than Constraints and Guidelines for Proper Societal Behavior?

Bill Schmarzo

Chief Innovation Officer, Hitachi Vantara

Twitter, when used for good, can be a marvelous sharing and learning environment. For example, one of my Twitter followers made an interesting statement in response to my blog post "AI Ethics Challenge: Understanding Passive Versus Proactive Ethics" (*https://oreil.ly/TTeZu*). They posted: "Reducing ethics reasoning to a utility function misses the level of abstraction that ethics provide to act across contexts and situations. Then you don't have ethics anymore, you have constraints."

Constraints? Interesting. Or put another way: *are ethics just the set of constraints, rules, and guidelines that dictate how one is expected to act or behave within a properly functioning society?*

While I don't feel qualified to talk about ethics from a general society perspective, the discussion of ethics from an AI perspective is certainly within my domain of experience and should be everyone's concern. And that means we need to have a discussion about the creation of the *AI utility function*. The AI utility function comprises the constraints, rules, and guidelines that guide the actions and adaption of the AI model.

When creating AI-enabled autonomous entities—entities that make decisions, take actions, learn, and adapt with minimal human intervention—the definition of the AI utility function is critical. The AI ethics challenge is to define and encode those ethics (constraints, rules, and guidelines) into the math that makes up the AI utility function and drives the operations of autonomous entities. The AI utility function must understand these ethics in order to take the most appropriate or "right" actions. If we are going to transform into a world of AI-enabled autonomous entities—cars, trucks, and so on—then we must master encoding these ethics into math.

Asimov's Three Laws of Robotics Ethics

Isaac Asimov (*https://oreil.ly/QuPJX*) was an American writer who was well known for his science fiction works. In a 1942 short story, Asimov first set forth his "Three Laws of Robotics," within which a robot must be expected to behave in order to have a properly functioning society. The three laws are:

First Law
> A robot may not injure a human being, or, through inaction, allow a human being to come to harm.

Second Law
> A robot must obey the orders given it by human beings, except where such orders would conflict with the First Law.

Third Law
> A robot must protect its own existence, as long as such protection does not conflict with the First or Second Law.

I postulated in the blog post "Isaac Asimov: The 4th Law of Robotics" (*https://oreil.ly/eEkMs*) that we might need to come up with a Fourth Law of Robotics.

There will be situations in which these autonomous entities will be forced to make life-and-death decisions about which humans to save and which humans to kill—for example, an autonomous vehicle deciding between saving its passenger or a pedestrian. Isaac Asimov didn't envision needing a law to govern robots in these sorts of situations, where it isn't the life of the robot versus the life of a human in debate but a choice between the lives of multiple humans!

Surveys have been conducted to understand what to do in a situation in which the autonomous car has to make a life-and-death decision between saving a passenger and sparing pedestrians. The article "Will Your Driverless Car Be Willing to Kill You to Save the Lives of Others?" (*https://oreil.ly/ m7caN*) found the following:

> In one survey, 76% of people agreed that a driverless car should sacrifice its passenger rather than plow into and kill 10 pedestrians. They agreed, too, that it was moral for autonomous vehicles to be programmed in this way: it minimized deaths the cars caused. And the view held even when people were asked to imagine themselves or a family member traveling in the car.

But hold on—while in theory 76% favor saving the pedestrians over the passenger, the sentiment changes when it involves *you*!

> When people were asked whether they would buy a car controlled by such a moral algorithm, their enthusiasm cooled. Those surveyed said they would much rather purchase a car programmed to protect themselves instead of pedestrians. In other words, driverless cars that occasionally sacrificed their drivers for the greater good were a fine idea, but only for other people.

Riddle me this, Batman: Would the "programmed" reaction of an autonomous car in these life-and-death situations impact your decision to buy a particular brand of autonomous car?

Another study published in the journal *Science*, "The Social Dilemma of Autonomous Vehicles" (*https://oreil.ly/f7w7H*), highlighted the ethical dilemmas self-driving car manufacturers are faced with. About 2,000 people were polled, and the majority believed that autonomous cars should always make the decision to cause the fewest number of fatalities. On the other hand, most people also said they would buy a self-driving car *only if it meant their safety was a priority*.

I'm not sure that we want individual companies or our political leaders programming the rules that guide these sorts of life-and-death decisions.

But if not them, then who?

Summary

Are ethics just the set of constraints, rules, and guidelines that dictate how one is expected to act or behave within a properly functioning society?

For some, the Bible may be the ultimate book on ethics. (I can't speak for any other religious books such as the Quran or the Tanakh or the Tripitaka because I have not been exposed to them.) The Bible is full of constraints, rules, and guidelines on the ethics that guide proper individual and societal actions and behaviors, encoded through commandments, stories, and parables.

If we can create constraints, rules, and guidelines—encoded in the AI utility function—that guide the proper actions and behaviors of AI-enabled autonomous entities, then maybe we have a chance to really pull this AI thing off. We just need to get the most qualified leaders in our society to start identifying, validating, valuing, and prioritizing those constraints, rules, and guidelines that will need to comprise the AI utility function.

Five Core Virtues for Data Science and Artificial Intelligence

Aaron Burciaga

Global Operations Director, Analytics & Artificial Intelligence,
HCL Technologies

Virtues should be digitized. As we speed toward reliance on machines to process more and more information in order to provide cognitive support for all types of decision making, we must consider ways to imbue automated processes, data machinations, and recommender systems with a sense of some of the finest human virtues.

We are at the crossroads of a moral decision in AI—what I call the codification of virtue (or not). We either both address historic biases and impose just standards for reality based on fair data and decision making that seeds an ever-better world, or we fail to jettison anachronistic social norms and business practices that are the antithesis of virtuous intelligence, independent flesh, or silicon.

The Greek philosopher Epictetus said, "One cannot learn what they think they already know." This is particularly relevant in AI and among its engineers inasmuch as the system, or the human(s) creating the system, must be thoughtful, methodical, and explicit in how they've embedded an algorithm. A machine will not, and in fact cannot, do this of its own accord.

This has been a common shortfall I've had to address throughout projects I've led, in programs and teams I've developed, and across solutions that my teams have delivered—so I will now codify five points for the "quants" to remember (which is a term I use liberally to include data scientists, AI engineers, machine learning engineers, data miners, statisticians, and those with neighboring skills).

I submit that the following "Five Core Virtues" should be as explicitly practiced by the quants as they are codified by the AI—it's necessary to consider these as both soft and technical terms that are compelling, if not compulsory, for both the quant and the AI.

1. Resilience

Both the quant and the AI:

- Adapt to situations and recover quickly.
- Engineer conditions with design of experiments and explore the full solution space and feasible scenarios.
- Account for effects of local constraints and overcome such conditions to mitigate premature stopping.

2. Humility

Both the quant and the AI:

- Take responsibility for results.
- Continually learn and adapt with reinforcement learning.
- Recognize and engineer outcomes that appreciate how little can be known or controlled.

3. Grit

Both the quant and the AI:

- Avoid getting stuck admiring the problem or preoccupied with developing the smartest solutions.
- Obsess on being productive and getting stuff done in new and innovative ways.
- Provide auditable and interpretable results.

4. Liberal Education

Both the quant and the AI:

- Welcome and work with complexity, diversity, and change.
- Review opportunities or business problems critically, analyzing data fully and considering feasible methods to formulate solutions.

- Communicate clearly, cleanly, and reasonably with documentation that develops healthy and accountable solutions for society.

5. Empathy

Both the quant and the AI:

- Recognize and account for social impact and the feelings of others.
- Develop objective functions or constraints based on perception, discernment, understanding, and compassion.
- Identify interdependence and direct connections with "higher purpose" or consciousness.

Conclusion

The points I've made here, tying both the quant and the AI to each virtue, are meant to be at once concise as well as provocative and open ended. I've explicitly followed each virtue with the line "Both the quant and the AI" for the purpose of encouraging us all to consider how it is as much the responsibility of the solution as it is that of the author to emulate the attributes of resilience, humility, grit, liberal education, and empathy.

AI will free up human thinking, but it should not be an excuse from thought or virtue.

We cannot afford or risk a world in which AI is filled with all the virtues we despise—let's instead be intentional about developing it, and ourselves, with all the virtues we admire.

PART VII

Case Studies

This section contains specific examples of situations in which an ethical consideration arises. From auto insurance to predictive policing and autonomous weapons, the situations described in these submissions help to make the broader concepts discussed in the book more tangible.

Auto Insurance: When Data Science and the Business Model Intersect

Edward Vandenberg

Business Consultant, Teradata

The business model of automobile insurance (and therefore of most large insurance carriers) is changing drastically. Seemingly every month, an innovation is announced that at some point will have all of us chauffeured around in autonomous vehicles that never have an accident and are never exposed to the weather. But there are clouds forming. Extreme personalization of underwriting risk, and therefore the premium charged, may not be fair and ethical for everyone.

When an accident occurs, people and societies depend on the financial backing of insurance to defray the cost of damages and injuries (yes, accidents and weather-related damages will still happen). The way this works today (in a simplified view) is that insurance companies create policies with generic ratings for different types of drivers and vehicles. The underwriting and rating are designed to spread the risk. That means that lots of drivers will pay a little bit more to cover the few who have accidents. This seems appropriate when you never know which driver will get into an accident.

But the way the industry has been moving for the last 10 years or so, with AI, machine learning, and lots more data, is toward individual rates that predict the frequency and severity of accidents and the specific drivers who will have them, or at least smaller and smaller segments of like drivers. Things get more complicated when considering usage-based insurance, or "UBI," powered by telematics. Again, this is now possible because of all kinds of technology and data that are the offspring of AI-related innovations.

There are two major problems with the application of AI technology for personal auto insurance: (1) the data can simply be wrong (in fact, some of the data is very likely to be wrong some of the time); (2) analysts must make lots of choices when considering historic data for rating, and some of those choices lead to data being wrongly interpreted. Human biases are in the mix of rates that can affect whether people can afford auto insurance and can drive legally, given mandatory insurance laws.

Driving is very often a necessity to make a living and take care of families. For some, auto insurance can cost more than rent, and the premium takes up a much larger share of the incomes of the lower economic classes who likely depend on their vehicles the most.

While we want insurance that fairly reflects our individual risk, pure usage-based insurance applied very granularly is not a great idea socially. As such, while the AI wave enables the extreme personalization of auto insurance, companies and regulators will have to determine what level of "individual" risk and what level of "shared" risk makes sense for all of us.

As for data curation and the fairness of noisy and interpreted data, someone must "wear the hat" of the data ethicists when this data is being curated. And this person must have the power to direct how the data should be interpreted or whether it should be used at all.

While the AI-powered world of insurance is exciting and beneficial to society overall, it must be guided and tempered by wise analysts who are formally coached in the ethical use of data and by wise executives and regulators who can figure out what's the fairest use of this amazing technology.

To Fight Bias in Predictive Policing, Justice Can't Be Color-Blind

Eric Siegel

Founder, Predictive Analytics World

Crime-predicting models are caught in a quagmire doomed to controversy because, on their own, they cannot realize racial equity. It's an intrinsically unsolvable problem. It turns out that although such models succeed in flagging (i.e., assigning higher probabilities to) both black and white defendants with equal precision, as a result of doing so they also *falsely* flag black defendants more often than white ones.[1]

But despite this seemingly paradoxical predicament, we are witnessing an unprecedented opportunity to advance social justice by turning predictive policing around to actively affect more fairness, rather than passively reinforcing today's inequities.

Predictive policing introduces a quantitative element to weighty law enforcement decisions made by humans, such as whether to investigate or detain, how long a sentence to set, and whether to parole. When making such decisions, judges and officers take into consideration the calculated probability that a suspect or defendant will be convicted of a crime in the future. Calculating predictive probabilities from data is the job of *predictive modeling* (a.k.a. *machine learning*) software. It automatically establishes patterns by combing historical conviction records (*https://oreil.ly/-5_sE*), and in turn these patterns—together, a *predictive model*—serve to calculate the probability for an individual whose future is as yet unknown.

Although "color-blind," crime-predicting models treat races differently from one another. Usually, the models don't explicitly incorporate race—or any

---

1 References for many specifics in this article can be found in Eric Siegel, "How to Fight Bias with Predictive Policing," *Voices* (blog), *Scientific American*, February 19, 2018, *https://oreil.ly/OT6py*.

protected class—into their calculations (I cover glaring exceptions to this policy in my article in Part V of this book, "*Blatantly Discriminatory Algorithms*, page 150"). Despite this, black defendants are flagged as higher risk more often than white ones.

This disparity is a direct consequence of the racially imbalanced world in which we live. For example, a defendant's number of prior convictions is a standard input for predictive models, since defendants that have previously been convicted of a crime are more likely to reoffend (after release) than those who have not. Since more black defendants have prior convictions, this means predictive models flag black defendants more often than white ones. A black defendant isn't flagged by race but is more likely to be flagged nonetheless.

Today's heated dispute, however, isn't about this higher rate of flagging—it's about a higher rate of *falsely* flagging. Predictive models incorrectly flag black defendants who will not reoffend more often than they do white defendants. In what is the most widely cited piece on bias in predictive policing, Pro-Publica reports (*https://oreil.ly/5JKDE*) that the nationally used COMPAS model falsely flags white defendants at a rate of 23.5% and black defendants at a rate of 44.9%. In other words, *black defendants who don't deserve it are erroneously flagged almost twice as much as whites.*

In opposition, advocates of COMPAS counter that each flag is equally justified for both races. Responding to ProPublica, the creators of COMPAS point out that among those flagged as higher risk, the proportion that is falsely flagged is similar for black and white defendants (*https://oreil.ly/AfNuK*): 37% and 41%, respectively. In other words, *among defendants who are flagged, COMPAS is erroneous for white and black defendants equally often.* Other data scientists agree (*https://oreil.ly/E-I60*) this meets the standard for exonerating the model as unbiased.

It appears each individual flag is racially equitable, but the overall rates of false flagging are not. Although these two assertions may seem to contradict one another, they both hold true:

- If you're flagged, the chances it was deserved are equal, regardless of race.

- If you don't deserve to be flagged, you're more likely to be erroneously flagged if you're black.

Who's right? On the one hand, all flags seem to be equally well deserved. For defendants who are assigned higher probabilities, the rate of subsequent prosecutions is the same for both white and black defendants. On the other hand, among defendants who won't reoffend, black individuals face a higher risk of being falsely flagged. A more nuanced position claims that to settle the matter, we must agree on how fairness is defined (*https://oreil.ly/gkWQc*).

But instead of crossing swords about whether the model is "biased," the enlightened resolution would be to agree on measures to combat racial inequity. Debate over the word "biased" distracts from the next course of action. Rather than evaluating only whether a model worsens racial injustice, let's enhance predictive policing to actively decrease injustice. The seeming paradox itself brings to light a normally hidden symptom of today's racial inequity: if predictive flags are calibrated to be equally precise for both groups, then given the higher overall rate of reoffense among black defendants, that group suffers a greater prevalence of false flags.

And what an astonishing inequity that is. For a defendant of any race, being flagged means enduring a substantial risk that the flag is false. This can result in additional years of incarceration, with no way of confirming whether it was warranted (since the jailed defendant loses the freedom to demonstrate a lack of future crimes). For the black population, enduring this risk more often than whites adds insult to injury: not only are black people more likely to become defendants in the first place, but black defendants are in turn more likely to be unjustly sentenced to additional years in prison on the basis of a false prediction of future crime.

To address this, let's educate and guide law enforcement decision makers on the observed inequity. Train judges, parole boards, and officers to understand the pertinent caveats when they're given the calculated probability that a black suspect, defendant, or convict will reoffend. In so doing, empower these decision makers to incorporate these considerations into their decision making.

Three crucial considerations to reflect on when working with reoffense probabilities are:

The probability you're looking at has been influenced by the defendant's race, via proxies.

> Although race is not a direct input into the formula, the model may incorporate unchosen, involuntary factors that approximate race, such as family background, neighborhood ("Is there much crime in your neighborhood?"), education level (only partially chosen), and the behavior of family and friends (*https://oreil.ly/iQ8Nt*).

The probabilities disfavor black defendants due to biased ground truth.

Since black individuals are investigated, arrested, and therefore convicted more often than white individuals who have committed the same crime, measures of model performance do not reveal the extent to which black defendants are more often unjustly flagged.

The black population is ravaged by false flags.

Taking this systematic issue into consideration contributes to the greater good. Acknowledging this issue provides an opportunity to help compensate for past and present racial injustices and the cycles of disenfranchisement that ensue. This is where predictive policing can de-escalate such cyclic patterns rather than inadvertently magnify them.

Crime-predicting models themselves must remain color-blind by design, but the manner in which we contextualize and apply them cannot remain so. Reintroducing race in this way is the only means to progress from merely screening predictive models for racial bias to intentionally designing predictive policing to actively advance racial justice.

When to Say No to Data

Robert J. Abate

VP & CDO, Global IDs Inc.

While I was working as the director of a large retailer, we started to build a data lake with all the information that could be collected (both inside and outside the enterprise) in order to get a 360-degree view of the customer (for marketing and other purposes). This would become a huge dataset incorporating customer data, syndicated sales data, shopping cart information, marketing (promo) data, demographics (from the US Census Bureau), store locations, weather, and so on.

This data lake would contain information on the who (shopper), what (product), where (location), when (time), how (transaction type), and why (external data such as weather, stock market, income around store locations, etc.). Its primary usage would be to support visualizations inside the Data CAFÉ (Collaborative Analytics Facility for the Enterprise). The Data CAFÉ was designed so that executives could enter this room with nine (9) large screen displays of information and make critical business decisions in real time (e.g., Black Friday sales on the East Coast allowed management to change distribution in the Mountain and West Coast time zones based on live feeds).

Inside the Data CAFÉ, we would slice and dice the data so that visualizations could be created with filters (specific store, state, region, etc.), and then simply by pushing this view to a different screen or dimension (e.g., from time to product), the executive could see whether something was a local trend or a larger one. We coined the term "Archimedes's Visualizations" (as Archimedes was regarded as one of the leading scientists in classical antiquity).

Imagine that you could visualize information for a specific location (store) and then move to the next higher grouping (local market, state, division) and finally to global. Now consider that you were looking with these filters and that you could easily move these filters across to another monitor with when (time) or who (consumer) or what (product). Executives would be able to find their own trends based on their market experience and also have the advantage of data-driven decisions.

As the data integration started to mature, we quickly learned that this information could be used to find out very sensitive information about an individual or a household—specifically, what a neighbor was buying in our stores. This was instantly recognized as a problem when it came to data ethics, as data engineers and data scientists were going to be given access to the dataset for analysis. This could rapidly turn into a liability without some forms of control placed on the data lake.

To address this issue, we decided to create a set of rules that would limit the return of datasets from queries made to the data lake:

- No query would be allowed that returned fewer than 30 results (since in the Midwest, small towns could have a population of 10, and thus the result set could be deterministic).

- No query would be permitted by name, address, phone number, or any other personally identifiable information (PII) such as loyalty identifier, IP address, and so forth.

- No query would be supported that tracked the data or patterns of a unique individual or household (to stop the limited result set restriction from being bypassed).

- All queries would be saved, so that if we found instances of ethical violations, we could stop them in the future while discussing with the query owner the reason for this type of interrogation (in case there was a real reason but the result set was deemed inappropriate).

As time went on, we were very surprised to learn that many attempts were made to access the data of individuals, and some used very innovative approaches, including multilevel queries and joined result sets. We did not understand why this was happening, as we had been very clear from the outset that this data lake would be used to find trends and determine how to improve the baskets of shoppers.

As it turned out, upon investigation we found that many attempts were actual mistakes made in the query design, resulting in small result sets. Very few were found to be intentional, and this was after we reviewed the entire population of suspect queries. We had observed that the data engineers and scientists were mostly acting ethically, and this was no surprise, as the culture of the corporation was one of trust and personal responsibility.

Many things were learned from this data lake, including the following interesting observations (provided purely for your viewing enjoyment):

- The items most commonly found in shopping carts included fruit (bananas, strawberries), gasoline, water, bread, and rotisserie chickens.
- Shoppers could be grouped into different categories, but their browsing behavior was similar.
- Bad weather's effect on shopping contradicted the assumption that it would cause more sales over the period.
- Placing items in prominent locations would increase their sales marginally.
- Shoppers would seek out sale items over their own brand choices.

The Paradox of an Ethical Paradox

Bob Gladden

VP, Enterprise Analytics, Highmark Health

Ethics in data and analytics is a critical field that fortunately is getting increased attention. From data aggregation firms that repeatedly demonstrate disregard of their data stewardship responsibilities to meet company objectives, to pandemic methodologies that invade individual privacy for the greater societal good, ethical paradoxes are seemingly everywhere.

Some technology firms have given the concept of data and analytics ethics serious consideration. Others put on a public show of creating a data ethics council, only to violate the articles of their own code of data ethics in that council's creation. There are few public examples paving a path for data and analytics ethics. It seems the grown-ups have all left the room.

To be fair, organizations are often faced with ethical choices that can, in the minds of leaders, be seen as ethical paradoxes. But are they? Let's consider a simple example: in early February a church treasurer receives a request from the pastor for a substantial donation. As a condition of accepting the gift, the pastor asks the treasurer, on behalf of the donor, to backdate the letter officially acknowledging the gift to December of the previous year. When confronted, the pastor said he saw it as an ethical dilemma. The choice was between more funds for the church to do good work versus the legality of the donor having a lower tax bill because everyone had "fudged" the timing.

This is *not* an ethical paradox, even though the pastor had convinced himself it was. It is not the choice between two diametrically opposed ethically appropriate decisions. Yes, the funds would have helped the church. Yet accepting the gift, however much we all may not like the IRS, was a clear violation of the tax code. In fact, if uncovered (and given the paper trail, that would have been easy), it could result in penalties, including the church losing its nonprofit status.

These same types of false ethical paradoxes face business leaders daily. The vast majority of the time the right decision is made. But there are too many examples in which thinking becomes muddled and the decision makers create a paradox that doesn't exist.

Examples of actual ethical challenges include:

- A health care payer establishes a function to contribute to the research community based on their book of business. One study strongly suggests that higher CAP scores (an NCQA [National Committee for Quality Assurance] measurement of customer health plan satisfaction) are directly related to members with a higher risk burden (higher response rate and a direct correlation of higher satisfaction to increased use of health care services). So the research is not published, avoiding public scrutiny over that plan's high satisfaction scores.

- A project within a health organization pulls consumer data into models that assess a patient's risk based on their buying habits. This could be an example of data used for good—a physician having information they can use to help guide a patient's care based on their food purchases. However, that same information, if collected by a health plan, could be used to adjust future premiums, even pricing the product out of reach for that member/group as a way for the health plan to shed higher-risk customers.

- In an effort to improve an asthma-related HEDIS measure, a health plan embarks on a program for everyone classified in the HEDIS denominator (those classified as having asthma per NCQA definitions) to get a specific medication (controller), even though there was no question many members were false positives as a result of a challenged methodology. Concerns over higher-quality scores resulted in moving forward with the effort, including those that were false positives, with the justification that the unnecessary prescription would "not hurt them."

These are all relatively simple examples...and the paradox is not a paradox at all. It is a choice between self-interest, clouded as the "right thing to do for the organization," and the seemingly obvious ethical course of action. If organizations struggle with these choices today, the challenges introduced as a result of AI elevate this to a far more complex conversation. As Yuval Noah Harari has noted, "Humans are always far better at inventing tools than using them wisely."

This should not be written off as the rantings of someone riding on a moral high horse. This is basic stuff. Ethical behavior is the cornerstone of a civilized society, professionally and personally. Yet ethics today is under attack everywhere, with falsehoods presented as "facts" to divert attention and achieve what some see as the "greater good." Having an ethical code of conduct that is carefully integrated into an organization's psyche is a great start to addressing these false paradoxes. We can all do better...

Foundation for the Inevitable Laws for LAWS

Stephanie Seward

Associate, Booz Allen Hamilton[1]

Advances in AI technology have led to justified calls for banning lethal autonomous weapons systems (LAWS). Governments worldwide answer these calls with silence. When countries, methods of governance, and lives are at stake, leaders resort to extreme methods to ensure survival and protect their citizenry. In the future of warfare, the ability of LAWS to assess and engage targets quickly will give a decisive advantage to the country that possesses the most advanced technology and a willingness to use it. In warfare, the technology required to win prevails. Considering these stark realities, what degree of certainty do AI machines require to engage targets autonomously? The following is a methodology that practitioners can use to dictate how much freedom to give autonomous systems in making or informing vital decisions.

Performance Expectation Methodology (PEM)

A model trained on one set of data and tested on a separate set of data has a baseline metric for accuracy that may not be representative of real-world scenarios. The PEM is designed to test LAWS in a manner representative of real-world scenarios and should serve as the baseline for testing requirements that LAWS must pass before they are deployed to make independent decisions. Much as a doctor who achieves excellent grades over the course of medical school must still complete a residency, so too should LAWS undergo a rigorous trial period.

The PEM consists of two components: testing environment (TE) and output accuracy metric (OAM). The TE is designed to mimic real-world scenarios. For instance, a LAWS built to identify enemy artillery could be tested in a TE

---

1 The opinions expressed in this document are the author's own and do not reflect the views of Booz Allen Hamilton.

containing friendly and enemy equipment, test dummies, and other non-enemy artillery objects. The performance of the LAWS in terms of correctly identifying targets is the OAM.

Additionally, a LAWS training in a TE must deploy to a similar environment when engaging in decision making. For instance, a LAWS completing PEM in a desert TE must be deployed in a desert environment upon completing PEM. Were the same LAWS to be deployed into a forested environment post-PEM, it may have diminished accuracy due to environmental deviations, requiring a reevaluation of performance.

LAWS Performance During PEM

Consider a scenario in which the artillery identification LAWS undergoing PEM obtained an OAM of 99.9%; out of 1,000 objects, the system correctly identified 999 as either enemy artillery or not enemy artillery. *Requiring LAWS to engage in a standardized PEM grants data scientists the ability to identify and determine a LAWS's strengths and weaknesses in identification and determine how well a LAWS must perform before it is deployed.* In this scenario, the LAWS performs with an accuracy of 99.9%, but it confuses friendly artillery with enemy artillery .1% of the time. To what standards does the .1% confusion dictate successful completion of the PEM? Should the LAWS be deployed when it may commit fratricide? What if the same LAWS incorrectly identified enemy artillery as enemy tanks .1% of the time? Is that more acceptable? Perhaps this same LAWS's accuracy outperforms that of humans. Is it acceptable to deploy?

The answers to these questions coincide with current laws of warfare and the level of warfare countries are engaging in. In total war, for example, the PEM standards may be lower, as the potential collateral damage is outweighed by the lives lost by continuing warfare. In counterterrorism scenarios, perhaps the PEM OAM requirement and TE conditions are much higher or else LAWS are banned completely, because the risk of even a small inaccuracy could have far-reaching strategic impacts. The PEM is an approach that gives countries the opportunity to create policies to ensure LAWS are used as ethically as possible.

PEM: Continuous and Cyclical

The PEM requires additional enforceable standards for implementation on an international scale. Additionally, the PEM determines only whether LAWS are initially deployable. LAWS must be monitored on a regular basis to ensure continued accuracy, or they can be "pulled off the line" and retested using PEM. LAWS that have undergone model retraining must also recertify under the PEM prior to deployment to ensure continued performance.

Extensions to PEM

The PEM is applicable to a variety of settings. As AI systems continue to enter and improve lives, metrics of success throughout the life cycle of AI systems must ensure they perform based on the intent for their use.

A Lifetime Marketing Analyst's Perspective on Consumer Data Privacy

Mike McGuirk

Faculty Member, Babson College

In today's business environment, more and more companies are adopting customer-centric business practices. According to marketing and customer experience experts Don Peppers and Martha Rogers, the authors of *Managing Customer Experience and Relationships* (Wiley), a customer-centric business ensures that the *customer* is at the center of the business's philosophy, operations, and ideas.

From my perspective, these customer-centric practices provide benefits to both consumers and businesses. Consumers benefit from companies setting up processes to listen to their needs and using analytics and insight-driven approaches to modify their business operations to improve the overall customer experience. Businesses benefit from implementing customer-centric practices by building consumer trust, value, and brand loyalty and by gaining more consumer advocates. I will once again cite Don Peppers and Martha Rogers to highlight some of the core traits of customer-centric businesses:

- They collaborate with customers.
- They use interactive communications to determine individual needs.
- They differentiate customers from each other to interact with consumers in a more relevant, customized manner.

Underlying these core traits of customer-centricity is a critical theme/topic: consumer data privacy.

Consumer data and feedback resulting from interactive communications with consumers is the fuel that enables businesses to adopt and implement innovative customer-centric practices. Without this data, businesses are blind to the ever-changing behaviors, preferences, and needs of consumers.

Therefore, it is critical that all businesses, customer-centric or otherwise, incorporate consumer data collection practices that encourage consumers to keep this pipeline of customer data flowing into businesses. The data collection and usage practices need to be completely transparent to consumers. These practices need to protect against data breaches and give consumers a greater level of control over what personal information is collected, stored, used, and shared by businesses. Without this, there will be more cases like Cambridge Analytica's misuse of Facebook member data (*https://oreil.ly/x7yTC*) for political campaigns that continue to erode consumer confidence and advance the perception that companies cannot be trusted to keep consumer data private and secure.

I also believe that marketers need to be very thoughtful about how they use the data and insights to communicate with consumers. *They need to put themselves in the shoes of the consumers.* Do you like being retargeted via Facebook Messenger for an item you abandoned in an online retailer cart? Maybe, if the retargeting message comes with an enticing offer. The point is that some consumers will be comfortable with retargeting tactics, while others will feel they are too intrusive and creepy and show their disapproval by taking their shopping elsewhere. If businesses want to truly improve the customer experience, they need to figure out solutions that make all customer segments comfortable with how their data is being used.

The European Union has its own approach to regulating consumer data privacy. As of May 2018, all retailers doing business with EU citizens must adhere to the laws outlined in the EU's GDPR (*https://oreil.ly/Z3TTM*). These laws set a new data privacy standard for this region and provide consumers with much greater access to and control over the personal data collected by businesses. The first major infraction of GDPR was levied against Google in January 2019 by a French regulator who accused the tech giant of securing consumers' "forced consent" to collect their personal information. That is, consumers would not be given full access to certain Google apps if they did not consent to Google's data collection practices. Not a good look for Google, and another potentially damaging incident for those companies that implement responsible data collection practices and rely on this data to operate their customer-centric businesses.

Also, closer to home, the California Consumer Privacy Act (*https://oreil.ly/tKK8C*) went into effect in January 2020, giving California residents greater control over the personal information that is collected and used by businesses. This shows that if US businesses can't self-regulate responsible consumer data collection and usage practices, then state and federal agencies will eventually do it for them.

Regulated data protection can be a bit of a double-edged sword for consumers. It certainly provides peace of mind to know that greater data protection practices are in place and being enforced. However, if the regulations are too onerous and restrictive, businesses will quickly begin to lose their ability to stay tapped into the behaviors, needs, and voice of the consumer, and this will impede the implementation of customer-centric business practices that benefit all consumers.

As someone who has worked in the marketing and data analytics field for 30 years, I understand the value that responsible data collection and analytics can provide to both consumers and businesses. It is time for all businesses to assess their own data privacy and usage policies and make changes, if necessary, so we can begin to regain the trust of consumers.

100% Conversion: Utopia or Dystopia?

Dave Cherry

Executive Strategy Advisor, Cherry Advisory LLC

It was a bright day in retail, and conversions were striking 100% yet again.[1]

Marketing had once more delivered hyperpersonalized offerings. These offers were not only unique to each individual customer, but also context-sensitive to the specific mindset of each customer at the time that they were delivered. Upon receipt of each offer, every customer had the identical reaction: "I'll take it."

Merchandising had the perfect amount of inventory on hand in every store and in the fulfillment center. So regardless of where the customer wanted to complete the transaction, the product was in stock. Additional shipping costs to fulfill out-of-stock items were a thing of the past.

Excess inventory, clearance, and returns were nonexistent. IT removed the clearance section from the website, and store operations eliminated labor hours for redlining and returns. Every transaction was productive, and operational costs had never been lower.

Financial planning and analysis continued its record of perfect forecast accuracy, as it nailed unit, margin, and revenue targets precisely. Stock prices soared, and incentive compensation targets were exceeded.

The chief analytics officer took pride in the amount of customer data gathered and stored from transactions, loyalty, and social media...as well as the new video analytics capability that used facial recognition to track visits, dwell time, and sentiment for customers in the store. This information fed advanced machine learning models that could accurately predict what each

---

1 This introductory statement is adapted from George Orwell's *Nineteen Eighty-Four* (Harcourt, Brace), which begins, "It was a bright cold day in April, and the clocks were striking thirteen."

customer would buy, at what price, through which channel, and when. It was astonishingly accurate.

The repeated chaos of Monday mornings was a thing of the past. Leaders spent time creatively developing plans for future seasons instead of digging for the root cause of sales missing expectations. Pricing was competitive, aggressive, and perfect—beating the competition and delivering profitable margins.

And what about the customers? Were they happy? That depends on which customer you asked.

The first customer was thrilled. "They know me—sometimes better than I know myself," she said. "Everything that they offer me works. It is always at a price that I think is fair, and they always have my size in stock. The colors and looks fit perfectly with my existing wardrobe and my style. In fact, I had just recently posted a comment that I needed new boots when they showed me the perfect pair!" She even shouted, "*It's utopia!*"

The second customer was furious and skeptical. "I don't like how much of my information they track. With every purchase, I need to provide my email address or phone number. Even when I'm browsing the website, they track me. It even seems like they track my social media activity and conversations —how else would they know what I discussed with my spouse last night and send me an offer on it today? And who knows what they're doing with all of my information or who they are selling it to!" She griped, "*It's dystopia!*"

And what about the retailer? Was it effective? Was it ethical? That once again depends on whom you asked.

For those of you who identify with either customer's evaluation, your opinions are likely set. But for those who have yet to decide, here's something to consider.

The rise of technical capabilities to gather, track, and analyze demographic, transactional, and behavioral customer data raises the bar on retailer performance expectations. It is no longer acceptable for a retailer to market a product that doesn't perfectly resonate with the customer—at the right size, price, and style. And if performance expectations rise, only the best retailers will survive, and the level of service and quality that customers experience will also rise.

Should retailers be required to gain approval from every customer in order to use their information? Doing so would surely increase costs and create significant inefficiencies in the timeliness and effectiveness of their analytical models at minimum and would also likely reduce the accuracy of those models. And if that happens, perhaps both retailers and customers lose.

But if retailers gather, track, analyze, and protect this data effectively, customers win.

Instead of a scenario resembling a dystopia with great suffering or injustice, customers would experience a more ideal state of fewer offers, more relevance, and better products, service, and quality. While 100% conversion ultimately is not practical or achievable, striving for this goal may yield the closest semblance of a perfect, utopian experience both for the customer and the retailer.

Random Selection at Harvard?

Peter Bruce

Founder, Institute for Statistics Education at Statistics.com,
an Elder Research company

Ethics in algorithms is a popular topic now. Usually the conversation centers around possible unintentional bias in a statistical or machine learning algorithm and the harm it could do when it is used to select, score, rate, or rank people. For example, a credit-scoring algorithm may include a predictor that is highly correlated with race, which could result in racially biased decisions.

There are contrary cases, though. The use of discretionary human judgment to admit students to highly selective universities is fraught with controversy and allegations of bias. Here's a proposal for a simple statistical selection technique to assure diversity while avoiding bias. It is best illustrated with Harvard University and a court case that has brought notoriety to the university's admission process.

"An art collection that could conceivably come our way..."

With 19 rejections for every acceptance, entry to Harvard can seem like a moonshot. The family art collection was one student's advantage in applying to Harvard. It's no secret that big donors, or potential donors, have a leg up when it comes to their kids getting into Harvard, Princeton, or any of hundreds of universities. Still, it was unusual to see the plain truth out in the open—the "art collection" reference came in an email from Harvard's admission director that was made public in a lawsuit brought by Asian Americans claiming discrimination by Harvard.

Big donations are only one fast track to Harvard. Athletics, obviously, is another. Being from a rural area helps. Admission officers have considerable discretion, much of which they exercise in the service of ethnic diversity. But tilting the scale in favor of one ethnic group inevitably tilts it against another, and pursuit of diversity, as currently practiced, runs right up against legal prohibitions against discrimination.

Another Way

Harvard and similar institutions rely on human judgment in favoring one group over another, which can leave them defenseless against charges of bias. A simple idea can extricate Harvard from this affirmative action bind while promoting diversity: choose students by random lottery, the time-honored statistical technique for eliminating bias and ensuring equal representation.

A minimum threshold of qualifications can be established, and the pool can be those applicants judged capable of academic success. According to the trial evidence, a large number of applicants—far more than the number admitted—meet this standard (children of alumni and donors are admitted at six times the normal rate, and Harvard says they do fine). Preferences for legacies, athletics, and so forth could be retained, but if too great, they could compromise the perceived validity of this suggested new method.

A key tweak will assure diversity in *all* respects, not just racial: choose from each zip code according to population. Applicants whose parents have the money and drive to push their kids into enriching precollege activities to boost their admission chances will no longer have an edge.

In stratified sampling, the population to be sampled is split up into strata to facilitate adequate representation of groups of interest. How will geographic stratification work?

Random Selection with Geographic Stratification

The new admission algorithm can work like this:

1. Divide the country into equal population zones (using zip codes, for the sake of argument).

2. Establish how many applicants will be accepted, and divide the allowance equally among the zones.

3. Establish the minimum qualifications (using numerical criteria such as SAT scores and grade point averages).

4. Select an equal number of applicants from each area, picking randomly from those above the qualification threshold, and staying within the zone allowance.

How will this ensure diversity? In the current judgment-based system, Harvard takes into account personal and social characteristics other than pure intelligence—participation in extracurricular activities, an engaging personality, performance in an interview, and so forth. Students in wealthy suburban neighborhoods absorb more of this college-bound ethos and ambience than those from poorer areas, whether urban or rural, where going to college is not the norm. If Harvard selects randomly from all geographic zones according to population, it will necessarily end up with a diverse student body since it will need to "dig deeper" in zones where the path to college is not so well trodden.

Harvard and its peers are uniquely positioned to try this experiment:

- They can well afford to risk potential diminution of alumni affinity and money (the income from Princeton's endowment alone would allow the university to give free tuition to every student, with plenty left over).

- Their reputations are so well established that they no longer need to rest on the achievements of "super-students."

- The pool of well-qualified applicants is so vast, relative to admissions, that lowering the admission bar in some geographic areas will still yield fully qualified applicants.

- As private universities, Harvard and its peers need not worry about politically appointed regents or meddling state legislatures.

Best of all, a sound map-based stratified sampling plan will extricate Harvard and its peers from the legal and political bind of affirmative action. There is nothing objectionable about selection in which geography (as opposed to race or ethnicity) is a factor. Moreover, reducing elite institutions' role in nurturing and heightening supposedly inherent distinctions of merit among individuals will also have a salutary democratizing effect.

To Prepare or Not to Prepare for the Storm

Kris Hunt

Partner and Cofounder, Hard Right Solutions

In August 2005, I was working in the analytics group for a major home improvement retailer based in North Carolina, and my father and his wife lived in New Orleans. When Hurricane Katrina hit the Southeast, I was able to see and assess the devastation from a personal, professional, and analytical perspective. Conversations with my family, my firsthand experiences volunteering, and visits to the New Orleans area after the storm gave my work more meaning by attaching names and faces to the results. I would remember the sights, sounds, and smells when I was back in my cube analyzing the data to capture the enormous impact of Katrina on our business. In addition, I found myself wondering what we as a company and as analysts could do to be more prepared in the future.

Prior to the storm and immediately after the hurricane made landfall, the business trends were typical, and our emergency teams responded according to the protocols. We were analyzing which stores were affected and quantifying the lost sales by department. What was unique about Katrina was that the storm did not subside after it first made landfall in Florida. Instead, it gained strength in the Gulf and then hit New Orleans, and the storm surge caused the levees to fail. The amount of land, property, and people experiencing damage and destruction grew exponentially. Employees and customers lost their homes and belongings. Stores were closed or had limited hours due to building damage, loss of inventory, intermittent power, lack of staff, compromised municipal support, and the limitation of replenishing supplies. This situation was a worst-case scenario.

Before Katrina, we had built a best-in-class database that supported predictive models for purchase patterns, product affinities, seasonality, regionality, and sales forecasts. My team was truly on the leading edge of retail analytics. Now we were tasked with determining what data needed to be excluded from our existing processes so that the rest of the company could operate as usual.

At the same time, we realized that we had a true treasure at our fingertips. The excluded data could not be used to predict the normal business; however, it could be used to determine the key products and new patterns that would present in the database, providing a playbook for how our business evolves through a storm. In short, Hurricane Katrina gave data scientists an opportunity to analyze an epic disruption in the retail world and the ability to identify when the new normal was established.

I realize that analyzing the "evolution of a storm" is making a huge jug of lemonade; however, it was a very exciting time and project. I started creating "bands" that identified the level of destruction in miles from the center of the storm outward to determine the line of normalcy. Over time, each band would reach its new normal. After four to five years, we had built a once-in-a-lifetime dataset—but what could we do with it?

Possible uses:

- Provide the public with a list of items to secure and protect property in the event of catastrophe.
- Create "mobile" stores, which are basically 18-wheelers with a built-in POS and outfitted with the items most needed immediately after the storm passes.
- As a goodwill gesture, fill empty trucks with the cardboard and "clean" trash from the stores, as trash removal is often suspended during these times, further straining a retailer's operations.
- Develop a playbook and adapt this process to use the method, taking different types of disasters, regionality, and seasonality into consideration.
- Integrate the data with the available weather data and create case studies for students, as this event beautifully illustrates how data evolves and how you must be as nimble as what you are analyzing to be effective.
- Improve current protocols for locations in disaster-prone areas.
- Outline methods used to isolate the storm impact and still forecast business projections to optimize the expected "new normal"—the demand after the storm spikes but is not sustainable....Be careful, as you could model a need for additional locations that are not going to thrive once the area recovers.

We ran into a corporate budget question of whether to continue capturing and analyzing this "data gift" with the expense of retaining and maintaining it. Given that these events are rare, hard to predict, and even harder to act on quickly, the decision was made to let the data start rolling off the database naturally, using existing data-retention policies. I wonder if that dataset could have been used to improve storm preparedness, save lives and property, and improve disaster logistics, as it seems powerful storms are not as rare today.

Ethics, AI, and the Audit Function in Financial Reporting

Steven Mintz

Professor Emeritus, Cal Poly San Luis Obispo

AI broadly refers to technologies that make machines "smart." AI has unleashed many practical applications that can enhance the decision-making process. AI is powered by algorithms, and algorithms are driven by large amounts of data.

The ethical questions in an AI system are: (1) is the data reliable? (2) can we trust that the data provides the information needed for managerial decision making? (3) how can auditors evaluate the data provided by the system?

In September 2019, Genesys released a research report that said 21% of employees surveyed had expressed a concern that their companies could use AI in an unethical manner. Therefore, an independent audit is essential to conclude that the data presents fairly the financial information and results of operation that are crucial to assessing the performance of an organization.

Without a reliable audit, it is virtually impossible to conclude that the data produced by AI systems can be relied on by the users of financial statements, the key ingredient in placing our trust in that data. In other words, the data must report what it is supposed to report and be unbiased.

Auditing is an essential function for organizations, but much of it is routine. The examination of financial statement information lends itself to the use of technology to analyze big data and decide which areas of the audit to focus on and how best to gather the data needed to ensure the audit meets professional and ethical standards. Accounting firms are experimenting with AI systems in which machines go beyond doing rote tasks and inform basic decision making.

There are many implications of AI for organizational ethics, including internal auditing, internal control over financial reporting, and the role of the external auditors. Moreover, unintended consequences may exist with respect to the potential for fraud in AI systems, and these need to be understood in conjunction with an effective audit. Accountants and auditors should be adequately trained to make these assessments.

What's missing from today's discussion of AI in the accounting and auditing arena is a clear understanding of what the ethical issues are in an AI system and how best to address those issues. Here are ten areas of concern:

- How can an organization establish accountability and oversight through corporate governance systems in an AI environment?
- How does the use of an AI system influence the role and responsibilities of the chief financial officer with respect to the certification of financial statements under Section 302 of the Sarbanes-Oxley Act (SOX) of 2002?
- What are the role and responsibilities of the system of internal controls over financial reporting in an AI environment?
- What must management do to assess whether internal controls in an AI system are operating as intended, which is a requirement under Section 404 of SOX?
- What are the possible threats to objectivity and integrity in an AI environment, and what safeguards exist to mitigate those threats and enhance the external audit function?
- What is the risk that AI systems might be used to promote a management agenda that may include occupational and/or fraudulent financial statements?
- If significant risk exists, then how can the integrity of the financial statements be protected?
- What is the risk that AI diminishes the data rights or privacy of individuals and communities, and how can that risk be managed?
- What are the role and responsibilities of the audit committee in an AI environment?
- Should there be a separate AI ethics committee to ensure that the corporate culture supports ethical decision making on AI matters?

The challenges for accounting, auditing, and financial reporting in an AI environment are substantial. One way to characterize them is to emphasize the need for transparency, accountability, and integrity. Another is to trust but verify.

The Gray Line

Phil Broadbent

Senior Manager, GCX Analytics, eBay

I stood in the amphitheater-shaped room presenting results from the latest machine learning model we had implemented. It would optimize prices at an online retailer that was embracing the novelty of data science in order to drive revenue. I looked up to face my accuser.

We'd had modest success to that point and were proposing a new metric to measure the impact moving forward. We avoided most of the usual political turmoil that exists in bigger companies by maintaining a relatively flat organization, both in hierarchy and in operation. Folks with good ideas that delivered results were consistently given room to make decisions and own strategic direction.

One drawback to this structure is the ability of folks with different agendas to derail progress that others make. Such was the case on this day, as a leader of a marketing team (which had been tasked with driving up demand and was struggling to do so) expressed doubt in the metric we were proposing. They accused my team and me of "misleading" the organization by showing the results in the way we were. Most of the folks in the room were not quantitatively minded and didn't see the attack for what it was: a political maneuver designed to position one group higher at the expense of another.

As a reader, you may react by questioning the details (they are many, and the history is long) and supposing that perhaps intentions were misinterpreted (they may have been). We can debate the accuracy or intent of each of the players involved, but the point is that these are the players (real humans) in the corporate battles we see across all companies today, in which customers, their data, and their actions and behaviors are used as weapons to get competitive edges over corporate colleagues, internal or external.

We have seen the start of government regulation with enactment of the EU's GDPR and similar measures worldwide, but what about within the corporate walls? When pressed for results (increased revenue, decreased cost, or some other insight to drive business strategy) and faced with severe penalties if results aren't delivered (annual bonus impact, salary, promotion eligibility, etc.), what levers will people reach for?

We are now in an environment in which actions and strategies are visible only underneath the algorithms/models/artificial intelligences that the designers/architects may or may not understand. There has been talk recently about how Google had swayed some nonzero number of voters, talk that has even reached the Senate floor for a hearing (*https://oreil.ly/s0Sov*). Does this result potentially come from an executive leader demanding results and corporate citizens delivering click-through rates, page views, and/or insights that come from manipulating customers' search results? If so, who is making the decision about when the line is crossed between legally campaigning and election meddling? Is it the employees who are driven to deliver results at the risk of losing a promotion/bonus/job?

Contributors

Aaron Burciaga

Aaron Burciaga is a data scientist, AI engineer, author, and advisor. As a seasoned technology and business leader in both start-up and enterprise settings, he has focused his career on delivering efficiency and value through automation, data science, machine learning, artificial intelligence, blockchain, quantum computing, and emerging concepts and innovative technologies. His development and implementation of programs and initiatives have enhanced multibillion-dollar programs and operational efficiencies across industries in commercial, federal, and defense sectors. Aaron's roles have included Global Operation Director for Data Science and Analytics at HCL Technologies, CTO at Analytics2Go, Vice President Data Science and AI at Booz Allen Hamilton, Global Analytics Platform Lead at Accenture, and Senior Research Scientist at Elder Research. Before turning his attention to the commercial and public sectors, Aaron was a Marine Corps officer and Iraq War veteran and was the head operations research analyst and director of operations analysis activity at the Pentagon, supporting the Marine Corps Headquarters. He is also a Marine reservist, where he supports the Chief Information Officer at Headquarters Marine Corps, Pentagon, as Lead Data Technologist. Aaron is a *Forbes* contributor, frequently invited keynote and speaker, and Certified Analytics Professional (CAP). He is an appointed member of the US Department of Commerce's National Technology Information Service advisory board. Aaron received his MS in operations research from the Naval Postgraduate School and his BS from the US Naval Academy.

Five Core Virtues for Data Science and Artificial Intelligence, page 237

Andreas Messalas

Andreas Messalas is an artificial intelligence researcher and developer with a special interest in machine learning transparency, fairness, and robustness. His work at Code4Thought focuses on rendering algorithms transparent and helping organizations become accountable. Andreas holds a master's degree in computer engineering and informatics from the University of Patras in Greece.

Use Model-Agnostic Explanations for Finding Bias in Black-Box Models, page 174

Anna Jacobson

Anna Jacobson is an engineer by training, a project manager by experience, and a data scientist by aspiration. She is passionate about the evolution of decisions, from data to information to insight to action—and she is fascinated by the potential this process has to change the world around us. As a student in UC Berkeley's Master of Information and Data Science (MIDS) program, Anna is rigorously pursuing the study of many facets of data analysis, while also serving as a student representative for both the MIDS Social Good initiative and the Women in MIDS initiative. As a professional in the construction industry, she is responsible for leading teams that create and implement strategies to help her clients plan and prepare for the complex process of designing and constructing a building.

Fairness in the Age of Algorithms, page 24

Arnobio Morelix

Arnobio Morelix is a Silicon Valley–based leader working at the intersection of strategy and data science. His work and analysis have been featured widely in national and global media, including the *New York Times,* the *Economist,* the *Wall Street Journal,* and the BBC. He is a frequent public speaker and has presented at South by Southwest, Facebook, the Federal Reserve Bank, and elsewhere. Arnobio has advised, worked with, and presented to CEOs, founders, current and former government ministers, and top academics, and he also serves in data science–focused roles at Stanford University and *Inc.* magazine. As Chief Innovation Officer at Startup Genome, Arnobio leads a global team conducting research and advising governments and private organizations across 35+ countries on their innovation policies.

Pay Off Your Fairness Debt, the Shadow Twin of Technical Debt, page 103
Algorithmic Misclassification—the (Pretty) Good, the Bad, and the Ugly, page 133

Bill Schmarzo

Bill Schmarzo, Hitachi Vantara Chief Innovation Officer, is responsible for defining Hitachi Vantara's analytics (AI/ML/data science) direction and driving "co-creation" efforts with select customers to leverage analytics to power digital transformation. Bill is a University of San Francisco School of Management (SOM) Executive Fellow and an Honorary Professor at the School of Business and Economics at the National University of Ireland–Galway, where he teaches and mentors students in his courses Big Data MBA: Driving Business Strategies with Data Science and Thinking Like a Data Scientist.

Bob Gladden

Bob Gladden is a veteran health care analytics leader with experience across multiple segments of the industry. He is the Vice President for Enterprise Analytics at Highmark Health and is also the CEO and owner of Front Edge Analytics, a health care insights advisory services organization. His experience includes leadership positions at CareSource Management Group, Ernst & Young in their Healthcare Consulting Practice, Northwestern Healthcare System, Advocate Healthcare System, McNerney Heintz, and CoMed. Gladden has over 35 years of experience in the fields of health care analytics, health care administration, health care research, data management, data governance, information systems, actuarial science, underwriting, and finance. His past positions have included CFO, CIO, and multiple executive roles for analytics. He holds a master's degree from Bowling Green State University.

Bonnie Holub

Bonnie Holub holds a PhD in artificial intelligence and has served in a variety of roles, including Practice Lead, Data Science at Teradata, VP Talent Analytics at Korn Ferry, Master Data Scientist at Cognizant, Analytics Director at PwC, and Enterprise Data Warehouse Program Manager at UCare Health Insurance. She has also been an entrepreneur, founding several companies. She has taught at the graduate level and been involved with the founding of successful Big Data, Data Science, and AI programs at several universities.

Silos Create Problems—Perhaps More Than You Think, page 93

Brendan Tierney

Brendan Tierney is a long-time developer of data solutions, including data warehousing, Big Data, machine learning, and data architecture. He is an independent consultant (Oralytics) and lectures on data science, databases, and Big Data at Technological University Dublin. He is an active blogger, writes articles for various publications, and is a regular presenter at various developer conferences, including Oracle User Group conferences, Devoxx, PyCon, and ODSC. Brendan has published four books—three with Oracle Press/McGraw-Hill (*Predictive Analytics Using Oracle Data Miner*; *Oracle R Enterprise: Harnessing the Power of R in Oracle Database*; and *Real World SQL and PL/SQL: Advice from the Experts*) and one with MIT Press (*Data Science*), the last of which has been translated into six other languages. These books are available on Amazon in print, ebook, and audiobook formats. Vist Brendan's website and blog, *www.oralytics.com*, and follow him on Twitter *@brendantierney*.

Facial Recognition on the Street and in Shopping Malls, page 142

Brent Dykes

Brent Dykes is Senior Director of Insights and Data Storytelling at Blast Analytics. He is also the author of *Effective Data Storytelling: How to Drive Change with Data, Narrative, and Visuals* (Wiley). Brent has more than 15 years of enterprise analytics experience at Omniture, Adobe, and Domo. His passion for data strategy and data storytelling comes from consulting with many industry leaders including Nike, Microsoft, Sony, and Comcast. He is a regular Forbes contributor and has written more than 35 articles on different data-related topics. In 2016, Brent received the Most Influential Industry Contributor Award from the Digital Analytics Association (DAA). He is a popular speaker at conferences such as Strata, Web Summit, Shop.org, Adtech, Pubcon, RISE, Crunch, and Adobe Summit. Brent holds an MBA from Brigham Young University and a BBA in marketing from Simon Fraser University.

Data Storytelling: The Tipping Point Between Fact and Fiction, page 39
The Ethical Data Storyteller, page 109

Brian T. O'Neill

Brian T. O'Neill is a designer, advisor, and founder of Designing for Analytics, an independent consultancy that helps companies turn analytics and ML into indispensable decision support applications. For over 20 years, he has worked with companies such as DellEMC, Global Strategy Group, Tripadvisor, Fidelity, JPMorgan Chase, E-Trade, and several SAAS startups. He has spoken internationally, giving talks at Strata, Enterprise Data World, the International Institute for Analytics Symposium, Predictive Analytics World, and Boston College. Brian also hosts the highly rated podcast *Experiencing Data*, on which he reveals the strategies and activities that product, data science, and analytics leaders are using to deliver valuable experiences around data. In addition to consulting, Brian is also a professional percussionist and has performed at Carnegie Hall and the Kennedy Center. Follow him on Twitter *@rhythmspice* and join his mailing list at *https://designingforanalytics.com/list*.

Introducing Ethicize™, the fully AI-driven cloud-based ethics solution!, page 5

Carole Piovesan

Carole Piovesan is a partner and cofounder of INQ Data Law, where her practice concentrates on privacy, cyber readiness, data governance, and AI. She regularly counsels clients on a wide range of matters related to privacy, data protection, data governance, ethical AI, and risk management for AI operationalization.

How to Innovate Responsibly, page 206

Cassie Kozyrkov

Cassie Kozyrkov is Chief Decision Scientist at Google Cloud, where she guides teams in data-driven decision process and AI strategy. She is the innovator behind bringing the practice of decision intelligence to Google, personally training over 20,000 Googlers.

The Truth About AI Bias, page 2
AI Ethics, page 106

Christof Wolf-Brenner

Christof Wolf-Brenner works as a consultant in the areas of AI and Big Data. Besides leading creative workshops, conducting training courses, and managing projects, he has taken up philosophy as an academic hobby. By combining work experience and a broad theoretical background, he started to immerse himself in the ethics of AI a year ago.

Rules and Rationality, page 16

Collin Cunningham

Collin Cunningham is a data scientist at Amazon Web Services. Outside of work, he founded the SpringForward Foundation, which helps underserved high school students apply to college, and he serves as principal architect at ATLFamilyMeal. While completing his master's degree at UC Berkeley, Collin was awarded the Jack Larson Data for Good Fellowship for his work in ethics and his contributions to his community through data science.

Ethical CRISP-DM: A Framework for Ethical Data Science Development, page 228

Damian Gordon

Damian Gordon has been a lecturer in computer science at the Technological University Dublin for over 20 years. He has authored more than 50 research papers, 40 of which are focused on his work as an educational researcher (looking at blended learning, universal design, ethics, and eLearning). Before starting as a lecturer, he worked in the computer industry, where he was employed variously in the roles of software developer, business systems analyst, technical team leader, and implementation consultant.

Anonymizing Data Is Really, Really Hard, page 77
Ethics Is the Antidote to Data Breaches, page 88

Dave Cherry

Dave Cherry is principal of Cherry Advisory, LLC. He is a thought leader, executive strategist, and speaker with over 25 years of experience. He helps clients in the customer experience industry (that's everyone with customers) define a customer experience strategy, enabled by innovation and measured/informed by analytics, that drives deep relationships and connections with customers. He has worked with and for leading organizations such as LBrands, Polo Ralph Lauren, Ascena Retail Group, Journeys, DSW, Disney, Alliance Data, Nationwide Insurance, AEP, Huntington Bank, Cardinal Health, OhioHealth, Deloitte Consulting, and Price Waterhouse. He holds a BS in economics from the Wharton School at the University of Pennsylvania, and he serves on the International Institute for Analytics Expert Panel and also as an advisory board member for the Women in Analytics Conference and CBUS Retail.

Data Science Does Not Need a Code of Ethics, page 204
100% Conversion: Utopia or Dystopia?, page 259

Dave Mathias

Dave Mathias combines his passions around customer, data, and product to bridge the gap between business and technology. He is founder of Beyond the Data, cohost of the *Data Able* podcast, and coleader of MinneAnalytics and TC Data Viz Group.

Ethics as a Competitive Advantage, page 53

Doug Hague

Doug Hague is the founding Executive Director of the School of Data Science at the University of North Carolina at Charlotte. Dr. Hague had more than 20 years of corporate experience in aerospace, telecommunications, and financial services prior to joining the university, including his role as Chief Analytics Officer for Bank of America's Merchant Services. Dr. Hague has authored more than 20 articles published in academic and professional journals and holds four patents.

Unbiased ≠ Fair: For Data Science, It Cannot Be Just About the Math, page 32
A Framework for Managing Ethics in Data Science: Model Risk Management, page 168

Edward Vandenberg

Edward Vandenberg is a business analyst for the insurance industry, specializing in data science. For the past 15 years, he has worked with major insurance companies to help them develop advanced quantitative models and deploy them into pricing, underwriting, and claims processes. He holds advanced degrees in business and technology and currently works for Teradata Corporation.

Auto Insurance: When Data Science and the Business Model Intersect, page 241

Eric Schmidt

Eric Schmidt has over 20 years of international experience structuring complex business questions, developing analytic tools and capabilities, and translating analytics into actionable insights and recommendations for senior stakeholders. His analytics career has spanned several industries, including banking, risk management, hospitality, and consumer packaged goods, where he has led credit risk model validation, pricing and revenue optimization, demand forecasting, and marketing and decision sciences. Currently, Eric leads a global data and analytics team for a major beverage company in Atlanta, Georgia, focusing on business intelligence and data science applications for finance, marketing, and strategy. Eric holds bachelor's, master's, and doctorate degrees from the Georgia Institute of Technology, where he studied mechanical engineering and fluid mechanics, and he has an MBA from Emory University's Goizueta Business School, where he focused on marketing and decision sciences. He received academic scholarships at both Georgia Tech and Goizueta Business School. In 2011, Eric received the Marketing Faculty Honor Award as the top marketing student in that year's graduating class.

Eric Siegel

Eric Siegel, PhD, founder of the Predictive Analytics World and Deep Learning World conference series, makes the how and why of machine learning understandable and captivating. He is the author of the award-winning book *Predictive Analytics: The Power to Predict Who Will Click, Buy, Lie, or Die* (Wiley), a former Columbia University professor, and a renowned speaker, educator, and leader in the field. Read his other writing on data and social justice at *www.civilrightsdata.com*, and follow him on Twitter *@predictanalytic*.

Evan Stubbs

Evan Stubbs is a partner and director at the Boston Consulting Group, has written a number of books on driving competitive advantage through data, and is a global leader in BCG's Data and Digital Platforms practice. He has worked at the intersection of strategy, engineering, and capability for over 20 years and works with his clients globally to turn technology into competitive advantage.

Fred Nugen

Dr. Fred Nugen is a researcher in predictive computational medicine and teaches data science at UC Berkeley. His focus is on building bridges between engineering and medicine to foster meaningful collaboration. He works to design, build, and improve new technology that can improve quality of living and save lives.

Securing Your Data Against Breaches Will Help Us Improve Health Care, page 96

Grant Fleming

Grant Fleming is a data scientist at Elder Research Inc. At Elder Research, Grant works with private and public sector clients to identify and pursue new avenues for analytics. His primary technical interests are in interpretable machine learning, reproducibility, and deep learning for text analytics.

The Ethical Dilemma of Model Interpretability, page 171

Hannah Kitcher

Hannah Kitcher is responsible for increasing awareness of the work of Ada Lovelace Institute, the independent body working to ensure data and AI work for people and society. Prior to this, Hannah was Communications Manager at the responsible tech think tank Doteveryone. Hannah has extensive experience in both research and communications at independent organizations, working to understand and find solutions to some of society's major social issues.

We're Not Yet Ready for a Trustmark for Technology, page 64

Hassan Masum

Hassan Masum is Senior Director of Analytics at Prodigy Education and a "progress strategist." He is passionate about working with innovative organizations and changemakers to tackle complex challenges, and he loves codeveloping sociotechnical solutions that marry quantitative and qualitative insights to make people better off. His experiences and publications are waypoints in a life journey to harness the power of analysis, collaboration, and servant leadership in pursuit of worthwhile goals.

Understand Who Your Leaders Serve, page 29
Build Multiperspective AI, page 50

Heidi Livingston Eisips

 Heidi Livingston Eisips is adjunct faculty in the Department of Marketing and Business Analytics at San Jose State University's Lucas College of Business, where she teaches a wide range of courses that span marketing, data science, and statistics. Dedicated to incorporating experiential learning and data ethics into her teaching, Ms. Eisips draws upon more than 30 years of experience as a marketing strategist with Fortune 100 companies, start-ups, and midsize companies across a variety of industries (such as enterprise software, biopharma, telecom, and more). Ms. Eisips holds BA (English) and MBA degrees and is currently pursuing her doctorate.

Algorithmic Bias: Are You a Bystander or an Upstander?, page 55

Hugh Watson

 Dr. Hugh Watson is a professor of MIS in the Terry College of Business at the University of Georgia. He is a leading scholar and authority on business intelligence and analytics, having authored 24 books and over 200 scholarly journal articles. Hugh helped develop the conceptual foundation for decision support systems in the 1970s, researched the development and implementation of executive information systems in the 1980s, and for the past 20 years has specialized in data warehousing, business intelligence, and analytics. Hugh is a Fellow of both the Association for Information Systems and the Data Warehousing Institute and is the Senior Editor of the *Business Intelligence Journal*.

Be Careful with "Decisions of the Heart", page 21
Avoid the Wrong Part of the Creepiness Scale, page 127

Irina Raicu

Irina Raicu is the director of the Internet Ethics Program at the Markkula Center for Applied Ethics. She is an attorney and a Certified Information Privacy Professional. Her writing has appeared in a variety of publications, including the *Atlantic*, *USA Today*, the *San Jose Mercury News*, the *San Francisco Chronicle*, and Recode.

Perceptions of Personal Data, page 73

James Taylor

James Taylor is founder and CEO of Decision Management Solutions and a faculty member at the International Institute for Analytics. He is a leading expert in digital decisioning and using advanced analytics, business rules, and AI to improve business results. He provides strategic consulting to companies in the Fortune 100 and top 100 companies globally, working with clients in all sectors to adopt decision-making technology. James is the author of *Digital Decisioning: Using Decision Management to Deliver Business Impact from Artificial Intelligence* (MK Press) and (with Jan Purchase) *Real-World Decision Modeling with DMN* (MK Press).

Trust, Data Science, and Stephen Covey, page 34
What Decisions Are You Making?, page 155

Janella Thomas

Janella Thomas is a data scientist at Cox Enterprises. She received her bachelor's degree in economics from Spelman College and her master's degree in analytics from Iowa State University. She lives in Atlanta, Georgia, with her fiancé and her miniature schnauzer.

Data Transparency: What You Don't Know Can Hurt You, page 186

Jennifer Lewis Priestley

 Dr. Jennifer Priestley is the Associate Dean of the Graduate College and Director of the Analytics and Data Science Institute at Kennesaw State University. She architected the country's first PhD program in data science, which launched in February 2015. She has authored dozens of articles on binary classification, risk modeling, sampling, statistical methodologies for problem solving, and applications of Big Data analytics. Prior to receiving a PhD in statistics, Dr. Priestley worked in the financial services industry for 11 years. Her positions included Vice President of Business Development for VISA EU in London as well as for MasterCard US, and a role as an analytical consultant with Accenture's strategic services group. Dr. Priestley received a PhD from Georgia State University, an MBA from Pennsylvania State University, and a BS from Georgia Tech.

Should Data Have Rights?, page 75
Ethics and Figs: Why Data Scientists Cannot Take Shortcuts, page 153

Jesse Anderson

 Jesse Anderson is a data engineer, creative engineer, and Managing Director of Big Data Institute. He works with companies ranging from start-ups to Fortune 100 companies on Big Data. He is widely considered an expert in the field and is well regarded for his novel teaching practices.

Automatically Checking for Ethics Violations, page 178

Jitendra Mudhol

Jitendra Mudhol is the founder/CEO of CollaMeta, an artisanal Silicon Valley firm at the intersection of human creativity and artificial intelligence, solving problems in the business and social sectors. His three decades in the industry span continents, cultures, and large enterprises such as Siemens, IBM, Toshiba, Fujitsu, Qualcomm, and Broadcom as well as scrappy start-ups. As an Executive Fellow at Santa Clara University's Miller Center for Social Entrepreneurship, he uses data science and machine learning to maximize social impact. In spite of his BS (EE) and MBA degrees, he considers himself a novice and a lifelong learner.

Algorithmic Bias: Are You a Bystander or an Upstander?, page 55

John F. Carter

John F. Carter, PhD, is an accomplished data and analytics executive and consultant with broad industry experience leveraging data and analytics to drive business impact. John's expertise includes enterprise data management, analytics, predictive modeling, digital transformation, and artificial intelligence. John is currently helping companies use data and analytics to strategically transform their organizations and capabilities to accelerate growth. Previously, John was Senior Vice President of Analytics & Business Insight at Charles Schwab, where he created a high-performance enterprise analytics organization and pioneered the use of unstructured Big Data and AI/machine learning capabilities. John also was Chief Data Officer at Equifax, Inc., where he established data strategy, data acquisition, and data governance best practices across Equifax's global business units. During his career, John has held senior level positions at Acxiom, Citibank, and Responsys. John received his PhD in statistics from the University of Connecticut.

Data Ethics—Three Key Actions for the Analytics Leader, page 196

John Power

John Power is a Wall Street executive with nearly 30 years' experience, holding financial operations positions with firms such as Spear, Leeds & Kellogg, Bank Julius Baer, E-Trade Financial, and Mellon Bank. John has been teaching in MBA programs for the past 10 years and is in his seventh year at

Mercy College. John is currently pursuing his doctoral degree in business at Wilmington University. He lives in Queens, New York, with his wife and two sons.

Ethics, Trading, and Artificial Intelligence, page 157

John Thuma

John Thuma brings 30 years of hands-on-the-keyboard experience in data and analytics. John currently works for FIS's Data Solutions Group, which is a newly formed, highly collaborative, and fast-paced team that is expanding to support FIS's growing data business. The Data Solutions Group is responsible for providing the next generation of data products and services to FIS clients. These tools provide transformative, data-driven insights and actions and empower their clients to succeed in an increasingly competitive, data-driven world. The group is passionate about its work and takes a client-first approach to everything it does. There are great opportunities for growth and learning within this group, including engaging in special assignments across the team and business.

Spam. Are You Going to Miss It?, page 60

Justin Cochran

Justin Cochran is an associate professor of information systems at Kennesaw State University. He earned a PhD in business administration from the University of Georgia and master's and bachelor's degrees in mechanical engineering from Auburn University. In addition to his professor responsibilities, he provides programs to challenge faculty in the College of Business to stay current with evolving technologies and business practices. In his spare time, he can be found renovating houses, educating people on basketball courts, or riding mountain roads on his motorcycle.

The Importance of Building Knowledge in Democratized Data Science Realms, page 123

Kenneth Viciana

Kenneth Viciana is currently the Director of Information Risk Management at Fiserv. He is recognized globally as an innovative data and analytics leader. A hybrid business and IT executive, Kenneth has successfully developed and mobilized strategies, capabilities, and programs that help companies leverage and harness the power of actionable data to enable business outcomes.

Ethical Issues Are Front and Center in Today's Data Landscape, page 90

Keri McConnell

Keri McConnell is the Executive Director of the Northwestern Mutual Data Science Institute (NMDSI) at Northwestern Mutual. In this role, Keri is leading the creation of the NMDSI, a unique and innovative partnership between Northwestern Mutual, Marquette University, and the University of Wisconsin–Milwaukee. She was a founding leader of the analytics practice at Northwestern Mutual during a time of tremendous organizational growth. Keri's early career was spent in telecommunications, filling various operations and technology roles. She earned her MEd from Northeastern University specializing in adult and organizational learning.

Framework for Designing Ethics into Enterprise Data, page 201

Keyur Desai

Keyur Desai is a global enterprise data management, data monetization, and analytics executive with 30 years of expertise in maximizing the impact of data, analytics, and data products on business results, operational efficiency, enterprise risk, and innovation. He is Chief Data Officer at TD Ameritrade.

Equally Distributing Ethical Outcomes in a Digital Age, page 193

Kris Hunt

Kris Hunt is an experienced data analyst with a demonstrated history of working/consulting in the IT industry and software development. She is skilled in statistical modeling, customer relationship management (CRM), databases, data warehousing, and financial analytics. Kris is a strong entrepreneurship professional with a BS focused in statistics from Rutgers University.

The Golden Rule of Data Science, page 136
To Prepare or Not to Prepare for the Storm, page 265

Laura James

Dr. Laura James is an engineer and leader who builds and grows responsible, sustainable, and collaborative products and organizations, with a focus on emerging internet technologies.

We're Not Yet Ready for a Trustmark for Technology, page 64

Leandre Adifon

Leandre Adifon is the founder and CEO of Pyramid Base Technologies LLC (a.k.a. PyBTech LLC), a company that was started to lift people and the planet by making earth-friendly high-techs affordable to those who live at the base of the socioeconomic pyramid. Until recently, he was Vice President, Engineering & Technology, at Ingersoll Rand. In that role, he oversaw systems engineering and advanced technology globally for the company. Before joining the company, he spent 20 years at United Technologies and was Vice President of Worldwide Engineering for Otis Elevator.

How to Determine What Data Can Be Used Ethically, page 85

Linda Burtch

Linda Burtch is an industry leader in quantitative recruiting and has dedicated her career to becoming a subject matter expert on the analytics and data science hiring market. Linda is a frequent speaker on quantitative career topics at luncheons, conferences, corporate meetings, and webinars and has been an active member of the Chicago chapter of the American Statistical Association and INFORMS for years, including holding several board positions. She has been interviewed by the *New York Times*, the *Wall Street Journal*, CNBC, Bloomberg, the *Economist*, and *InformationWeek*, among others, and has maintained a blog on the analytics and data science hiring market for over 10 years. Burtch Works has also been recognized by Forbes as one of America's Best Recruiting Firms.

Ethics Must Be a Cornerstone of the Data Science Curriculum, page 37
Ethics: The Next Big Wave for Data Science Careers?, page 199

Majken Sander

Majken Sander is a data nerd and business analyst who also advocates for data literacy and the ethics in how we put data to use. Majken has worked with IT, management information, analytics, business intelligence, and data warehousing for more than 20 years. Armed with strong analytical expertise, she is keen on "data-driven" as a business principle, data science, and all other things data. Read more at majkensander.com.

How Can I Know You're Right?, page 166

Marc Faddoul

Marc Faddoul is an algorithm designer and researcher and a specialist in the field of computational propaganda. He gained his technical expertise at France's leading computer science engineering school, Télécom Paris, from which he graduated with an MS in data science. He then worked as an algorithmic designer in industry before being drawn to the School of Information at UC Berkeley, where he has sought to deepen his understanding of the social consequences of new technology.

Toward Algorithmic Humility, page 188

Mario Vela

Mario Vela is a data scientist with more than 20 years in the telecommunications industry and a passion for philosophy and mathematics.

Data Science Ethics: What Is the Foundational Standard?, page 27

Marty Ellingsworth

Marty Ellingsworth is an analytics professional and entrepreneur. He uses data, AI, advanced analytics, and cloud to address critical business problems and public concerns. He specializes in risk assessment, risk selection, pricing, marketing, claims service, and sales in property and casualty insurance. And he is a frequent author and speaker on crafting culture to include innovation and data-driven continuous improvement. Marty received his BS in operations research from the US Air Force Academy and his MS in operations research from the Air Force Institute of Technology. He is a long-time member of INFORMS, a past board member of American Risk and Insurance Association, and a frequent industry track member of KDD.

Is It Wrong to Be Right?, page 62

Michael Hind

Michael Hind is a Distinguished Research Staff Member in the IBM Research AI department in Yorktown Heights, New York. He has authored over 50 publications, served on over 50 program committees, and given several keynotes and invited talks at top universities, conferences, and government settings. Michael has led dozens of researchers to successfully transfer technology to various parts of IBM and helped launch several successful open source projects, such as AI Fairness 360 and AI Explainability 360. His 2000 paper on adaptive optimization was recognized as the OOPSLA'00 Most Influential Paper, and his work on Jikes RVM was recognized with the SIG-PLAN Software Award in 2012. Michael is an ACM Distinguished Scientist and a member of IBM's Academy of Technology.

Don't Generalize Until Your Model Does, page 117

Mike McGuirk

Mike McGuirk is a lecturer and full-time faculty member at Babson College, where he teaches undergraduate and graduate-level courses that focus on the successful use of analytic practices in marketing and closely related business functions. Prior to joining Babson in January 2020, Mike taught at Emerson College for four years, where he was also the Graduate Program Director of the new Digital Marketing and Data Analytics master's program. Before transitioning to academia, Mike had been working in the analytics field for over 25 years as a data-driven marketing and analytics consultant. He has always been interested in developing solutions that utilize data, technology, and analytics to help business executives make more informed, insight-driven decisions. Mike has extensive experience helping Fortune 1000 companies identify customer insights that lead to highly profitable marketing programs and superior customer experiences. He has deep expertise in descriptive, predictive, and prescriptive analytic techniques. He was recently a partner at iKnowtion (acquired by TTEC) and has also led analytic consulting departments at Epsilon and multiple start-ups.

Ethics and Reflection at the Core of Successful Data Science, page 222
A Lifetime Marketing Analyst's Perspective on Consumer Data Privacy, page 256

Miroslava Walekova

Miroslava Walekova is an enterprise performance improvement architect with 10+ years of experience in the financial services industry, focusing on leveraging the latest technology to drive responsible and sustainable organization transformation and growth.

"All Models Are Wrong." What Do We Do About It?, page 183

Naomi Arcadia Kaduwela

Naomi Arcadia Kaduwela is an innovative, ethical AI creator. As the head of Kavi Labs, the innovation arm of Kavi Global, Naomi partners with clients across industries to cocreate business value leveraging AI, advanced analytics, and IoT. Prior to joining Kavi Global, Naomi was a founding member of GE Healthcare's analytics team and graduated from GE's Digital Technology Leadership Program. Naomi is an academic researcher and a conference speaker. Naomi holds an MS degree in analytics from Northwestern University and joint BS degrees in computer science and applied psychology from Ithaca College.

Should Chatbots Be Held to a Higher Ethical Standard than Humans?, page 180

Nenad Jukić

Nenad Jukić is a professor of information systems at the Quinlan School of Business at Loyola University Chicago. He conducts research in various information management–related areas, including database modeling and management, data warehousing, business intelligence, data mining, business analytics, Big Data, ebusiness, and IT strategy. His work has been published in numerous management information systems and computer science academic journals, conference publications, and books.

Imbalance of Factors Affecting Societal Use of Data Science, page 112

Nick Hamlin

Nick Hamlin lives to make social good data accessible, understandable, and actionable for everyone. As GlobalGiving's first data scientist, Nick wears many hats, including leading the organization's data strategy, building and maintaining core infrastructure, and designing experiments to evaluate program impact. He's also a Data Ambassador for Datakind's Impact Practice in community health; the developer of Pando, Root Change's platform for exploring networks in the social sector; and part of the team behind Aidsight, an app allowing nontechnical users to easily explore international aid transparency data to unpack hidden relationships between organizations and validate data quality. In his past life, Nick worked as a reliability consulting engineer for Fortune 500 companies around the world and held National Science Foundation research positions in China and Thailand. Outside the office, he is a folk music street performer, amateur coffee nerd, and former worm farmer. Find out more about Nick on Twitter (*@nicholashamlin*) or at *nickhamlin.com*.

Using Social Feedback Loops to Navigate Ethical Questions, page 225

Pamela Passman

Pamela Passman founded and was president of the Center for Responsible Enterprise and Trade (CREATe.org), which developed and disseminated leading practices on how companies manage key risks internally and with their global supply chains. Prior to that, Pamela spent 15 years with Microsoft Corporation. She is a Senior Associate at the Center for Strategic and International Studies (CSIS).

> *Responsible Design and Use of AI: Managing Safety, Risk, and Transparency*, page 146
> *Artificial Intelligence: Legal Liabilities amid Emerging Ethics*, page 211

Peter Bruce

Peter Bruce is the founder of the Institute for Statistics Education at Statistics.com, an Elder Research company in Arlington, Virginia. Previously, in partnership with the noted economist Julian Simon, Peter continued and commercialized the development of Simon's Resampling Stats, a tool for bootstrapping and resampling. In his work at Cytel Software Corp., he developed Box Sampler along similar lines, and he helped bring XLMiner, a data mining add-in for Excel, to market. He is the author of *Introductory Statistics and Analytics: A Resampling Perspective* (Wiley), and a coauthor of *Data Mining for Business Analytics* (Wiley, 11 editions, versions, and translations, with Galit Shmueli, Peter Gedeck, Inbal Yahav, Nitin R. Patel, and Mia L. Stephens) and *Practical Statistics for Data Scientists* (O'Reilly, 2nd ed., with Peter Gedeck and Andrew Bruce).

> *Triage and Artificial Intelligence*, page 130
> *Random Selection at Harvard?*, page 262

Phil Bangayan

Phil Bangayan is Principal Data Scientist at Teradata, where he helps partners solve business problems by applying machine learning. Prior to working at Teradata, he applied analytics to grow revenue through data science, marketing, and finance roles at NBCUniversal and the Walt Disney Company. Phil holds an MBA from the MIT Sloan School of Management and an MS in electrical engineering from UCLA.

Rethinking the "Get the Data" Step, page 83

Phil Broadbent

Phil Broadbent has spent his entire career in some form of retail analytics, ranging from pricing to forecasting to operations and merchandising. His resume includes solving problems at some of the world's biggest companies: Best Buy, Toys"R"Us, eBay, Home Depot, and more.

The Gray Line, page 270

Polly Mitchell-Guthrie

Polly Mitchell-Guthrie is the VP of Industry Outreach and Thought Leadership at Kinaxis, a supply chain and analytics software company. Previously, she was Director of Analytical Consulting Services at the University of North Carolina Health Care System and worked in various roles at SAS, in Advanced Analytics R&D, as Director of the SAS Global Academic Program, and in Alliances. She has an MBA from the Kenan-Flagler Business School of the University of North Carolina at Chapel Hill, where she also received her BA in political science as a Morehead Scholar. She has been very active in INFORMS (the leading professional society for operations research and analytics) and cofounded the third chapter of Women in Machine Learning and Data Science (which now has more than 60 chapters worldwide).

Ethical Data Science: Both Art and Science, page 218

Rachel Thomas

Rachel Thomas is founding director of the Center for Applied Data Ethics at the University of San Francisco and is cofounder of fast.ai, which created the most popular deep learning course in the world (as far as we know), available for free online with no ads. She was selected by *Forbes* as one of "20 Incredible Women in AI," earned her math PhD at Duke, and was an early data scientist at Uber. Rachel is a popular writer and keynote speaker.

Algorithms Are Used Differently than Human Decision Makers, page 100

Rado Kotorov

Rado Kotorov is a seasoned technology innovator, digital transformation leader, and software executive with broad international experience. Rado leverages deep understanding of data, business intelligence, analytics, machine learning, and AI to solve today's business challenges and identify untapped revenue opportunities. Rado is a proven leader in developing vision, strategies, and data-driven business models for the digital economy and has authored two management books on the use of data and analytics in business: *Organizational Intelligence: How Smart Companies Use Information to Become More Competitive and Profitable* (Information Builders) and *Data-Driven Business Models for the Digital Economy: How Great Companies Run on Data* (Business Expert Press). Rado is the recipient of the 2019 NJ Digi-Tech Innovators Award.

Leadership for the Future: How to Approach Ethical Transparency, page 13
The Ethics of Communicating Machine Learning Predictions, page 125

Randy Guse

 Randy Guse is Director of Artificial Intelligence Organizational Learning, Research and Strategy for Optum Enterprise Analytics at UnitedHealth Group. He is responsible for AI knowledge development, advancing the analytic maturity of the organization. Prior to joining UHG, Randy designed and managed delivery of analytic solutions for clients in a variety of industries, including financial services, retail, hospitality, transportation, communications, and technology. You can learn more about Randy at his LinkedIn page (*https://www.linkedin.com/in/randyguse*).

Algorithmic Impact Assessments, page 220

Rasmus Wegener

 Rasmus Wegener is a partner in Bain & Company's San Francisco office. He is a leader in Bain's Business Transformation and Advanced Analytics Practices.

How to Ask for Customers' Data with Transparency and Trust, page 68

Richard Hackathorn

 Dr. Richard Hackathorn of Bolder Technology is currently pursuing the mission of ensuring that deep learning systems at scale are manageable, both technically and ethically. For several decades, Richard has been globally known as an industry analyst, technology innovator, high-tech entrepreneur, university professor, and international lecturer in data analytics and business intelligence. He has pioneered innovations in database management, decision support, database connectivity, data warehousing, and immersive analytics.

Business Realities Will Defeat Your Analytics, page 163

Robert J. Abate

 Robert J. Abate has been in data for longer than he cares to admit—starting in development, moving to architecture, then to business intelligence visualizations, on to Big Data science, and finally to Chief Data Officer. Robert gained experience in delivering visionary data management, governance, and analytic solutions by utilizing strategic collaboration with technology partners and experts. By combining a deep technical understanding of leading-edge technologies and architectures with people skills, he has been fortunate to impact F100 corporations—improving competitive edge, empowering data-driven decisions, and turning raw data into information assets. Robert is fortunate to be considered a Big Data and analytics thought leader by his peers and has learned from such greats as John Zachman, Dr. Peter Aiken, David Marco, Martha Dember, and too many more to name. He authored the "Big Data and Data Science" chapter in *DAMA-DMBOK*, 2nd ed. (Technics), and was given the nickname "The Data Whisperer" by *Toggle* magazine in 2017. He is one of the cochairs of the 2020 MIT CDOIQ Symposium. His team received the Walmart 2013 Technology Innovation Project of the Year for the Data CAFÉ (Collaborative Analytics Facility for Enterprise).

Limit the Viewing of Customer Information by Use Case and Result Sets, page 81
When to Say No to Data, page 247

Robert J. McGrath

 Dr. Robert J. McGrath is the director of Graduate Programs in Health Data Science and Analytics and Chair of the Department of Health Management and Policy at the University of New Hampshire. His research focuses on the foundations of knowledge generation, collaborative science, and public good.

Data Science and Deliberative Justice: The Ethics of the Voice of "the Other", page 58

Ron Bodkin

Ron Bodkin is a serial entrepreneur focused on beneficial applications of AI. Ron leads Retail Industry AI and Responsible AI for the Google Cloud CTO office. He also leads AI innovation experiments and works with Google Product Management and Engineering to develop AI and analytics products, co-innovating with customers, and he is the technical executive sponsor for key customers working with Google Cloud. He has contributed articles on machine learning and artificial intelligence to Medium (*https://medium.com/@ronbodkin*).

Toward Value-Based Machine Learning, page 119

Scott Radcliffe

Scott Radcliffe is managing director of the Master of Science in Business Analytics program at Emory University's Goizueta Business School. In this role, he is focused on developing industry partnerships that provide students with hands-on learning experiences that integrate foundational training with application to a real business problem, with real data and the latest technology. He is passionate about experiential learning in business analytics education, as it drives the ability to understand how, when, and why to use it. Prior to joining Emory, Scott served as Executive Director, Operations and Customer Experience Analytics at Cox Communications. A career business analytics practitioner, Scott has extensive experience in applying analytics in various industries ranging from packaged goods, energy, and mobile telecom to data analytics product development. Scott is also cofounder and VP of Data Science at Vajra Partners. He is a Certified Analytics Professional (CAP) as granted by the Institute for Operations Research and the Management Sciences (INFORMS).

Causality and Fairness—Awareness in Machine Learning, page 139

Sébastien Paquet

Sébastien Paquet studied physics (BS) and received a PhD in computer science from Université de Montréal. He has worked on gamma-ray detectors, medical imaging, RF equipment, computer graphics, virtual reality, and social and collaboration software and is an experienced facilitator and

Contributors

organizer. As the first applied research scientist at Element AI, he is the originator of several initiatives in the company and has contributed to setting up
various processes and programs, including the applied research scientist hiring process. He has been managing the continuous improvement team and
the multiskilling program that accelerates the learning of technical employees. He is especially interested in AI businesses from the standpoint of culture and social impact.

Build Multiperspective AI, page 50

Sherrill W. Hayes

Dr. Sherrill W. Hayes is Director of the PhD in Analytics and
Data Science and professor of conflict management in the
College of Computing and Software Engineering at Kennesaw State University. Dr. Hayes has over 20 years of experience as a respected educator, researcher, and practitioner in
the areas of conflict management, program development, and evaluation
through his work with families, organizations, court systems, and higher
education in the US, the UK, and Germany.

Cautionary Ethics Tales: Phrenology, Eugenics,...and Data Science?, page 9
Informed Consent and Data Literacy Education Are Crucial to Ethics, page 41

Stephanie Seward

Stephanie Seward is a former US Army officer with two
deployments and over six years of experience in service. Following her time in the army, Stephanie joined Booz Allen
Hamilton as an associate focused on machine learning and
data science applications. She completed her master's degree
in information and data science through the University of California, Berkeley, in April 2020.

Foundation for the Inevitable Laws for LAWS, page 253

Steve Stone

Steve Stone is an accomplished executive and author with over 36 years of experience in the technology services and retail industries. He is an innovative, highly respected leader who has spearheaded the adoption of digital technologies and advanced analytics. In addition to serving on multiple technology boards, Steve currently operates an executive advisory firm, NSU Technologies, LLC, which he founded in August 2017.

Just Because You Could, Should You? Ethically Selecting Data for Analytics, page 79
Implementing AI Ethics Governance and Control, page 208

Steven Mintz

Steven Mintz, PhD, blogs under the name *Ethics Sage*. His blog has been recognized by Feedspot as the 21st best in philosophy among thousands of top philosophy blogs in their index using search and social metrics. His *Workplace Ethics Advice* blog is listed as the 3rd best in the 30 Exceptional Corporate Social Responsibility (CSR) blogs by Market Inspector based on spreading awareness about sustainability and CSR. Dr. Mintz is the recipient of many awards for his work as a college educator and researcher, including the prestigious "Accounting Exemplar" award given by the Public Interest Section of the American Accounting Association.

Ethics, AI, and the Audit Function in Financial Reporting, page 268

Steven C. Myers

Steven C. Myers is an educator in applied econometrics and data analytics, an evangelist for economists in data science, a presenter at SAS conferences, a former CIO, and the 2020 SAS Distinguished Educator. He specializes in combining economic and business acumen with rigorous statistical and programming techniques to solve problems and relate solutions. He is an associate professor of economics and teaches in the Economics and Business Data Analytics degree programs at the University of Akron. He blogs at *econdatascience.com.*

Ethics Rules in Applied Econometrics and Data Science, page 231

Stuart Buck

Stuart Buck has a JD and a PhD in education policy. As a Vice President at Arnold Ventures, he has funded renowned work showing that scientific research is often irreproducible and how to use open science and transparency policies to improve it. He has advised DARPA, IARPA (the CIA's research arm), the Department of Veterans Affairs, and the White House Social and Behavioral Sciences Team on rigorous and transparent research processes, and he has published in top journals (such as *Science*) on how to make research more accurate.

Why Research Should Be Reproducible, page 47

Thomas Casey

Thomas Casey has nearly 25 years of experience working with, designing solutions around, and helping Global 2000 customers to better leverage analytics. He has authored the Automating Intelligence framework, defining a pragmatic approach toward driving personalized decisioning using a common set of analytical guiding principles. Thomas has an MBA from Arizona State University and a BS from the University of Massachusetts. He is currently enrolled in the Harvard Business Analytics program and is a regular presenter at various analytically themed conferences and customer symposiums.

Probability—the Law That Governs Analytical Ethics, page 114

Tim Wilson

Tim Wilson has been working with digital data full-time since 2001 in a variety of roles, from managing a web analytics platform migration and developing analytics processes as the head of the business intelligence department at a $500 million high-tech B2B company, to creating and growing the analytics practices at three different agencies that worked with a range of large consumer brands. Tim also consults with the digital analytics teams at Fortune 500 companies on their strategies, processes, and tactics for effectively putting their digital data to actionable use. He is a long-time creator of pragmatic content for analysts and marketers, including cohosting the biweekly *Digital Analytics Power Hour* podcast (*https://www.analyticshour.io*) and cocreating *dartistics.com*—a site dedicated to encouraging analysts to learn the R programming language and apply statistical methods to their data.

"Ethical" Is Not a Binary Concept, page 7

Yiannis Kanellopoulos

Yiannis Kanellopoulos has spent the better part of two decades analyzing and evaluating software systems in order to help organizations address any potential risks and flaws related to them. (In his experience, these risks or flaws are always due to human involvement.) With his start-up, Code4Thought, Yiannis is turning his expertise into democratizing technology by rendering algorithms transparent and helping organizations become accountable. He's also a founding member of Orange Grove Patras, a business incubator sponsored by the Dutch embassy in Greece to promote entrepreneurship and counter youth unemployment. Yiannis holds a PhD in computer science from the University of Manchester.

Use Model-Agnostic Explanations for Finding Bias in Black-Box Models, page 174

Make Accountability a Priority, page 215

Index

Symbols

A

Arkansas, health care benefits software in, 100

Arnold Ventures, 47

ART (accountability, responsibility, and transparency), 184

Article 15 of GDPR, 174

Article 22 of GDPR, 22, 51, 174

artificial intelligence (AI) (generally)
    automation of the ineffable, 107
    bias, 2-4
        (see also algorithmic bias)
    building multiperspective AI, 50-52
    ethics, 106-108
    ethics, AI, and audit function in financial reporting, 268-269
    five core virtues for, 237-239
    levels of distraction, 106
    opaqueness of, xiv

Asian Americans, 262

Asimov, Isaac, rules for robot ethics, 16, 235

Association for Computing Machinery (ACM), 22

Athey, Susan, 233

attention optimization, fairness debt and, 103

AUC (area under the curve), 131

audits
    AI ranking of tax returns, 131
    ethical compliance, 209
    ethics, AI, and audit function in financial reporting, 268-269

automated decision making, accountable design and, 217

Automated Decision Systems (ADSs), 55-57

Automating Inequality (Eubanks), 55

automation
    analytical processes and, xiv
    Ethicize™ (imaginary software), 5

automobile insurance, 241

autonomous cars
    AI decision-making in, 130
    human overriding of algorithms, 115
    insurance issues, 241
    life-and-death situations made by, 235
    probability and analytical ethics, 114
    responsible design and use, 147
    utilitarian decisions and, 14

autonomous weapons, 213

autonomy, as medical research principle, 194

awareness, fairness and, 4

B

babysitters, risk-scoring of, 132

banking (see credit; financial services) (see financial services)

Baum, L. Frank, 21

behavioral research, 194

Belmont Report, 194

beneficence, as medical research principle, 194

Berk, Richard, 151

Bezos, Jeff, 132

bias
    AI and, 2-4, 219
    algorithmic misclassification and, 134
    audits of AI applications for, 209
    blatantly discriminatory algorithms, 150-152
    causality and fairness-awareness in machine learning, 139-141
    chatbots and, 180
        (see also chatbots)
    CRISP-DM and, 229
    data bias as replication of human biases, 11
    data storytelling and, 110
    deliberative justice and, 59
    distinction between "unbiased" and "fair", 32

HIPAA (see Health Insurance Portability and Accountability Act of 1996)

Hippocrates, 45

Hippocratic oath, 45, 218

hiring
    algorithmic misclassification and, 134
    ensuring diversity in, 209
    ethics as competitive advantage, 53
    medical history and, 137
    negative publicity's effect on, 199

Hitler, Adolf, 19

Hobbes, Thomas, 45

Hoffman, Anna Lauren, 227

Holmes, Oliver Wendell, 153

housing vulnerability, 72

human decision making, algorithms compared to, 100-102

human factor, responsible innovation and, 207

humans
    AI biases caused by, 3
    anthropomorphization of AI by, 106
    attempts to interject ethics into algorithms, 115
    as ethical actors, 204

humility
    algorithmic humility, 188-191
    as core virtue, 238

Hurricane Irma, 128

Hurricane Katrina, 265-267

hypotheses, verifying with data, 40

I

IBM Principles for Trust and Transparency of AI, 148, 212

IBM Watson
    data analysis at Memorial Sloan Kettering, 212
    mass surveillance systems, 101

IMDB, 77

impact assessments, 220-221

incarceration, 245

independent oversight, of analytics supply chain, 195

individual data (see personal data)

individual investors, 157

information asymmetry, 158

informed consent, 41-44, 74

innovating responsibly, 206

insight, decision making and, 205

instances, data breaches and, 88

institutional reforms, 57

insurance
    for autonomous cars, 241
    health insurance and ethical paradoxes, 251

intellectual property, 174

internal politics, 270

Internet of Things (IoT), 164

interpretability
    black-box models and, 171
    ethical dilemma of model interpretability, 171-173
    model-agnostic explanations for finding bias in black box models, 174-177

intuition, decision making and, 205

investors, institutional versus individual, 157

Ioannidis, John, 47

IQ tests, 134

"Isaac Asimov: The 4th Law of Robotics" (Schmarzo), 235

J

jobs (see recruitment)

Jones, Doug, 104

justice
    bias in predictive policing and, 243-246
    as medical research principle, 194

justice system (see criminal justice)

prescription records, 137

pretrial risk assessment tools, 188-191

"pretty good" mindset, 133-135

pricing model, 84

Priestley, Jennifer Lewis, 233

Principles (Dalio), 54

Principles for Trust and Transparency of AI (IBM), 148, 212

Principles on Artificial Intelligence, OECD, 174

privacy, 212

  (see also data privacy)

  anonymizing data, 77

  as barrier to health care research, 113

  data science teams and, 198

  determining what data can be used ethically, 85-87

  as obstacle to progress in beneficial use of data, 112

  personal data use and, 74

  protected health information, 212

  right to be forgotten, 22

proactive ethics, 18-20

probability

  analytical ethics and, 114-116

  ethical implications of nonhuman decision making, 115

profit

  consumer-generated data and, 112

  ethical pressures posed by, 30

  ethical system design, 161

profitability optimization, 104

ProPublica, 244

protected health information, 212

proxies, 245

proxy data, 84

psychographic profiling, 14

psychometric tests, 134

Public Safety Assessment (PSA), 188-190

public school teachers, algorithmic rating/firing of, 101

Q

Quantcast, 119

R

racial discrimination/racism

  algorithmic misclassification and voter disenfranchisement, 135

  bias in predictive policing, 243-246

  bias in pretrial risk assessment tools, 190

  blatantly discriminatory algorithms, 150-152

  discrimination in mortgage refinancing, 104

  facial recognition technology and, 219

  recidivism models and, 32

racial equity, 243

random selection college admission proposal, 263

ranking, of records, 131

rationality, rules and, 16

Receiver Operating Characteristics (ROC) curve, 131

recidivism models, 32

recommendation systems

  regenerative versus extractive recommendations, 120-122

  unintended consequences of ML bias, 119

  values-based machine learning and, 120-122

Recommendations on Artificial Intelligence, OECD, 213

records, ranking of, 131

recruitment

  algorithmic misclassification and, 134

  ensuring diversity in, 209

  ethics as competitive advantage, 53

  negative publicity's effect on, 199

redlining, 104

reflection, 222

regulation
  consumer data privacy laws, 257
  fairness debt and, 104
  federal data laws, 136
  multiperspective AI and, 51
  personal data laws, 38
  spam, 60
reproducibility, 47-49
Reproducibility Project in Psychology, 47
research
  AEA ethics guidelines, 233
  anonymizing data, 77
  as basis for data stories, 40
  data rights and, 75
  informed consent, 41-44
  principles outlined in Belmont Report,
    194
  reproducibility of, 47-49
resilience, as core virtue, 238
respect for persons, 194
responsibility
  in absence of unbiased and objective
    technology, 4
  innovation and, 206
  trustmarks and, 64
responsible design and use, 146-149
result sets, limiting viewing of, 81
results, delivering, 35
retail
  customer data and, 113
  facial recognition as marketing tool,
    143
  limiting viewing of customer informa-
    tion, 82
  100% conversion fantasy, 259-261
  preservation of storm-related sales data
    after Hurricane Katrina, 265-267
  video analytics of shopping traffic, 79
reuse of models, 169
right to be forgotten
  GDPR and, xv

perceptions of personal data and, 22
  reasonable exceptions to, xv
right to explanation, 154
rights
  of data, 75
  privacy (see privacy)
risk
  democratized data science tools as
    source of, 123
  PII storage as risk factor, 91
risk management/mitigation, 91
  (see also model risk management
    (MRM))
  auto insurance and, 241
  data and analytics for, 91
  responsible design and use, 147
  responsible innovation and, 207
robots
  Asimov's ethical rules for, 16, 235
  need for Fourth Law, 235
ROC (Receiver Operating Characteristics)
  curve, 131
Rogers, Martha, 223, 256
rules, rationality and, 16

S

Sarbanes–Oxley Act (SOX), 136, 269
Science (journal), 47
scientism, defined, 11
Securities and Exchange Commission
  (SEC), 157
security
  health care and, 96-98
  responsible design/use and, 147
self-defense, killing in, xv
self-driving cars (see autonomous cars)
"Selling Your Bulk Online Data Really
  Means Selling Your Autonomy" (Morozov), 73
sentencing, 245
Shapley values, 172, 175

About the Editor

Bill Franks

Bill Franks has spent his career focusing on analytics, data science, AI, and big data. He began his career in hands-on roles coding and building models, and then advanced to chief analytics officer positions in both large public company and small private organization environments. Franks is also the author of the books *Taming the Big Data Tidal Wave* (Wiley) and *The Analytics Revolution* (Wiley). He is a sought-after speaker and frequent blogger who has been ranked in multiple global influencer lists tied to big data, analytics, and AI, and he was an inaugural inductee into the Analytics Hall of Fame. His work has spanned clients in a variety of industries, for companies ranging in size from Fortune 100 companies to small nonprofit organizations. You can learn more at *http://www.bill-franks.com*.

O'REILLY®

There's much more
where this came from.

Experience books, videos, live online
training courses, and more from O'Reilly
and our 200+ partners—all in one place.

Learn more at oreilly.com/online-learning